AWADH UNDER THE NAWABS

POLITICS, CULTURE AND COMMUNAL RELATIONS

1722-1856

Awadh under the Nawabs

Politics, Culture and Communal Relations 1722-1856

SURENDRA MOHAN

Foreword by
IRFAN HABIB

MANOHAR
2026

First published 1997
Reprinted 2021, 2022, 2023, 2024, 2025, 2026

ISBN 978-81-7304-203-4

Published by
Ajay Kumar Jain for
Manohar Publishers & Distributors
4753/23, Ansari Road, Daryaganj,
New Delhi-110002

Printed at
Replika Press Pvt. Ltd.

Contents

List of Plates

Acknowledgements

This book is based substantially on my Doctoral thesis—*The Communal Relation in Awadh—1754-1857*. The idea of this research originally came from Late Prof. K.C. Srivastava, Head, Department of Western History, Lucknow University, Lucknow. I am greatly indebted to Prof. S.N. Qanungo, my guide, for his great interest and valuable advice. Not only for the thesis, but for the major part of the book also. The idea of utilising Indian sources and concepts to dispel many of the wrong impressions, which have been propounded about Awadh and the Nawabs, was basic to this research. I got lot of help from Dr. Saiyad Athar Abbas Rizvi, who presented his two learned volumes—*Shah Wali-Allah And His Times* and *Shah Abd al-Aziz*. He is unfortunately no more, but on his visits to Lucknow, I had detailed discussions with him on Islamic concepts of Awadh in the eighteenth century. Mr. Alvi, who was an officer in the Transport Department, Lucknow, was in the I.N.A. and had seen the communal harmony in its best ramifications, brought to me a rare insight of what might have happened in Awadh during the Nawabi times. Yogesh Praveen with his keen mind and undoubted talent of diction, gave me various historical facts which reflected the happy routine of *Lucknow-walas*. I also had the pleasure of meeting Ali Mian Saheb of Nadwa, who took a lot of interest and readily offered help of institute's library. Dr. Nayyar Masud gave me indigenous sources of the history of Awadh. My friend from the Urdu Samaj, Dr. Abbasi, provided me with the basic source materials. My friends from Lucknow University—Dr. R.N. Mehra and N.K. Zutshi, provided me with lot of Library support. Dr. S.N. Sinha, Former Director, U.P. State Archives, was a great help in providing primary source materials for this book. Dr. Sheema Rizvi and her mother, gave me help in reading and explaining some Persian and Arabic manuscripts. Dr. Pankaj Kumar, Vidyant College, Lucknow, was also a great help. I owe a lot of gratitude to the Libraries of

U.P. Secretariat, U.P. Legislative Assembly, Amiruddaula Public Library and Tagore Library, University of Lucknow, Lucknow. From Raza Library, Rampur, Dr. Siddiqi, sent me the hand-written passage of the manuscript, along with the Arabic text and Urdu translation of *Risala-Fi-Ahkam al-Arzin* of Sayyad Dildar Ali Nasirabadi. Dr. S.P. Singh, Vice-Chancellor, University of Lucknow, Lucknow, was able to get me the photocopy of a very rare book—*Private Life of an Eastern King*, from the University Library. State Museum, Lucknow, has given me copies of some rare photographs of pre-1857 days. Hakim Safdar Nawab of Lucknow, has been able to give me some valid explanation about the life-style of Nawab Wajid Ali Shah. I am indeed grateful to Prof. Irfan Habib of Aligarh University, with whom I have been in touch since the days of my research. He gave me some copies of original and rare manuscripts from the University Library. His greater contribution to this book, is his painstaking reading and invaluable suggestions for authenticity an improvement in the text of the book. He brought to bear his immense scholarship and deep knowledge of the subject. His foreword has given me a lot of satisfaction and confidence, in what I have written. His complimentary note is for me a great morale booster and most readers will find it very gratifying.

Sayyad Kutubuddin, my Law-Advisor in the Board office, for his help in various things, including appendices on *Baradaris* and *Imambaras.* I am also thankful to Ali Kausar, Scientist, Central Drug Research Institute, Lucknow, for giving his consent to use the photographs on Chattar Manzil, taken by him, for the cover page of this book.

This book would never have been completed without the help from my young friend Dr. Anupam Roy Chowdhury. He was able to take the long dictations on his computer. I have almost lost the habit of writing by hand, after long years in service. He made cross-referencing possible and his documentation has been perfect.

I am indeed thankful to my publishers, Manohar Publishers, for the interest they have taken in bringing out this book.

Need one thank one's family. My wife, Deepashree, who has been associated with this research. My children, Mitali and Manas, and my nephew Anand Adhikari, have been a great source of encouragement.

SURENDRA MOHAN

Foreword

Dr. Surendra Mohan, I.A.S., who has recently retired as Chairman, Revenue Board of Uttar Pradesh, a position with a long history of its own, has a deep attachment to the past and the traditions of the vanished state of Awadh. In the following pages he offers a wide-ranging interpretation of what he obviously considers to be the golden age of Awadh during its appearance as a distinct political unit under Saadat Khan and his descendants, who ruled it from 1722 to 1856.

Dr. Mohan believes that by circumstance as well as by design, the Nawabi regime of a hundred and thirty-five years gave full reign to the indigenous tradition of communal amity and folk culture, while adding the veneer of Mughal and Iranian cultures which the rulers were heirs to. The court at Lucknow patronised Insha, with his contribution to standardization of literary prose in both Hindi and Urdu, and Mir, the great Urdu lyricist; it encouraged *kathak* as a new form of classical dance and *thumri* as the style of music; and it created an interesting, if not necessarily magnificent, variant of Mughal architecture. That this cultural renaissance should take place under the shadow of British power, threatening, appropriating and yet insatiable, gives to the renaissance an air of particular tragedy. Dr. Mohan is far from asserting that Nawabi regime had no serious flaws; but he argues that the British themselves were responsible for both aggravating and exaggerating such flaws. They put the Awadh rulers in a position that was essentially one of responsibility without power; and this could not but bring about a deterioration in the administration of that emasculated polity. Dr. Mohan's sympathies are clear and unconcealed; but they are not without a strong factual basis.

Given his assessment of the Nawabi regime, Dr. Mohan's criticism of the annexation of Awadh by the Company in 1856 is strong and unqualified. But let us remember that another man, who could be expected to have no sympathy with princes of any sort, was also driven to describe the British treatment of Awadh in these indignant words:

> This denying the validity of treaties which had formed the acknowledged base of intercourse for twenty years; this seizing violently upon independent territories in open infraction even of the acknowledged treaties; this final confiscation of every acre of land in the whole country; all these treacherous and brutal modes of proceeding of the British toward the people of India. . . .

So wrote Karl Marx in 1858.

Dr. Mohan feels that with Annexation the 'prosperity' of Awadh departed too. His focus being on political and cultural developments, economic conditions have not naturally received the same degree of attention. Yet, as against Sleeman's portrayal of Awadh peasantry ravaged by baronial brigandage, one can draw a less unfavourable balance sheet by comparing its lot with that of the peasants of the adjacent British territories, pauperised by the rent-enhancements of the Mahalwari system, so tellingly described by Eric Stokes. That Awadh had a flourishing urban sector is evidenced by the large population of Lucknow, estimated *c.*1850 at a million; it was certainly no less than 5,50,000, to judge from the more precise house-statistics collected by the police early in 1857, and now studied by F. Anjum Taban. The city's population underwent a rapid decline after Annexation, being only 3,58,000 in 1869/72. Donald Butter's survey of southern Awadh shows a much larger number of urban settlements with a larger average size in 1838 than in the period beginning with the census of 1869-72. Such data bear out Dr. Mohan's judgement of an economic decline setting in with the Annexation; and no contrary picture has yet been drawn with any measure of conviction.

The literature on Nawabi Awadh, both contemporary and more recent, is massive; and, as his citations show, Dr. Surendra Mohan has read widely and drawn on all kinds of sources, not leaving out newspaper articles for any clues to oral tradition. For students of Awadh history, his is a noteworthy contribution that needs to be read with all due care.

IRFAN HABIB

Introduction

In my mind the idea of this book began with a question—if Lucknow symbolised an effete culture, why did we have to fight the battles of 1857 and 1858, in each house of the city of Lucknow. If nothing was left of our heritage, if everything had been lost in decadence, then why did the people of Lucknow fight at all—and that too together as a group, Hindus and Muslims alike. Most Western writers have condemned the times of the *nawabs* of Awadh as degenerate. Lucknow and Awadh have ever since been misrepresented in the West on the lines of a book—*Private Life of An Eastern King*, published in London, 1855, just before the annexation. An objective reading of history does not support the idea of decay at that time. It was definitely a time of awakening. The more I thought about it, the more I was convinced that the battles of 1857 and 1858 were basically the War of Independence for India—the first Indian effort to break out of the cocoon of colonialism, and the next ninety years were a follow-up of this effort—the Freedom Movement. If that was so, where did the strength lie in the culture of Awadh to fight that war? Somewhere in the recesses of history a music has remained dormant because of some artificial cacophony of discordant noises created by vested interests. The gaps have been left where they were for a long time. Now let the music come out of its depth. The search for that lost submerged melody is my quest—the reason to embark on my research on *Awadh's Ambience*.

In this book, the history of Awadh has been traced from 1722. The beginning of the real conflict of the State of Awadh with the East India Company came in the year 1764—the year the battle of Buxar was fought and lost for India. In this battle the nascent power of the East India Company defeated the combined forces of *nawab* Shuja-ud-daula of Awadh, Mir Qasim of Bengal and the fugitive Mughal emperor, Shah Alam. More than the battle of Plassey, it was the battle of Buxar which was decisive for the history of modern India. In this battle three different streams of Indian history came together face to face in a confusing confrontation.

The first stream is of the ancient Indian history which spins its way from the earliest tribal settlements and then making it the Aryavarta—the land of the Ancient Aryans. Vedas and Upanishads were conceived perfected and handed down by memory (*Shruti*) from generation to generation till Rishi Vyas gave it a written form. In this land of Aryavarta, Lord Ram Chandra, an incarnation of Vishnu was born in the ruling dynasty of Ikshvaku. This legend has remained an integral part of the history of Awadh. It has set the standard of social morality and family ethics of the people living in this area. Rulers may come and rulers may go but the concept of Ram remained the basic principle of their mundane existence. More and more tribes came and settled in this subcontinent but all of them became a part and parcel of Hindu thought and philosophy. Whenever kings and rulers of other parts of the country were inspired by religious sentiments they constructed a temple in Ayodhya. It was their ladder onto the other world. For individuals Ram was the beacon and the pathfinder of relief from this worldly existence. When the soldiers made their final assault they thought of *raja* Ram. The last journey was accompanied by the chanting of *ram naam satya hai*—'Ram is the ultimate truth'. In social life, caste became a very important factor. All rulers adopted a social framework dependent on caste system with its theory of some people ranking above the others in society. The urbanity of the area was provided with three important towns—Ayodhya, Saket and Shravasti. Kashi was also a great centre of Hindu thought but it was on the outskirts of Awadh and had a separate cultural identity.

Islam entered Awadh in 1192 with Malik Hasam-ud-din-ugul Bak, a representative of the House of Ghor. Awadh was conquered. For a brief spell between 1399 to 1479, Awadh remained under Sharqui dynasty of Jaunpur. When Babar defeated Ibrahim Lodi in 1556, Awadh became part of the Mughal empire. In *Babarnama*, Awadh and Baharaich are listed as *sarkars* of the Mughal empire. Ayodhya was the seat of the provincial administration. Akbar, Jehangir, Shah Jahan and Aurangzeb retained the primacy of Awadh and made regular appointments of important persons as *subedars* of Awadh. After the death of Aurangzeb in 1707, his successors proved totally incompetent to retain the integrity of such a big empire. The outlying portions slowly emerged independent. In 1722 Saadat Khan was appointed the *subedar* of Awadh by the Mughal emperor. He consolidated his position against the small rulers and *taluqdars* because of his military power. After him Safdar Jang was appointed the *subedar* of Awadh and a perception grew that it was a hereditary office. When Shuja-ud-daula came to power in 1754, it was almost clear that *subedari* of Awadh had become hereditary. During the time of Shuja-ud-daula, the Mughal Prince Ali Gauhar had to leave Delhi because of the court conspiracies and he had taken shelter in Patna and Allahabad. Later he assumed the title of the Mughal emperor as Shah Alam. In the battle of Buxar in 1764, the armies of Awadh and Mughal empire fought almost as equals.

The most important factor of the 1764 war was the appearance of the East India Company. The East India Company was created by a Charter granted by Queen Elizabeth in 1600. The merchants of London came together under this Charter and obtained monopoly of trade with India and the East. In a hundred years starting from 1600, the East India Company was in constant conflict with Spain, Portugal and Holland and later with France. By the year 1700, they had established their factories and urban population centres in Calcutta, Madras, Bombay and Surat. In the year 1765, the East India Company gained the *diwani* of Bengal and this was the beginning of their political dominance of northern India. The Company was forced to evolve new relationships with its Board of Directors in England and also with Parliament. Whenever the Company asked for a new Charter, the King and the Parliament of England imposed their own conditions. During 1757-65, East India Company took advantage of internal conflicts between Mir Jafar and Mir Qasim and began to acquire political power. East India Company was created under a national commitment. In the hundred years, since the beginning of the East India Company, England had grown to be the most important maritime power in Europe and was also controlling its colonies in Canada and America. She had acquired new techniques of war and had developed a tremendous fire power. Their army was disciplined and fought with a certain national objective. The East India Company represented a country which had a national mission. In India such a commitment was lost after the death of Aurangzeb.

In 1764 the armies which fought in the battle of Buxar had Indian soldiers on both sides. On the Indian side their understanding of war was limited to the Mughal perceptions. Their generalship was divided. Most people were pursuing selfish ends. There was treachery during the battle which as usual has remained an essential factor of Indian history. On the other side was the East India Company which had an undisputed generalship and they pursued a national aim. Englishmen by this time had adopted the basic concepts of imperialism. For them the people of Asia and Africa were *white men's burden*. The objective of this book is to study the interaction between these three streams of history. From 1722 to 1857, they were basic and essential components of the history of Awadh.

In 1856 the last King of Awadh, Wajid Ali Shah was deposed. It provoked sadness and an empty emotional outcry. The British rulers thought that they had won the day. There were no ripples and there was no call to arms. But the British were mistaken. There was no denying the fact that India had lost the sense of any mission. In 1707, Aurangzeb died as the emperor of India. In 1803 the Mughal emperor had become a pensioner of the East India Company. But the symbol remained. In 1857 it was again the Mughal emperor who was projected as the leader of the 1857 War of Independence. Awadh which was surreptitiously made to break away from the Mughal empire in 1819 joined the war and again accepted the Mughal emperor as the leader. From 1722 to 1857, Awadh remained the crucible for a harmonious blending of cultures. People of various religious faiths came together. They adopted what they thought was the best among the others. Beginning from the eighth century to the eighteenth, Islam had lived in India for a thousand years and had come to stay. Perhaps more than in any other part of this country Hindus and Muslims lived together in Awadh with a basic instinct of mutual respect. It was this togetherness which gave them the strength and the idea of a national mission to fight the *firangis*. It does not mean that smallness of minds did not show up in Awadh. It did in ample measure but people did rise above the selfish interests for a higher cause. In spite of these vicissitudes if this book is able to bring out the tonality of the music of unity, my objective will be served.

One of the concerns which prompted me to write this book was the idea that the history of Awadh has been misrepresented by the

Western Historians. This was not limited to the nineteenth century. Even as late as 1989 J.R.I. Cole, has followed the same line in his book. He wrote

> Syed Dildar Ali Naseerabadi harboured an almost violent animosity towards Hindus arguing that the Awadh Government should take stern measures against them.[1]

Further, he allegedly make Sayyad Dildar Ali opine that

> Muslims could only grant infidels personal security (*Aman*) in a country they rule for one year, lamenting that the Government had long treated as grantees of personal security, the Hindus of north India, who openly followed their idolatrous religion, drinking wine and sometimes even mating with Syed women.[2]

In the next paragraph, he goes on to write quoting Sayyad Dildar Ali that 'Legally, none the less, the lives and property of Hindus could be licitly taken by Muslims.'[3] I acquired an authentic copy of the document quoted by Cole in his book from Raza Library, Rampur.[4] A mere reading of this document, which is in Arabic, will disclose how grossly Dildar Ali has been misrepresented. Nowhere in this document the word Hindu has been used. The word used is '*mushrikin*'—meaning those who believe in many gods. Hinduism cannot be represented as such a religion. In Hinduism there is only One Authority and He is *parmatma*. Everybody draws his power from Him. The story of Krishna lifting the Govardhan mountain on his small little finger of the left hand in the playful display of his supreme power proves the point. My idea here is not to write a treatise on Hinduism, I merely wish to state in the most direct way as to what has been written by Sayyad Dildar Ali and how it has been misconstrued by Cole. Cole wishes to convey that according to Sayyad Dildar Ali Hindus and Infidels mean the same thing and that is why he has commanded that the lives and properties of the Hindus could be taken licitly by Muslims. This is totally wrong. In the original document this statement has been made about *nasibs*. The narration is like this 'Take the property of *nasib* wherever it be, and send one-fifth portion of this to us.' Then a further query is raised, 'What about killing a *nasib*', the reply was 'It is *halal*'. Now *nasib* is actually that sect of Muslims who are strongly opposed to Shia thought and religion. This sect is viciously opposed to Hazrat Imam, and has been mentioned as such in the famous Shia book *Sahi Mana-e-Kamila*. The Hindus are nowhere involved.

Another fact worthy of mention about this particular document *Risala-e-Fiq* is that this has been quoted by Cole from a book called *Nuzhatul Khawatir*, written by a Sunni *alim*, Sayyad Abdul Hai. According to Shia scholars, this is not an authentic statement of the philosophy of Sayyad Dildar Ali.

There is another point where I would like to touch on another mis-statement in Cole's narrative. Cole writes, 'The Sunni *Naqsbandi* thinker Shah Vali-ullah wanted the Moughals to ban Hinduism'.[5] For this inference Cole has cited *Shah Wali-Allah and His Times* by Sayyad Athar Abbas Rizvi. When Sayyad Athar Abbas Rizvi visited Lucknow, he personally presented a copy of his book to me and also had a discussion with me. So what I write is closer to the correct perspective. The actual text is as follows:

> The eighth point of *Kalima-i Hashtum*—Strict orders should be issued in all Islamic towns forbidding religious ceremonies publicly practised by infidels (such as the performance of Holi and ritual bathing in the Ganges). On the tenth of Moharram, Shias should not be allowed to go beyond the bounds of moderation, neither should they be rude nor repeat stupid things (that is recite *tabarra*, or condemn the first three successors of the Prophet Muhammad) in the streets or bazaars.[6]

Where does the sentence carry the meaning that Shah Wali-Allah wanted the Mughals to ban Hinduism? *Kalima-i-Hashtum* quoted above merely restates the Muslim judicial precept that religious ceremonies should not be practised in public. According to this principle, the ritual of the celebration of Holi and bathing in the Ganges, has been put on the same pedestal as Shias not being allowed to go beyond the bounds of moderation on the tenth of Moharram. The recitation of *tabarra* on streets has always been deplored by all Sunni thinkers. An illusion has been projected that dissensions have existed between the Hindus and Muslims in India and efforts to bring about unity have never succeeded, 'The two have remained disparate as ever.'

The authenticity of this document *Kalima-i-Hashtum* is itself a matter of doubt, has been pointed out by Sayyad Athar Abbas Rizvi himself—

> There are significant gaps in the text of other letters published by Nizami, and comparison of these letters with the Rampur copy indicates annoying omissions, thus undermining the utility of this edition.[7]

But J.R.I. Cole has to derive the unseemly conclusion that Sunni Naqshbandi thinker Shah Wali-Allah wanted the Mughals to ban Hinduism! The life span of Wali-Allah was 1703-62. The Mughal rulers always followed a policy of religious tolerance with the sole exception of Aurangzeb. The downfall of the Mughals was the outcome of Aurangzeb's policies. When the Mughal empire was tottering after 1707, where was the occasion for any one to say that Walli-Allah wanted the Mughals to ban Hinduism. S.A.A. Rizvi has very correctly described the situation prevailing at that time in these words:

> The low state to which the political, economic and social life of Delhi had sunk naturally turned the attention of both the Hindus and the Muslims to religion. A number of the Muslims religious leaders called for a return of true Islam, and of these decidedly the most important was Shah Wali-Allah,[8]

and Shah Wali-Allah could never think of banning Hinduism.

A very significant factor of this era was the influence of the growth of Hindi and its poetry in which the personage of *bhagwan* Ram and Krishna played so important a part. Krishna is the *avatar* of Vishnu with all the sixteen attributes of a perfect human being. John Pemble described him as the erotic hero—

> The erotico-mystical cult of Krishna became widespread in southern India and Bengal, while in Avadh and the Ganges valley, the puritan cult of Rama predominated.[9]

Krishna is the author of Gita. He is the Eternal Hero. He is the *purush* (the Man) and Nature is *prakriti* (Female) of which the mortal beings are a part. The mortal human beings are in constant endeavour to reach their *Beloved* for the continuity of creation. The effort of trying to come together between the *purush* and *prakriti* is marked by deepest emotions and the highest passions. Of this Romance, Krishna is the Eternal Hero. The West has gone in raptures over its small little heroes who starting from Byron and coming down to Jackson of the present-day. These little ones had their ephemeral appearance and were soon put on the shelves of time. Krishna is the ever living, ever present Supreme Being. Nobody like him was ever there, no body like him will ever be there. The philosophy of Hinduism as enunciated in *Gita* is the reason of the undying culture called Bharat. The reasons of decay of Hindu civilization and culture have to be found somewhere else. But the thought of Ram and Krishna have always brought it back after some aberrations and its worst national disasters.

The inferences drawn by Cole in his chapter on Communal Relations in Awadh are highly illusory and misleading. Nowhere does he mention the undisturbed role of Hindus in the area of revenue and financial administration, which was the basis of the prosperity of Awadh. Nowhere does he mention the perennial existence of mutual respect. The expression *pahley aap* which is the hallmark of Lucknow was not merely an outward expression of social etiquette. It had a deeper meaning: understand and respect the views of others, before putting across your own. It was a philosophy of co-existence. For a multi racial society like we have in India, nothing else will suit more than the idiom of *pahley aap*. That is the basic *ambience of Awadh*.

State Formation

The book is basically a study of communal relations under the *nawabs* of Awadh. The evolution of Awadh as a State came through a process of consolidation of small principalities lying between Gorakhpur and Lucknow. It grew as an administrative unit without any racial or religious bias. This was a time when the new regional states were coming up in different parts of this country. These days there is a debate initiated by some eminent historians which seeks to revaluate the question of the collapse of the Mughal empire and the emergence of a variety of regional political orders in the early eighteenth century. There is a tendency to view the early eighteenth century emergence of regional polities like Awadh as the culmination of an endemic conflict between the regions and the Mughal empire. The debate has also brought out the question of specificities of state formation in the long interlude between the collapse of the Mughals and the emergence of the British regime. The developments of this period have been viewed as a phase where Indian economy and society underwent major realignments. It has also been suggested that Upper India experienced economic prosperity which provided political stability to the new regional formations! The economy was characterised by growing commercialisation of agriculture which triggered major social reconfiguration. More revenue was required both for agricultural investments and to meet the military and political threat from the Company. This led to increased revenue farming and maintenance of large armies. Both these factors became the new pivots around which regional elites sought to consolidate themselves. This argument is however applicable only to a brief period of the eighteenth century after the death of Aurangzeb. The native states went on fighting against each other. In the process they became so weak that the Company could gobble them up, or reduce them to subordination.

To write about the emergence of the regional states during this period of history will be going much beyond the scope or idea of this book, but some thoughts may be offered to bring things to a perspective.

In the country that we live in, India that is Bharat, what should be considered as 'the state'. Is it the beacon of power that is located in the centre, in and around Delhi (Indraprastha), or the breakaway groups who defy the centre and create their separate identities? The question further is whether these regional states were being created by a spurt of local economy or were part of a natural formation. Was the Mughal empire the only central rule created in India or there were precedents for it? If we do not delve deeper into the history of India, going back to the days of *Ramayana* and *Mahabharat*, let us at least begin our analysis from the days of the Mauryan empire. Every time, when an all-India figure has arisen, there has been a tendency to look inwards towards consolidation of a system and concentration of power. Whenever people of smaller stature have taken the lead, the process has been reversed, sometimes ensuring the success of the external aggression.

It will be worthwhile to quote from some recent writers of history—

> Generations of Europeans regarded the Mughals as a magnificent predatory horde. Mughal rulers seemed to be operating a vast system of plunder which frustrated the development of a landed gentry or a secure mercantile society in south Asia. The historians of Aligarh University have laboured to correct this tenacious view. As they point out, the states right to tax did not extinguish other rights over land, least of all, that of occupancy cultivation. The Mughal military elite (*Mansabdars*) had some features of classic bureaucracy.[10]

This idea has been put across, because perhaps the knowledge or information about the laws of agricultural land in India stops here. In this country the agricultural land has always been under the ownership of the state. The individuals are given only tenurial rights.

This has been there from the ancient times. The systems of control on agricultural land have varied from time to time with the various empires and the regions. The power of landed aristocracy has depended entirely on the policy of the state. The landed aristocracy has been named differently at various periods of time in history as *thakurs*, *jagirdars*, *taluqdars*, *ijaredars* or the zamindars, as may have been decided by the overall-authority of the State. It is perhaps known to the modern historians that the Revenue Law in India has been a totally non-religious law. It has always been secular. It does not recognise the personal religion of anybody. The succession to the agricultural land is decided by the ability of the person to stay closest to the land and his capacity to put it to agricultural use. That was why in Free India it was easy to abolish *zamindari* and distribute the land among the less fortunate people of the earlier period. The tradition of India had won. In Russia, the persistence of large landownership led to Revolution.

It has also not been a very correct statement that Mughal was an agrarian economy. In fact, at no time in the history of India, our economy was insular or isolated. The national economy of this country has also not been merely agrarian. It has always had large industrial and commercial sectors. From the first to the seventh century India traded with south-east Asia. After the end of the reign of Harshavardhan, two superstitions developed. One was that, if you sail across the sea, you incur *paap* (sin). The second was that if you are not born a Hindu you cannot become a Hindu. It reversed the outward and outgoing trend of this country. The first affected the trade across the seas so that the contact with the outside world became increasingly limited through the land routes. With the second decision, Hindus became a closed society. Before that time, everybody who came to India with whatever religious belief or faith had become a Hindu. Later with the advent of Islam, Indian trade went westward through the land routes. The traders carried the stories about the Indian economy from tenth to the fourteenth century to Arabia and Europe. India was known as the *Golden Bird*. When Columbus set sail from a port in Spain, he had a vision to reach India and the land he touched was named Indies. Coming back to Mughal empire, Bayly writes—'It was more like a grid of imperial towns, roads and markets which pressed heavily on society and modified it, though only at certain points. The towns came up with heavy urban population centers. The empire lasted so long as the Hindus, the majority population felt that the King could maintain their religion and the order of the caste. When the Mughal emperor could no longer fulfil this concept, the social order began to liquidate.'[11]

In Mughal times, the international trade was through land routes and sailing ships. In the eighteenth century, when the East India Company succeeded in establishing its grasp over India's foreign trade India was impoverished. Bayly acknowledges that India 'was the most populous and sophisticated of Europe's formal colonial domains'.[12] Mentally nobody in India at that time was prepared to face this situation. Smaller people could think of only smaller things. Bayly in his book further raises the question,

> What is the meaning of *raj*, kingdom to the societies of warriors and cultivators? Eighteenth and early nineteenth century Hindi genealogies and poems on the duties of kings suggest only a limited set of functions: warfare, the service of the Gods and arbitration between clansman and castes.[13]

This was what the great Hindu philosophy had come to be understood in the eighteenth century! The inter-regional relationship in a vast country like India has always engaged the attention of thinkers in India. Nagendra Singh's has very succinctly defined the real concept in his book, *Juristic Concepts of Ancient Indian Polity*,

> Moreover, a study of the ancient polity of any civilised human community cannot be in relation to a single State or built round a sole political entity. Human existence spread over a geographical area would give rise to several political-cum-social entities whether tribal, city-based, or State-wise. Once this entity-wise diversification takes place the growth of inter-unit relations becomes inevitable. The juristic concepts of *Rajya*, or State, and *Rashtra* or territory, were so well developed in ancient India that a study of Aryan polity cannot ignore the inter-tribal and later inter-Statal relationship which went to develop many juristic concepts in another field of law. This was the result of historical evolution of centuries of political relationship between *Rajyas* with their separate political heads in the form of monarchs, or presidents of republics, functioning as the veritable mouthpiece of their respective political units for the conduct of inter-State intercourse. Whenever the inter-statal relationship have been ignored there has been dissipation of organised authority.[14]

To say that after the fall of the Mughal empire there has been rise of regional 'States', is to describe the situation in a very superficial form. The Hindu philosophy of the formation of the State has been deeper and has given a lot of thought to the constitutional authority of the King or the ruler or the ruling system of the State. The philosophy has been in some ways more comprehensive than the political thinking in West. Nagendra Singh maintains:

> The constitutional organism of the sabha and the samiti as the sister institutions of the Vedic age led to the inviolability of the State and to its greatness. The concept of these two institutions which evolved and got elaborated in centuries of Indian history furnishes another achievement of the political life of ancient India which influenced the present generation to readily to accept in modern times the concept of Parliamentary Democracy and to inscribe it in the Republican Constitution of 1950 as the ultimate safeguard of the Indian citizen today. The reason being that it was the fruit of rich inheritance and hence not alien but a plant true to the soil. India could, therefore, rightly claim to be not only the largest and the most populace democracy in the world today but also one of the most ancient.[15]

To say that the regional *Satrapies* was an experiment in the State formation will mean minimisation of India as a country and as a thinking nation. Only the rise of Marathas was based on the concept of *Hindu Pad-Padshahi* as the only alternative to the Muslim kingship of India, dominating the country from the eleventh century. The fall of *peshwai* underwent the same pangs of bereavement as the fall of the Mughal empire. The idea that the rise of regional powers was an evolution of the State formation, is totally out of place with the general context of Indian history. One historian has observed that, 'the deportment of the Sipahi constituted one of the few ideological bridges between the Company and the Indian society and formed a major source of legitimacy for it'.[16] Legitimacy can never be a right word for colonial rule. Its very specific dispensation was paramountcy and imperialism. The Indians came to realise the fallacy of a foreign rule only slowly and in polities like Awadh the realisation came on the strength of its native understanding.

According to Bayly,

> Sir John Seeley in 1880 warned his audience against the chauvinistic belief that Britain had conquered India in any simple sense. The East India Company, he said, had merely taken advantage of the disturbed conditions after the end of the Mughal empire in 1707, and that was mainly by dint of the support of important groups of Indians. This change of perspective was slow in establishing itself. The history of non-European peoples was held back for a generation by the imperial bluster of the interwar years. But after 1945 Indian history was drawn along in

the train of the vast amount of scholarly writing on Asia and Africa which insisted that imperialism was created as much by events and interests in the non-European world as by the driving force of industrialization and national conflict in Europe itself.[17]

The history of Awadh during this period was a case of drifting away from the main stream and then coming back to it in 1857. Bayly maintains,

The Victorian desire for orderly administration and bigger revenues impelled them to swallow the last 'reserved dominions' of the Awadh ruler. This final annexation provided one of the main grievances fuelling the great rebellion which broke out throughout north India in the following year.[18]

Calling the events of 1857 as *The Great Rebellion* is quite an advance among the historians. It was earlier named as *Sepoy Mutiny* and then a neutral nomenclature *1857*. If the Hindu-Muslim relations are studied in their proper perspective, the real character of 1857 will be much more clearly understood as the War of Independence.

NOTES

1. J.R.I. Cole, *Roots of North Indian Shi'ism in Iran and Iraq: Religion and State in Awadh, 1722-1859*, Madras: O.U.P., 1989, p. 226.
2. Ibid.
3. Ibid.
4. See Appendix-I.
5. J.R.I. Cole, op. cit., p. 226.
6. Sayyad Athar Abbas Rizvi, *Shah Wali-Allah and His Times*, Australia, 1980, p. 227.
7. Ibid.
8. Ibid., p. 3.
9. John Pemble, *The Raj, the Indian Mutiny and the Kingdom of Avadh*, New Delhi, 1977, p. 142.
10. C.A. Bayly, *Rulers, Townsmen and Bazaars: North Indian Society in the Age of British Expansion—1770-1870*, New Delhi: O.U.P., 1983, pp. 9-10.
11. Ibid., p. 10.
12. Ibid., p. 4.
13. Ibid., p. 19.
14. Nagendra Singh, *Juristic Concepts of Ancient Indian Polity*, Delhi, 1980, pp. 6-7.
15. Ibid., p. 177.
16. Seema Alavi, *The Sepoys and the Company: Tradition and Transition in Northern India—1770-1830*, Delhi: O.U.P., 1985, p. 1.
17. C.A. Bayly, op. cit., p. 2.
18. Ibid., p. 1.

CHAPTER I

Crossing the River (1722-40)

Awadh is beyond the comprehension of any single historian. Here geography has deep roots in history because of the long interaction that has taken place between man and his environment than in most other places on this earth. For a fair understanding of human society, dual approach of history and geography becomes necessary. Since times immemorial Awadh has played a very significant role in the political, social and cultural history of India.

In the words of R.W. Bird, the Assistant Resident at the court of Awadh, during the reign of Wajid Ali Shah,

> The kingdom of Oude is situated at the root and in the heart of the Indian Peninsula. Interposed between the Ganges and the Himalayas, it comprised about 24,000 square miles. Its population is bold and war-like and furnished the best constituents of our Indian armies. Its fertility is so remarkable amongst the principalities of this prolific land that it is commonly spoken as the *Garden of India.*[1]

The *suba* of Awadh lay between 49°45' east and 84°15' east and between 26° north and 29° north. It extended for about 260 miles latitudinally, while its average width was about 150 miles.[2]

In prehistoric days 'Awadh' and 'Kosala' (the popular form of 'Ayodhya') were synonymous and these names were employed for a great kingdom whose capital was Ayodhya. In a very famous *bhajan* of Tulsi Das, Lord Ram is addressed as Kosal Chandra. In those days Ayodhya was a large, flourishing and magnificent city which according to Valmiki extended over 12 *yojana*. It was the seat of the great Kings of Surya dynasty of which the fifty-sixth emperor was Raja Dashrath, the father of legendary Ram.[3] With the fall of the last Suryavanshi ruler, Raja Sumitra (the one hundred and thirteenth monarch) Ayodhya turned into wilderness and the royal family diffused.[4] In that remote antiquity Lakshmanpuri, the present Lucknow, was a suburb of this great kingdom.[5]

In the sixth and fifth centuries BC there were sixteen kingdoms (*janapadas*) in India, Kosala being the most important. Its northern frontier was probably in the hills of present Nepal, the southern boundary was formed by the Ganges and the north-eastern boundary was the eastern limit set by the Sakya territory. The total extent of Kosala was therefore a little less than that of France today.[6] According to R.C. Majumdar,

> It was bounded by *Sadanira* (Gandak) river on the east, *Panchala* on the west the *Sarpika* or *Sandika* (Sai) river on the south and Nepal hills on the north. The country of Kosala was divided north and south, evidently by the river Sarju. Sravasti was the capital of northern Kosala and Kusawati, the capital of southern Kosala.[7]

Ṣimilar are the findings of H.C. Raychaudhuri who observed that

> the east Kosala then extended up to river Gandak separating Videha. In the west, it was bordered by the river Gomti. The three great cities of Ayodhya, Saket and Sravasti were within the province of Kosala.[8]

The city of Ayodhya was the earliest capital of the northern Kosala, which roughly corresponds to modern Awadh. Saket which is often mentioned in early literature as the capital of Kosala, is sometimes taken to be another name of Ayodhya,[9] though it is probable that the two cities were contiguous. Sravasti, on the border of Gonda and Baharaich districts was possibly the capital of this *janapada* in the age of the Buddha. But Saket seems to have been reinstated to its position soon after.[10]

The kingdom of Kosala became a paramount power after the conquest of Kashi, Shakyas of Kapilvastu in Nepal Terai, Kalamas of Keshputta (on the Gomti river) and the other neighbouring kingdoms. Its king Prasenjit, one of the most important rulers of Kosala, was a contemporary of Buddha and a rival of Magadha Kings, Bimbisara and Ajatshatru.[11] There exists scanty information about Kosala after Vidudabha who succeeded Prasenjit. The previous sixteen kingdoms were eclipsed by the rise of the Magadha empire. In the words of W. Crooke,

> Thus in Oudh, apparently, after the fall of Sravasti, a state in alliance with or subject to the Imperial Gupta Dynaṣty, the northern districts fell for a time into the hands of a tribe whom traditions call Bhars.[12]

During this time Kosala included the northern part of Awadh, that is, the trans-Ghagara region and the southern part had two divisions, that is, the western state and the eastern state.[13]

Ayodhya increased in its importance during the Gupta period and probably it was the second capital of Gupta emperors during AD 330 to 472. In the seventh century Awadh was a part of Harshavardhan's empire and in the ninth century it was included within the dominion of Gurjara-Pratiharas.[14]

Malik Hasam-ud-din-ugul Bak, a commander of Muizuddin of Ghor conquered Awadh in AD 1192.[15] Thereafter it remained an integral part of the Sultanate. For a brief spell (1399-1479), it was a part of the Shirqui kingdom of Jaunpur, but again came under Delhi during the period of Lodi dynasty. When Babur defeated Ibrahim Lodi (1526), Awadh became a part of Mughal empire.[16] *Babarnama* mentions that Awadh and Baharaich were in the occupation of Babur who appointed Shaikh Bijid in Awadh. Again, Ayodhya was the seat of provincial administration.[17]

The complete absorption of Awadh was delayed till Akbar became the ruler. It became a *suba* when Akbar organised his empire in 12 *subas* in 1580.[18] Before him the Hindu *rajas* had remained much more free and undisturbed. As such Awadh played a prominent role in the political, cultural and economic spheres of Mughal empire. Due to its strategic location and rich agricultural potential this *suba* had a privileged position. The province of Awadh during the Mughal period was of considerable size. The limits of the province roughly were the Himalayas in the north, Bihar in the east, Manikpur (in the province of Allahabad) in the south and Kannauj in the west. The length of the province was about 270 miles and the breadth was about 230 miles. The province was unevenly divided into five *sarkars* or districts: Haveli Awadh (Faizabad), Gorakhpur, Baharaich, Lucknow and Khairabad.[19] Since the rivers traverse the region from west to east, the administrative units had been usually so shaped that they had a greater lateral extension as compared to their longitudinal expanse.[20]

The northern boundary ran along the foot of Himalayas.[21] It is interesting to note that the boundaries of Akbar's empire ran much further north in this section than the boundaries of modern India. A study of the extent of some of the northern *mahals* would make this point clear.

(i) The *mahals* of Tilpur and Binayakpur were the southern extensions of Butwal territory. Their history began in the fourteenth century with the establishment of the Chauhan principality of Butwal. Binayakpur, in fact, takes its name from a village now in Nepal. A considerable portion of this territory (lying between the present Indian frontiers and the foot of the hills) was handed over to Nepal after 1857.[22]
(ii) The *mahal* of Bahrah originally comprised 142 villages in Nepalese territory, which were ceded to the British by the treaty of Sigauli in 1816 and made over to the Awadh rulers, under whom they were held by the *raja* of Tulsipur as the Banki *ilaqa* until 1860 when they were restored to Nepal.[23]
(iii) Rajhat, which now lies almost entirely in Nepal, was ceded to the British in 1816 and held by the *raja* of Tulsipur till 1860, when it was restored to Nepal.[24]
(iv) Sujhauli included the Padampur Mahalwara estate of 72 villages, which was restored to Nepal in 1860.[25]
(v) Sultanpur included 21 villages, which in 1816 belonged to the *raja* of Saliana and were subsequently held by the *raja* of Tulsipur, until 1860 when they were restored to Nepal.[26]

This shows that Akbar's empire extended up to the foot of Himalayas, and that the northern boundary in this sector was decided by the physical features.

It should, however, be noted here that the political, administrative and fiscal control exercised by the imperial authorities on the northern submontane tracts situated near the foothills was probably quite weak. The *suba* was bounded in the east by the main channel of Gandak.[27] The southern boundary up to the Naipur and Anhonah *mahals* of *sarkar* Awadh skirted the turbulent Ghagara.[28] From this point westwards, it had a zigzag course till it met the Ganga in the Deorakh *mahal* of *sarkar* Lakhnau. It is of interest to note that the boundary of *suba* Awadh does not follow any significant physical feature in this sector only. This may perhaps be explained by the fact that this portion of Ganga-Ghagara Doab, unlike the forested trans-Ghagara tract, was highly developed politically, culturally and economically by the standards of those times. During the period of the Delhi Sultanate, three centres seem to have grown in this region—

Jaunpur, Ayodhya and Kara. Political boundaries thus tended to follow the boundaries of the areas of influence of these three centres.[29] Physical factors were relegated to the background. Historical and perhaps ethnic factors played the decisive role in the determination of boundaries. This was also partly due to the fact that there was no effective physical barrier in the Ganga-Ghagara Doab, the Gomti and the Sai being, from the physical point of view, insignificant streams, as compared to their neighbours, the Ganga and the Ghagara.

The south-western boundary of *suba* Awadh ran along the Ganga from Deorakh *mahal* of *sarkar* Lakhnau in the south-east to *mahal* Khankhat Mau of *sarkar* Khairabad in the north-west. The north-western sector of the boundary of *suba* Awadh lay in thickly forested tracts and joined the north-western tip of *mahal* Khairgarh of *sarkar* Khairabad, situated at in the foot of the hills, with *mahal* Khankhat Mau on the Ganges.[30]

Shahjahan (1627-58) reorganised the empire and divided it into four large regions—Hindostan (northern India), Dakhin (southern India), eastern Hindostan (eastern India) and north-west India, with ten, six, five, and one *subas* respectively.[31] Awadh was in eastern Hindostan and was subdivided into five *sarkars*: Haveli Khas, Khairabad, Baharaich, Gorakhpur and Lakhnau. These five *sarkars* had 119 *mahals*.[32] The extent of the *suba* on its east was *suba* Bihar, on the west was Kannauj—a *sarkar* of *suba* Akbarabad (Agra) of the Hindostan region; it extended in the south up to Manikpur (in Allahabad) and on the north, it was bounded by the Himalayas. From 'Gorakhpore' to Kannauj, it was 260 miles and from the mountains in the north to Handia (in Allahabad) it was 230 miles.[33] From the Mughal period up to the rise of *nawabi* rule the boundaries of the *suba* remained almost the same.[34]

Death of Aurangzeb and Break-up of Empire

In the year 1707 Aurangzeb died. After his death, the political unity of the Mughal empire came under great pressure. Among the Mughal emperors he was perhaps the ablest as a politician and an administrator. As a statesman he was a total failure. He destroyed the vision of Akbar, who had realised that India was a *crucible of cultures* and mutual respect and tolerance was the right policy for this country. Aurangzeb wanted to provide domination to Sunni

Islam and created a situation in which the innate forces of historical diversities of this country came out into the open. Aurangzeb had ruled an empire which was vast powerful and strong and his fiat ran through the empire. The *subedars* were changed and transferred on merit or administrative convenience. Nobody thought of hereditary *subedari.* Shivaji had died in the year 1680 and his newly created kingdom had been taken over by the Mughals. Guru Gobind Singh carried on his fight against Aurangzeb but later made peace with Bahadur Shah (1707-12). The Rajput kingdoms were totally subjugated and were loyal officers of the state. But the idea of domination of a single creed, viz. Islam, had left the fires simmering and burning. At the ripe age of 80 years Aurangzeb died leaving behind him aged and infirm princes as his successors. His Will, dividing the empire into three parts did not find favour with his three sons. They fought against one another and Muazzam ascended the throne under the title of *Shah Alam Bahadur Shah.* But the treasury in Delhi was empty and intrigues were galore. To add to the misfortune, Sayyad Brothers took over the role of king-makers. From 1708 to 1719, five emperors made their ephemeral appearance and disappeared. In 1719 Roshan Akhtar ascended the throne as emperor Mohammad Shah. The new emperor did not pay obeisance to the Sayyad Brothers and found among the court of Mughal emperor a band of loyal supporters. It took him two years to do away with the Sayyad Brothers the so-called king-makers. But the Mughal nobility had plunged into terminal disability and the empire was breaking into pieces.

The *subedars* of Bengal, Hyderabad and Awadh were inching away from the Mughal court and were setting up independent kingdoms. They were all appointees of the Mughal emperors and were also bound by the bonds of religion. But they took advantage of the weakness of Mughal court and slowly assumed independence. In Bengal, Murshid Quli Khan was first appointed *diwan* of Bengal by Aurangzeb in 1700. In 1713 he became Bengal's *naib-subedar.* In 1717, he was made the *subedar.* His successors assumed the style of hereditary *subedars* and the *masnad* of Bengal passed from one to the other with only a perfunctory nod from the Mughal emperor. In the south, the *suba* of Deccan became independent under Chin Qilich Khan, popularly known as Nizam-ul-mulk. He was once called to fight the Sayyad Brothers in 1722. After his victory he found the atmosphere so vitiated in the Mughal court that he returned to the south. In 1724 he defeated and killed the Mughal General Mubariz Khan who was sent to subjugate him in the battle of Rohankheda. Thereafter the Mughal emperor was obliged to recognise him as the *subedar* of Deccan and conferred upon him the title of Asaf Jah. The *subedari* of the Deccan had become hereditary. Saadat Khan having failed as the *subedar* of Agra in controlling the Jats was transferred to Awadh in 1722. While crossing the Gomti at a point beyond Gau Ghat a fish jumped into his lap as a rare gesture of welcome. When he crossed Gomti, a new kingdom had been created and the fish—a pair of them arched against each other forming a semicircle became the insignia of the new kingdom. But Awadh remained closely linked with the politics of the court of Delhi.

The Rajputs, Jats and Sikhs who were brought under subjugation at one time or another started raising their heads. They were never an integral part of the Mughal empire or its ethos. The Rajputs assumed independence in their respective fiefs in Rajputana. Sikhs became dominant in Panjab right up to the north-west frontier. The Jats did the same in and around Delhi, Agra, Kol (Aligarh), Hathras, Rohtak, Rewari and Gurgaon. The area of actual control of Mughal emperor was thus reduced considerably.

RISE OF MARATHAS

The Rajputs, the Jats and the Sikhs were merely throwing away the yoke of subordination to the Mughal throne. But the real challenge came from the Marathas. Shivaji had raised the banner of revolt and had set up an independent kingdom for himself. After his death his territory was taken over by Aurangzeb by superior arms and administration. On the death of Aurangzeb, the Marathas renewed their war of independence. In 1713, Sahuji Maharaj was released by the Mughals and became the successor of Shivaji. After some initial internal struggle Sahuji came out successful and was accepted as their ruler by the Marathas. In 1713, Sahuji appointed Balaji Vishwanath as his Peshwa—a Chithpawan Brahmin from Konkan. Later he came to hold the supreme power among the Marathas. In 1714, Balaji Vishwanath came to terms with the Mughal emperor. The main terms of the agreement were as follows:

1. Sahuji was to get back all the territories conquered by Shivaji in his life time. In addition Marathas were granted Khandesh, Gondwana, Berar and some districts of Hyderabad and Karnatak.
2. The Marathas were assigned the *chauth* (25 per cent of revenue) and the *sardesh-mukhi* (10 per cent of revenue) of the *subas* of Deccan.
3. The Marathas accepted the over lordship of the Mughal emperor. Although this went against the ideal of absolute independence of Shivaji, the Marathas became co-partners of Imperial administration. It gave them a dignity and prestige which was a new experience for them. When Marathas came to Delhi in 1719 as allies of Hussein Ali to destroy the ascendancy of the anti-Sayyad party at the Delhi court, they added a very significant chapter to their history.

Balaji Vishwanath was succeeded by Baji Rao as *peshwa*—the brightest star of the Maratha history. He promulgated the idea of Hindu *Pad-Padshahi* or the Hindu empire. This was the first challenge in the modern history of India to the idea of Muslim monopoly as a symbol of India's supreme kingship. After Baji Rao defeated Nizam-ul-Mulk in 1739, in the battle of Baroda, Marathas became the supreme power in the country and had acquired an undisputed authority even in the northern and western India. The Nizam was left to nourish his constituents in the south. In the same year Baji Rao entered into a treaty of friendship with Sawai Maharaj Jai Singh II of Amer and also with Chhatrasal Bundela. Baji Rao also conquered Salsette and Bassein from the Portuguese. When he died a premature death in 1740 Marathas had an undisputed sway from the Panjab to the south of Krishna in Mysore.

Baji Rao I also decided to set up semi-independent principalities in Berar, Baroda, Gwalior, Indore and Dharwar under the Bhonsles, Gaikwads, Scindhias, Holkars and Pawars. These principalities ultimately challenged the power of the Peshwa and led to the decay of the Maratha empire. But during the time when the Peshwa was in full command, these principalities gave a lot of native strength to the overall Maratha power. Baji Rao I was succeeded by Balaji Baji Rao. He made two changes in the overall setup. One, the ideal of Hindu *Pad-Padshahi* was diluted and the army became a composite force. Mercenaries found their way into the various formations of the Maratha fighting forces. Arcot, Srirangapattnam and Mysore came under the sphere of influence of the Marathas. He also suppressed the Angres—sea captains on the western coast of India—with the help of the English. The only resistance to the Maratha expansionism during this time came from Haider Ali of Mysore and the Nizam of Hyderabad under the able guidance of the French General Bussy.

The period from 1722-40 saw the steady decline of the Mughals. Although Mohammad Shah lived to rule until 1748, he became a placid ruler lingering on the periphery of events. The administration of Panjab and north-west had became weak and invited the covetous ingress from the Persian and then Afghan marauders. The Mughal nobility was divided between Hindustani, Turani and Irani parties. They had lost the idea of any mission, and were constantly trying to seek favours and petty advantages to themselves. Even occasions of external aggression, they were trying to utilise for their selfish ends. At this time the most devastating blow to the Mughal throne came from Nadir Shah.

Sayyad Brothers and the Emergence of Saadat Khan

Mir Muhammad Amin, better known in history by his title Saadat Khan, belonged to a celebrated Sayyad family of Najaf. His ancestors had served the Safavid dynasty of Iran for more than two centuries.[35] He was born in about 1680.[36] Nothing is known about his early life and education; but to his military exploits and other accomplishments in India glowing tributes were paid by contemporary authorities;[37] and these clearly suggest that his education and training were zealously looked after.[38]

Mir Mohammad Amin came to India in 1708-9, to meet his father and brother who had migrated earlier. His father died before his arrival. He and his brother went towards Delhi to get some position.[39] He got a job in 1710 with Sarbuland Khan, who was then *faujdar* of Kara-Manikpur and later became the Governor of Gujarat. He served him for more than two years and then left his services after quarreling with him.[40] Soon thereafter he became commander of some forces in the Walashahi regiment with the *mansab* of *yak-hazari* (commander of 1000 horses) due to the patronage of an Irani named Muhammad Jafar *alias* Ganj Ali Khan, who was *karori* of Ganj.[41] Some time later, he became the *naib* of his new patron[42] and served on this post for about three and a half years.

In the meantime, the Sayyad Brothers, Abdulla Khan and Hussein Ali Khan, gained complete ascendancy at the Mughal court. Mir Muhammad Amin who had managed to reach the Mughal court impressed them with his talents, and was able to secure the *faujdari* of Hindaun and Bayana on 6 October 1719.[43] His new assignment was further rewarded with an elevation of his rank to 1500 *zat*.[44]

The real test of his courage and cunning came when the Mughal court became embroiled in various conspiracies and counter-conspiracies in dealing with the Sayyad Brothers—the king-makers.[45] Mir Muhammad Amin had a well-trained and well-equipped body of troops with him. The possession of a bevy of forces was an essential requirement of the nobles during those days. It helped them to extract money from wherever they could lay their hands on and also to show their power in dealing with the Mughal court. The Conspiracy against Sayyad Brothers provided a test of his mental capacity to seize the right opportunity at the right time. The series of events started with the rebellion of Nizam-ul-mulk in the Deccan.[46] The emperor Muhammad Shah himself led the forces and moved southwards. Hussain Ali Khan, one of the Sayyad Brothers accompanied the emperor on this mission. They camped at Bahadurpur, about four miles north of Hindaun. Mir Muhammad Amin joined them, paraded his fully accoutred and disciplined retinue before Hussain Ali Khan, who was impressed with their performance and granted his request to let him accompany the emperor and his forces. The Sayyad Brothers had made enemies at the court and during the march to the Deccan a conspiracy was hatched by some nobles to eliminate Hussain Ali Khan. The Emperor himself became a party to it. Despite the patronage granted by the Sayyad Brothers to him, Muhammad Amin joined this conspiracy. The plot was executed between Juind and Buind, about 75 miles to the south-west of Agra and Hussain Ali Khan was murdered. The followers of the Sayyad Brothers offered tough resistance but Mohammad Amin displayed exemplary bravery and soon wiped them out. The Emperor raised his rank to 5000 *zat* and 3000 *savars* and also gave him the title of Saadat Khan Bahadur.[47]

After the above event the expedition to the south was quite naturally given up and the emperor and his party marched towards Delhi to deal with Abdulla Khan, the other Sayyad Brother. Muhammad Amin persuaded the emperor to raise him to the rank of 6000 *zat* and 5000 *savars*. He was also appointed *subedar* of Akbarabad (Agra) and *faujdar* of the *parganas* under its jurisdiction.[48] He immediately sent Neelkanth Nagar as his Deputy to the new assignment and himself accompanied the emperor in the fight against the other Sayyad Brother (Abdulla Khan). The two armies fought at Hassanpur, about nine miles to the north-west of Hodal (Haryana State). Mir Muhammad Amin fought valiantly and defeated the forces of Abdulla Khan, who was captured and later killed. As a reward, the emperor conferred the title of Bahadur Jang on Mir Muhammad Amin and the insignia of *mahib martib* (fish insignia) on him.[49] On 12 January 1721, he was made *darogha-i-khawasan* (Superintendent of Personal Attendants) with a *khilat* and a jewelled *sarpech* and was allowed to go to Agra towards the end of February.[50]

The province of Akbarabad (Agra) was in chaos and confusion. The Jat zamindars in the area of Agra and Mathura were in league with the clansmen of the Jats of Bharatpur. They were all in rebellion against the Mughals. Saadat Khan subdued them after a vigorous campaign. Meanwhile he was called to Delhi to deal with Ajit Singh of Marwar, who was also the Governor of Ajmer and Gujarat. Ajit Singh had close relations with Sayyad Brothers and he did not like the way they had been eliminated. Mir Muhammad Amin was asked to deal with him. He made a request for money and war equipment, but the jealousy of the court nobles came in the way of his getting full patronage from the wavering emperor. It was the quality of the man that he knew when he would succeed and when he was likely to fail. So he withdrew from taking the chance of a conflict with Ajit Singh and returned to Akbarabad. Meanwhile his *naib* Neelkanth Nagar was surprised by a force of Jats and was killed.[51] Saadat Khan carried out systematic warfare against the rebels for about six months, but could find no answer to the guerrilla tactics of his adversaries and failed in his mission. The emperor shifted him from Akbarabad and appointed him the *subedar* of Awadh and *faujdar* of Gorakhpur[52] on 9 September 1722.[53] The history of modern Awadh starts on that day.

SAADAT KHAN COMES TO AWADH

On the eve of Saadat Khan's appointment to Awadh, it was a simmering volcano of numerous big and petty chiefs and zamindars, who were semi-independent in their jurisdictions. They did not pay the revenue unless compelled to do so and indulged in highway robberies to such an extent that even the roads in the vicinity of Lucknow were not safe.[54] Some of these notable chiefs and zamindars were Mohan Singh, *raja* of Tiloi, in the Rae-Bareli district; the *raja* of Bansi, Rasulpur and Binayakpur in Basti; Chhatradhari Singh Sombansi, *raja* of Partapgarh; Chet Rai Bais of Baiswara; *raja* Dutta Singh of Gonda; and *raja* Narain Singh of Balrampur in the Gonda district.[55]

Lucknow and its adjoining areas were then under the control of the Shaikhzadas of Bijnor, who had reportedly got it as *jagir* from emperor Akbar and had held it since then. They had built a cluster of palaces called *panchmehla* and a fort on the bank of river Gomti. This fortified complex was built by Lakhna—one of the Shaikhzadas. One legend has it that the name Lucknow is derived from Lakhna. On the gate of the palace a naked sword was hung as a symbol of their power. They had such an influence in the area that every incoming Governor had to bow before it to avoid trouble from the Shaikhzadas. Another branch of these Shaikhzadas resided at Kakori, near Lucknow. They were always at daggers drawn with their counterparts in Lucknow.[56]

From Agra, Saadat Khan proceeded to Awadh and, on his way, halted at Farrukhabad. The ruler of Farrukhabad advised him to befriend the Shaikhzadas of Kakori and seek their help. He did the same and suddenly crossed the river Gomti at night much beyond Lucknow and camped near Kakori. After full preparation, he attacked the Shaikhzadas at Lucknow in a surprise move. The hanging sword was cut off. The Shaikhzadas, surprisingly, submitted after a very feeble resistance and vacated the *panchmehla* for the new *subedar*. The sudden, but comparatively easy, capitulation of the Shaikhzadas of Lucknow, had a profound effect on the whole of Awadh and it prompted other *rajas* and zamindars to offer their allegiance and submission to Saadat Khan. But some of them remained intransigent.[57]

In 1724 Saadat Khan engaged Mohan Singh Kanhpuria, *raja* of Tiloi (district Rai-Bareli) in battle and inflicted a crushing defeat on him. Mohan Singh was killed. Saadat Khan then proceeded to Awadh (Ayodhya) and made the ancient town the seat of his government. It brought back the territories of the Ayodhya district to its original fold. He pitched his tents on a high hill overlooking the banks of the river Ghagara far away from any inhabitation. Saadat Khan had no desire for spacious residences and so houses with unbaked bricks were built for his entourage to live in. When he was not touring, the ruler of Awadh lived in peace in his mud bungalows. In common parlance this abode came to be known as the *bangala*.

Saadat Khan Burhan-ul-Mulk

The above-mentioned actions of Saadat Khan enhanced the revenues of his *suba* considerably. Pleased with this the Mughal emperor conferred on him the title of Burhan-ul-mulk.[58]

Saadat Khan was also worried about the marriage of his daughter, Sadrunnisa. After some family confabulations, she was married to Mirza Muhammad Muqim, the son of his eldest sister, in 1724. Mirza Muhammad Muqim, who later received the title of Safdar Jang, was thereafter appointed *naib-subedar* (deputy Governor) of Awadh.[59]

In 1725, Saadat Khan gave his attention to Basti and Gorakhpur districts, where Tilak Sen of Tilakpur (Gorakhpur district) was resorting to plunder and loot. It went on till Safdar Jang occupied the *masnad* of Awadh when some semblance of peace and respectability was restored in the area after a protracted display of force.[60]

Another refractory clan of the Rajputs were the Bais of Baiswara. Saadat Khan marched with a massive force and select artillery against them. Much to his surprise, all the *rajas* and land-owners meekly surrendered and agreed to pay double the previous assessment of revenue. During the course of this expedition, Saadat Khan also defeated and subjugated the *rajas* of Tiloi and Amethi.[61]

Raja Narain Singh of Balrampur in Gonda district headed a large and powerful chiefdom and was semi-independent. Saadat Khan marched against him also and made him pay the revenues after he was routed in two hotly contested battles. However, his successors did not like this subordination and it always required a show of arms to make them pay up.[62] Prolonged warfare had to be resorted to against *raja* Dutta Singh of Gonda until both the contenders got tired and Dutta Singh agreed to pay a fixed tribute, which was accepted by Saadat Khan.[63]

Some historians have observed that many nobles, who had their *jagirs* in and around Awadh and were not able to get their dues because of the turbulence of the zamindars leased them out to Saadat Khan.[64] A very interesting example was the case of Mir Murtaza Khan, a noble of Delhi. He had Benares, Jaunpur, Ghazipur, Chunargarh, Azamgarh, Ballia and the eastern areas of Mirzapur as a *jagir* from the Mughal court. The *jagir* was managed by his relative, Rustam Ali Khan, on the condition that he would pay him five lakh rupees annually and retain the rest of the revenues. But Rustam Ali was unable to keep the trouble-making zamindars in check or to make them pay their dues. Impressed with the achievements of Saadat Khan in Awadh, Murtaza Khan leased these territories to him for an annual sum of seven lakh rupees in 1728. Saadat Khan handed them back to Rustam Ali on the condition that he would pay him an annual sum of 8 lakh of rupees.[65] It transpired that the very mention of the name of Saadat Khan created such an awe in the minds of the trouble makers that, except one, all agreed to honour their commitments. The exception was Mahabat Khan, a hereditary *raja* of Azamgarh, who continued to evade payments as usual. This led to the invasion of Azamgarh by Saadat Khan with a massive force. It brought Mahabat Khan to his senses and he offered to pay the dues. But Saadat Khan wanted to set an example and sent him to jail and installed his son, Iradat Khan, in his place.[66]

In 1729, Saadat Khan marched against Sachendi—twelve miles to the south-west of Kanpur, which was the stronghold of Hindu Singh, who was ravaging the territories of Awadh. By a stratagem, Saadat Khan and the *raja* of Bhadawar took over his fort. Hindu Singh made a bold attempt to retake it; but in vain. In sheer disgust he fled to Chhatrasal Bundela and thus the western frontier of Awadh was pushed up as far as Kannauj.[67]

Similarly Bhagwant Singh was also a rebellious zamindar of Ghazipur and Asothar in *sarkar* Kara Jahanabad, *suba* Allahabad. He was also occasionally seeking help from Marathas.[68] In 1735, when Saadat Khan was made *faujdar* of Kara Jahanabad, in addition to his *subedari* of Awadh, he organised a campaign to bring him under discipline. He marched with a force of 40,000 and a large park of artillery towards Kara, which he reached on 6 November

1735. Bhagwant Singh fought valiantly but was killed in action. Roop Singh, son of Bhagwant Singh, fled to Bundelkhand and tried to enlist the support of the Marathas and the Bundelas. In the beginning, they showed an inclination to help, but when Saadat Khan marched again towards Kara Jahanabad in February 1736, they changed their mind and refrained from interfering. Thereafter, the area remained under the peaceful possession of Saadat Khan.[69]

After the treaty of 1714, the Marathas began to extend their control over most parts of north India under the spirited leadership of Peshwa Baji Rao. The Marathas wanted to wrest Gujarat, Malwa and Bundelkhand from the hands of the Mughals. The nobles of Delhi were divided on the issue of checking their onslaught. Khan-e-Dauran and Jai Singh of Jaipur were in favour of reconciliation, but Saadat Khan, Qamaruddin, Muhammad Khan Bangash, Zafat Khan Turra-i-Baz, Sarbuland Khan, and Abhay Singh of Jodhpur advocated resistance.

There were so many currents and cross-currents that no concrete steps could be taken against the Marathas in an organised manner. The Mughal emperor was weak and indecisive. Saadat had taken the field against the Marathas once at Jalesar (in Firozabad district) in Doab and even chastised them. In retaliation Baji Rao suddenly appeared in Delhi and then moved towards Rajputana.[70] At this point Saadat Khan proposed that the *subedari* of Agra, Gujarat, Malwa and Ajmer be granted to him to enable him to drive the Marathas out of northern India; but Khan-e-Dauran and Jai Singh opposed his plan and even accused him of being responsible for the sudden dash of Baji Rao to Delhi. Emperor Muhammad Shah concurred with their views and hence the proposal of Saadat Khan was turned down. Disgusted with this situation, he returned to Awadh.[71] A.L. Srivastava has rightly remarked:

> It may be admitted that Saadat Khan and his friends did not realize the magnitude of the danger and dreamt the impossible dream of effectually stopping the Maratha expansion northwards . . . yet, there is little doubt that had Saadat Khan been given supreme command and had he been fully backed by Muhammad Shah and all the resources of the empire, Baji Rao would have been obliged to lower his ever-increasing demands.[72]

While Saadat Khan was still in Delhi, about 20 Rajput chiefs leagued together under Kewal Singh of Tiloi and rebelled. On hearing about it, Saadat Khan commissioned his son-in-law Abu-ul-Mansur Khan with a force of 12,000 horse and a strong park of artillery, to open a vigorous campaign against Tiloi. While he was getting ready, the confederates began to amass their forces at Amethi, so he at once turned his attention towards Amethi and defeated them after a siege of 16 days.[73]

The narrative of the military exploits of Saadat Khan in the area of Awadh is impressive. He was the maker of modern Awadh. He subdued and subjugated all the refractory *rajas* and landlords from Lucknow to Gorakhpur and Allahabad. All the clan leaders from Unnao, Amethi, Gonda, Balrampur and Kara paid obeisance to him. Awadh had been organised as a well run *suba*. He confronted the powerful Marathas at the peak of their power and came out as an equal in the conflict. Ayodhya was the seat of his government and his succession was decided well in time. Safdar Jang was to succeed him and was appointed *naib* in his lifetime. The policy of Saadat Khan towards the Rajput principalities was one of reconciliation but keeping the upper hand himself. He did not change any hereditary ruler; he merely subjugated them. The stream of local traditions continued unabated and slowly an understanding percolated down among the masses that a new master had come who provided them safety and security and protection of their native customs and religious faith. There were no conversions. He sought help of all native officers and the local population and laid the foundation of communal harmony.

Saadat Khan and Nadir Shah

The intrigues in the Mughal court continued to engage Saadat Khan's attention and enforced his repeated presence in Delhi. Nothing came out of the internecine conflicts of selfish court parties and the attitudes and policies towards the Marathas remained indecisive and lowered the prestige of the Mughal court. It weakened the defence of the north-west frontier, from where a scourge came in the form of Nadir Shah which destroyed the power and prestige of the Mughal court for all time to come. Saadat Khan was drawn into the vortex of these agonising developments.

The Safavid dynasty of Iran was destroyed by the Afghans in 1722. Nadir, a Persian free-booter, suddenly rose to power, cleared the Afghans from Persia and crowned himself the Shah of Iran in 1736. He then launched aggression against the Afghans of Qandhar, who began to flee to India. Nadir Shah repeatedly asked Muhammad Shah to check the inflow of the Afghans into his territories but to no avail. Annoyed with it, Nadir Shah burst in on northern India. After capturing Lahore on 21 January 1739, he advanced towards Delhi. Alarmed, Muhammad Shah and the nobles of Delhi, including Nizam-ul-mulk, *wakil-i-mutlaq*; Qamaruddin Khan, *wazir*, and Khan-e-Dauran, *mir-bakhshi*, marched forward and encamped at Karnal with their 75,000 men.

Summons were issued to Saadat Khan to join the emperor in the field of battle. He left Awadh in the third week of January 1739 with 30,000 horses, a strong artillery and huge stores. He joined the imperial army in the night of 22 February.

In the meantime, Nadir Shah had also advanced to about six miles from the camp of Muhammad Shah. As soon as he came to know about the approach of Saadat Khan, he sent a detachment to surprise him; but it missed him narrowly. Nadir Shah's forces took possession of some parts of the baggage train of Saadat Khan after killing some troops and herding away 500 camels.

In the morning of 23 February, a Council of War was held in the camp of Muhammad Shah and it was proposed that the attack on the Persian army should be delivered two days later. But Saadat Khan opened his attack without full preparation, on the Persian army on that very day as a hasty retaliation for the attack on his detachments. He was helped by Khan-e-Duaran, but the Khan was wounded in the ensuing battle. Saadat Khan was captured alive and was presented before Nadir Shah. He told Nadir Shah that the skirmishes so far were only from the army of just one noble and that there was a very large army in tow to help the Mughal emperor. Nadir Shah agreed to go back on payment of an indemnity of 55,00,000 rupees. Meanwhile Khan-e-Duaran died and the Nizam persuaded the emperor in the war camp itself to make him the *mir-bakhshi*—a post which Saadat Khan had cherished. When he saw his ambition dashed, he had it conveyed to Nadir Shah that a march to Delhi could easily get him two crore rupees and a lot of jewellery. Nadir Shah marched to Delhi. The rest is well-known history, the plunder of the Kohinoor and *takht-e-taus* (the Peacock Throne).

When leaders of state surrender national objectives to selfish ends such things must happen.

Saadat Khan had thought that by his act of inviting Nadir Shah to Delhi he would be able to score a victory against his adversaries. But after the massacre in Delhi, when Saadat Khan failed to redeem his promise, he was rudely insulted by Nadir Shah. In the night of 19 March 1739, Saadat Khan retired to his house and died before dawn.[74] The cause of his death has remained a moot question. He either died of shock or committed suicide. Either way the end was inglorious. He may not have realised then, but the invitation to Nadir Shah to come to Delhi was an act of national treachery which India will never forget or forgive. But that cost him his life and also rightly his reputation.

An Assessment of Saadat Khan

Saadat Khan was a man of an age, when self-interest dominated everything else. Yet he was capable of undertaking actions unmindful of his personal safety. He commanded his forces well and was able to turn the tables on his adversaries. His subjugation of the refractory princes in Awadh was more in the nature of small, unorganised engagements. Where he really showed his mettle was against the Marathas whom he repulsed in the battle of Jalesar in Doab. In the battle of Karnal against Nadir Shah his were the only detachments which gave the marauder a taste of Mughal armies, their training and techniques. But he had seen the vicissitudes of politics in the Mughal court and was adept at changing sides at the right moment. He was like the proverbial weather-cock in politics. Some historians have described him as a regular turn-coat—a remark which is uncharitable. Survival was the name of the game and the country was passing through a period where its leading lights had lost the sense of a national mission. On Awadh, his services had a lasting impact. He was the first generation noble in the Mughal court who had found his way up the ladder by his merit. He had laid the foundations of modern Awadh brick by brick. The struggle for *wizarat* at the Mughal court came only in the time of his successors. His success in Awadh was the success of the Mughal arms under his command. He was far too busy with the politics of the Mughal court to be able to devote time to the administration of Awadh. But he succeeded in creating an awesome atmosphere which made the collection of revenues easy and automatic. Prior to him, the native stream of history lay scattered and segmented in various small and insignificant principalities. Although they were associated with legend and history of this country for the longest period of time, it is ironic that a foreigner—Saadat Khan was responsible for bringing them together as part of an organised administration. It is also ironic that Awadh which got reassociated with the Mughal court under Saadat Khan broke away from the Mughal court to find its own niche in history at a later date. Saadat Khan Bahadur Burhan-ul-Mulk justified the titles conferred on him and gave to Awadh what it needed most at that time: a brave leader (Saadat Khan) and good administrator (Burhan-ul-Mulk). From this time the foundations of a new state of Awadh were laid which was more secular than many regimes in the rest of the country.

NOTES

1. R.W. Bird, *Dacoitee in Excelsis, or The Spoilation of Oude by the East India Company*, Allahabad, 1924, p. 1.
2. Moonis Raza, 'Delimiting Suba Awadh—1550-1605: A Study in Historical Geography', *The Avadh Geographer*, Vol. I, 1975, Lucknow, p. 3.
3. R.S. Dixit, 'Avadh: An Historico Geographical Analysis', *The Avadh Geographer*, Vol. I, 1975, Lucknow, p. 3.
4. *Imperial Gazetteer: Uttar Pradesh, Faizabad*, 1905, p. 13.
5. *Census Report Oudh: Allahabad*, Vol. I, 1869.
6. E.J. Rapson, *The Cambridge History of India*, Vol. I, Delhi, 1955, pp. 158-9.
7. R.C. Majumdar, *History and Culture of Indian People*, Bombay, 1968, p. 1.
8. H.C. Roy Chowdhury, *Political History of India*, Calcutta, 1972, pp. 88-9.
9. *Imperial Gazetteer: Uttar Pradesh, Faizabad*, 1905, p. 34.
10. T. Chand, *The Administration of Oudh*, London, Vol. I, 1971, p. 24.
11. R.S. Dixit, op. cit., p. 8.
12. W. Crooke, *North Western Frontier Provinces of India*, Varanasi, 1971, p. 75.
13. Ibid., p. 76.
14. R.S. Dixit, op. cit., pp. 10-11.
15. Ibid., p. 11.
16. H.C. Roy Chowdhury, op. cit., pp. 91-2.
17. Ibid., pp. 92-3.
18. A. Bhattacharya, *A Dictionary of Indian History*, Calcutta, 1967, pp. 67-74.
19. H.S. Jarrat and Sir J. Sarkar (tr.), *Ain-i-Akbari*, Calcutta, 1942, 2nd edn., Vol. II, pp. 181-5.
20. Moonis Raza, op. cit., pp. 3-4.
21. Ibid., p. 4.

22. *District Gazetteer: Gorakhpur*, pp. 216-17.
23. Ibid., *Baharaich*, p. 125; see also Beams, *Oudh*, p. 223.
24. Ibid.
25. Ibid.
26. Bahlol Lodi (AD 1450-88) is stated to have pushed the frontiers of his empire up to the foot of the Himalayas. The zamindars of these territories did owe allegiance to the emperor. But the terrain was such that Imperial interference would have been restricted to occasional tribute collecting expeditions. As far as Tilpur-Binayakpur territories are concerned, even as late as the days of the East India Company, they were 'wholly covered with forests and little attempt was made to demarcate the boundaries of Tilpur and Binayakpur *parganans*, wherein the Company authority was little more than nominal.'—*District Gazetteer: Gorakhpur*, p. 139.
27. Since the boundary line, separating Gorakhpur from Saran, ran through thickly forested tracts, it may be safely assumed that it was indefinite in character—a broad north-west-south-east zone rather than a definite line. Scholars are not agreed on the extent of *suba* Avadh to the east. The controversy relates to the extent of obscure twin *mahals*—Devapara and Kotla. C.A. Elliot asserts that this is Devapar Kohana, the old name of Salempur-Majholi, Shahjahanpur and Sidhua Johna, which were parts of great Majholi Raj. In some old writings the *mahal* is entered as Navapar Kohana Devapar. (C.A. Elliot, *North Western Frontier Policy*, p. 120). He further says that 'I have seen it somewhere mentioned that Salempur-Majholi, Sidhua Johna and Shahjahanpur were in Saran but this statement seems to rest on no authority.'—C.A. Elliot, op. cit., n.y., p. 121. Beams says that Devapar Kotla 'covered all the east of the Gorakhpur district.'—(Beams, *Oudh*, p. 221) that is, Salempur-Majholi, Sidhua Johna and Shahjahanpur. Nevil agrees with the above view (*District Gazetteer: Gorakhpur*, Table X). But in another place (*District Gazetteer: Gorakhpur*, p. 179) contradicts himself and says 'It represented the country beyond Deva or Ghagara, corresponding to modern Salempur-Majholi.' The latter view seems to be correct for Sidhua Johna and Shahjahanpur were transferred as one *parganah* from Saran to Gorakhpur as late as 1743 (*District Gazetteer: Gorakhpur*, p. 178). This is, however, not true of Salempur-Majholi which was and continues to be a part of Gorakhpur. In the light of this evidence it is safe to presume that during Akbar's reign the eastern portion of the present Gorakhpur was divided as follows:
    Parganah Salempur-Majholi—*mahals* Devapar Kohna,
    Sarkar Gorakhpur, *suba* Avadh.
    Parganah Sidhua Johna and Shahjahanpur—*mahal* Juwainah, *sarkar* Saran, *suba* Bihar.
    As has been shown later, Gandak flowed in the channel of the little Gandak, which today separates Sidhua Johna from the rest of Gorakhpur.
28. Changes in the course of the Ghagara, especially along the present Gorakhpur-Azamgarh boundary are frequent. For example, in 1876 the Ghagara broke into the Chhoti Azamgarh and scoured out a bed far into Sagri (*District Gazetteer: Azamgarh*, p. 232). It is therefore very difficult to establish the

actual boundary of *suba* Awadh in this sector comparing the measured area of the *mahals* Sagri and Gopalpur of *sarkar* Jaunpur and of *mahal* Daryaparh of *sarkar* Gorakhpur, the writer is inclined to believe that during Akbar's reign, the latter extended further south than the present Ghagara bed and therefore concludes that the Ghagara had broken into the Chhoti Sarju during the period 1550-1605, as it did in 1876.

29. Moonis Raza, op. cit., pp. 4-5.
30. Ibid., pp. 7-8.
31. W.H. Sleeman, *Journey Through the Kingdom of Oudh*, Vol. I, London, 1858, p. 22.
32. Ibid., p. 26.
33. W. Hoey, *Memoirs of Delhi & Fyzabad*, Vol. I, Allahabad, 1888, p. 25.
34. R.S. Dixit, op. cit., p. 1.
35. Ghulam Ali, *Imad-us-Saadat*, Lucknow, 1897, pp. 5,30; Kamal-ud-di Haider, *Salatin-i-Awadh*, Lucknow, 1879, pp. 19-20.
36. A.L. Srivastava, op. cit., Agra, 1954, p. 2.
37. Murtaza Hussein, *Hadiqat-ul-Aqalim*, Lucknow, p. 385; Ghulam Ali, *Imad-us-Saadat*, Lucknow, 1897, p. 5; Ghulam Hussain Khan, *Sier-ul-Muntakhirin*, Lucknow, n.y., p. 475.
38. Ghulam Ali makes such a claim—op. cit., 1897, p. 5.
39. Ibid.
40. Murtaza Hussein, op. cit., p. 383; Shah Nawaz Khan, *Maasir-ul-Umara*, Persian Text, Asiatic Society of Bengal, Vol. III, p. 802; A.L. Srivastava, *The First two Nawabs of Awadh*, Agra, 1954, p. 6-8.
41. Ghulam Hussain Khan, op. cit., Vol. II, p. 483; Khafi Khan, *Muntakhab-ul-Lubab*, Persian Text, Asiatic Society of Bengal, Vol. II, p. 902.
42. Shah Nawaz Khan, op. cit., Vol. I, p. 463.
43. Kunwar Khan, *Tarikh-i-Chaghtai*, Amir MS Amir-ud-Daulah, Public Library, Lucknow.
44. Khafi Khan, *Muntakhab-ul-Lubab*, Persian Text, Asiatic Society of Bengal, Vol. II, p. 902.
45. Kunwar Khan, op. cit.
46. A.L. Srivastava, op. cit., p. 13.
47. Kunwar Khan, op. cit.; Khafi Khan, op. cit., Vol. II, pp. 906-8; Murtaza Hussein, op. cit., p. 134; A.L. Srivastava, op. cit., p. 13-20.
48. Kunwar Khan, op. cit.
49. Ghulam Hussain Khan, op. cit., p. 443.
50. A.L. Srivastava, op. cit., pp. 26-7.
51. Khafi Khan, op. cit., Vol. II, pp. 944-5.
52. A.L. Srivastava, op. cit., p. 29.
53. R.C. Majumdar, H.C. Roy Chowdhuri & K.K. Dutta, *An Advance History of India*, London, 1963, p. 57.
54. Bhupat Rai, Insha-i-Roshan, MS Tagore Library, Lucknow: Lucknow University, pp. 2-21; C.A. Eilliot, *The Chronicles of Oonao*, Allahabad, 1862, pp. 107-8, 123.
55. A.L. Srivastava, op. cit., p. 31.

56. Ibid., pp. 34-7.
57. Ibid., pp. 36-9.
58. Ghulam Ali, op. cit., p. 8.
59. Ibid., pp. 8-9.
60. *District Gazetteer: Gorakhpur*, p. 182; *District Gazetteer: Basti*, p. 153.
61. C.A. Eilliot, op. cit., pp. 68, 73-4.
62. *District Gazetteer: Gonda*, pp. 78-9.
63. Ghulam Ali, op. cit., p. 23.
64. Khairuddin (tr.), *Bulwuntnamah*, Allahabad, 1875, pp. 2, 8.
65. Ibid.
66. *District Gazetteer: Azamgarh*, p. 171.
67. Eilliot & Dawson, *The History of India As Told By Its Own Historian*, Allahabad, 1964, Vol. VIII, pp. 46-7.
68. A.L. Srivastava, op. cit., pp. 44-6.
69. Ghulam Hussain Khan, op. cit., p. 468.
70. A.L. Srivastava, op. cit., p. 55.
71. Shamsulla, Tarikh-i-Hind, Urdu MS 12046, Allahabad: Regional Archives, p. 35; *Selections From Peshwa Daftar*, Vol. XV, pp. 29, 39, 47.
72. A.L. Srivastava, op. cit., p. 55.
73. Ibid., p. 56.
74. Ibid., p. 70.

CHAPTER II

The Suicidal Wars (1740-75)

Decline of the Mughal Court

The period between 1740 and 1775 was the turning point of modern Indian history. Nadir Shah had come, shocked Delhi and sapped the strength of the Mughal empire beyond repair. The territories of once great Mughal empire were reduced to the peripheries of Delhi. Later the Afghans tasted blood and made four invasions into northern India. But the resistance came from the Sikhs and then Marathas. The Afghans under the leadership of Ahmad Shah Abdali fought indecisive battles against the Sikhs and was frustrated by the brave opposition put up by them at different places at different times. Ahmad Shah Abdali finally made his way to Delhi and the town was plundered once again in January 1757, reminiscent of Nadir Shah's invasion. Imad-ul-mulk, the *wazir*, surrendered and a formal secession of Kashmir, Sindh and Sirhind districts was obtained from the Mughal emperor. After ransacking some more areas in and around Delhi, Abdali went back in April 1757 with immense booty. He appointed Najib-ud-daula as his supreme agent in Delhi to oversee the working of the Mughal court. In Lahore he appointed his son Timur Shah as his Viceroy. After some time the Marathas came and conquered Panjab, occupied Lahore and expelled the Afghans. The collision between Afghans and Marathas had become inevitable. Both were contending for the supremacy in Hindustan. Between 1758 and 1759 Ahmad Shah Abdali defeated Marathas in various battles and propagated the idea of Hindu-Muslim conflict, getting the support of the Ruhela Afghans and even Shuja-ud-daula, the *nawab* of Awadh. Najib-ud-daula, who was earlier pushed out of Delhi by the Marathas, naturally joined forces with Ahmad Shah Abdali at the battlefield of Panipat in 1761. The Marathas failed to elicit support of Rajput chiefs and even Suraj Mal, the Jat king.

The failure had more to do with the objectives and attitude of the Marathas and a total lack of any sense of national mission. The battle of Panipat in 1761 was hotly contested and was a disaster to the Marathas. Although the Marathas re-grouped soon thereafter, the idea of a Hindu king as a symbol of India had been lost for almost a century and a half thereafter. In 1857, when the forces of Indian nationalism rose against the British imperialism, it was again the upholstered Mughal emperor who was setup as a symbol of the Indian nation. Only in the beginning of the twentieth century, when Lokmanya Tilak proclaimed 'Freedom is my birthright and I will have it', a genuine national consciousness including Hindu rulership could said to have arisen in India.

England as World Power

Far away on the island of Britain, England and Scotland came together by an act of Parliament in 1707. Together they consecrated, formed and adopted the name of Great Britain. Between 1701 and 1713, the wars of Marlborough had ushered England on to the path of primacy on the continent of Europe. The Treaty of Utrecht in 1713 set a seal on the success of the British arms. The ambition of Louis XIV had been thwarted. The union of France and Spain had been prevented. France had finally recognised the claim of Mary and William as the Queen and King of England. England obtained the confirmation of its claims on the colonies in the East, America and Latin America. Great Britain became the supreme naval power in the world. The thrust and turbulence on the history of India in the eighteenth century came floating on the big sail-ships of England bugling their way on the waves of the Atlantic, Cape of Good Hope and the Indian Ocean.

In the beginning of the eighteenth century, England had become a country which had sorted out its internal struggle between King and Parliament. With the Glorious Revolution (1688), Parliament became supreme and held the purse-strings. Nationalism became the main factor behind policy formulation. The seeds of the party system had been sown and were growing into fruition and maturity. Whigs were the masters for more than 50 years after the Revolution of 1688. Walpole had assumed the name and functions of the Prime Minister of England in 1721 during the reign of George II.

The war of Austrian succession was brought to a close by the Treaty of Aix-la-Chapelle in 1748, giving England considerable concessions. The war between England and France had extended to India. The French Governor of Pondicherry, Dupleix, forcibly occupied Madras but was forced to give it back to the British by the above treaty.

Origin and Growth of East India Company

Early in the sixteenth century the world trade through the sea routes had been divided between Spain and Portugal by a Papal decree. In the last decade of the fifteenth century, there was a spurt of long and well organised sea voyages under the patronage of the kings of Spain and Portugal. In 1488, the Portuguese sailor Bartholomew Diaz sailed up to the Cape of Good Hope. In 1497, Vasco da Gama set sail from Portugal, and rounding the Cape of Good Hope, reached Calicut, in India in 1498. On the other side, under the patronage of the Spanish royal couple—Isabella and Ferdinand, Columbus started his famous voyage in 1492 towards west, which led to the discovery of the New World.

The sea voyages continued. Magellan, a Portuguese sailor reached the southern tip of South America, conquered the waves of the Pacific Ocean and reached Philippines. Magellan died in Philippines and is buried there. The fleet of ships which accompanied Magellan managed to reach Portugal, crossing Indian Ocean and Cape of Good Hope. This was the first circum-navigation of earth. All hitherto unknown continents were now discovered and our earth became one entity. Between 1500 to 1600, the entire sea trade was dominated by Spain and Portugal which was later joined by Dutch, French and English fleets.

The reign of Elizabeth-I (1558 to 1603) was an age of constant rivalry between England and Spain. In 1588 the defeat of Spanish Armada by the English established an equal status for the English Navy. In 1600 the Queen granted a charter to a Society under the title of 'the Governor and Company of Merchants of London trading into the East Indies'. The charter was renewed at regular intervals. But every time, the Kings and later Parliament sought or extracted more financial benefits from the Company as a share of the spoils in the trade with the east. Over a period of time the East India Company lost interest in the trade with the Spice Islands controlled by the Dutch, and began to give increasingly more attention to its trace with India. James I sent Sir Thomas Roe as the King's Ambassador in Jehangir's time. At this time first regular trade links were established between England and India. Shahjahan was not happily disposed towards the Portuguese and so he gave more concessions to the English traders. By the beginning of the eighteenth century, Portuguese rivalry had been over come. English factories have been established at Surat, Madras and Calcutta. Bombay was a territorial acquisition for the East India Company, having been acquired by purchase from King Charles II. Charles had got it in dowry from Portugal.

East India Company as Total Eastern Trade of England

East India Company held the monopoly trade with the east. London had become the financial capital of the world. Ordinary shareholders of the East India Company were reaping the profits of its monopoly. A fortuitous circumstance gave East India Company added advantage. In 1720, a treaty with Spain, opened the English trade with Spain. The business suddenly grew up like a bubble and like a bubble it burst. The episode is known as the *South Sea Bubble.* Thereafter the East India Company became the sole arbiter of the total external trade of England in the East. East India Company contributed a substantial amount in the equity base of the Bank of England, established in 1694. The coffers of British treasury was full and it supported the wars on the continent of Europe. Slowly and surreptitiously, Great Britain took over the naval strength of Holland and Belgium. British Navy became the most powerful instrument of the financial prosperity of England. They were controlling the slave trade with American and Latin American countries. This England united, organised and prosperous came to India on the strength of its ambition and its team power. India was broken, divided and unsure of its place in history.

Anglo-French Rivalry in India

On the Indian sub-continent during 1740-60, the most important series of events was the struggle between the English and the French.

English factories had been set up in Bombay, Surat, Madras and Calcutta. French factories were set up in Pondicherry and Chandernagore to rival Madras and Calcutta. The conflicts of succession between the various claimants to the throne of Arcot brought the English and French armies face to face. In 1751, Clive defeated the French forces and the challenge of French in India, all but vanished. Clive went back to England in triumph, rich and respected. Dupleix was recalled to France in disgrace. Later during the Seven-Years War (1756-63), England and France again confronted each other in India. This time it was the English who conquered Pondicherry. In 1760, in the battle of Wandiwash, Sir Eyre Coote conclusively defeated the French forces. French influence as an independent entity disappeared for ever. On the conclusion of the Seven-Years War, the Treaty of Paris (1763) gave Pondicherry back to the French in India but without any right to fortification. French had only a symbolic presence thereafter. Their officers kept on helping the Indian kings and princes like the fire-flies, sprinkling spots of light sometimes here, sometimes there. But the domination of Indian sub-continent passed into the hands of the British.

East India Company as a Political Power in India: Plassey and Buxar

The East India Company was gaining supremacy in Bengal because of the internal conflicts between the *nawabs* and the pretenders. In 1757, Clive defeated in a brief skirmish at Plassey the forces of Siraj-ud-daula, the *nawab* of Bengal. The battle of Plassey was fought more by treachery than by the force of arms. Mir Jafar who was commander-in-chief of the forces of *nawab* deserted him at the crucial moment and joined the English forces. As a reward of his treachery, Mir Jafar was made the *nawab* of Bengal. The ignominy of this act has remained an abominable chapter of Indian history. Soon thereafter, events led to another confrontation where the combined forces of the Mughal emperor Shah Alam, the *nawab* of Awadh and the ex-*nawab* of Bengal fought against the armies of the East India Company in Buxar in 1764 and were defeated by the superior British arms and strategy. In India during the eighteenth century the courtiers of the Mughal empire or anybody else had little time to think about the preparations of war. The British had learnt a lot by their experiences in the various theatres of war in Europe. It was perhaps only the Marathas who had acquired the resources and had the opportunities to update their knowledge and expertise in waging a war and winning it. Among the Indians they were the most powerful having repeatedly defeated the *nizam* of Hyderabad. But the decline of the Marathas left the British arms without a challenge. They acquired supremacy and command of the whole of this country at the end of the second Maratha War (1803-5).

The British Parliament took its role seriously after the battle of Buxar and the Treaty of Allahabad (1765), by which the *diwani* of Bengal, Bihar and Orissa had been granted by the Mughal emperor to the East India Company. The East India Company had acquired a certain semblance of territorial sovereignty. By the Regulating Act of 1773, the overall control of the Indian dominions in Calcutta, Madras and Bombay was given to the upgraded Governor of Calcutta who was rechristened as Governor-General. Warren Hastings made the most of it. Pitts' India Act of 1784 completed the process of organisation of command and administration.

Safdarjang and Awadh

Let us now return to Awadh. After the death of Saadat Khan in Delhi, Abu-ul-Mansur Khan was granted the *subedari* of Awadh in 1740, on payment of two crores of rupees to Nadir Shah. Accordingly, a contingent of Persians came to Awadh under the direction of Nadir Shah with robes of *subedari* for Mansur Khan. Soon after the departure of Nadir Shah from Delhi, emperor Muhammad Shah conferred the title of Safdar Jang on Abu-ul-Mansur Khan and confirmed his appointment to Awadh. A tactful handling of the situation by his *vakil* Lakshmi Narayan also helped in getting this appointment for Safdar Jang. He renamed the original site of *Bangla* as Faizababad about seven miles from Ayodhya.

In 1724, when he was married to Sadrunnisa Begum, Abu-ul-Mansur Khan was sixteen-year-old. He was brought up by Saadat Khan's second sister after the death of his mother. A study of the Persian letters written by him and preserved in the Tagore Library of Lucknow University, reveals that he had a complete command of the Persian language. His civil and military training commenced when he began to serve as Deputy Governor of Awadh from 1724 onwards. He soon acquired such practical knowledge of the state affairs that Saadat Khan had no hesitation in leaving the entire civil and military administration of Awadh in his hands during the last years of his life. He fought in all the wars with his father-in-law. In 1737 he was sent independently to help the besieged *nizam* at Bhopal; but Holkar intercepted him on the way and he had to retreat. In 1738, he marched to Jaunpur and defeated *raja* Balwant Singh of Benares. The *raja* was allowed to retain the zamindari of Mirzapur and Benares on an assured payment of thirteen lakh rupees to the State of Awadh. Ghazipur was given to one Shaikh Abdulla for three lakh rupees. He was enriched by these experiences in the art of negotiations with various chiefs and groups, which were part of Awadh conglomeration at that time.

Control of Awadh

The news of the death of Saadat Khan encouraged the refractory elements to raise their heads again. Nusratullah and Farhatullah, zamindars of Amethi Bandagi, were soon joined by the zamindars of Hasanpur, Tiloi, Garh Amethi and the Afghans of Jagdishpur. All of them took the field together. In the beginning, Safdar Jang hesitated a bit, but with encouragement from his wife, Sadri Jahan Begum, marched against the rebel forces, who were all dispersed within a short time. The *begum* proved great asset for him in later life also. Soon after *raja* of Tiloi re-assembled a strong force in his fort. Safdar Jang again marched against him. The forces of Tiloi could not withstand the artillery and better disciplined Mughal soldiers of Safdar Jang and lost the battle. After enforcing a complete surrender and obligation to pay revenues, Safdar Jang left the *raja* in possession of his territories and returned to Faizabad. Once again, *raja* Newal Singh Gaur, zamindar of Nabi Nagar and Katesar, refused to pay revenues. Safdar Jang besieged the forts in March 1741 and forced him to surrender. By a later agreement he was allowed to retain his territories on surety of regular payment of dues.

In Ruhelkhand, the involvement of Safdar Jang came about in a very circuitous manner. In Moradabad and Chandausi, an Afghan upstart—Ali Mohamad Khan—fought cleverly and valiantly and brought the entire Ruhelkhand area under his command and even extended influence into Kumaun region. Ultimately the forces of the Mughal emperor were obliged to take the field and defeated Ali Mohamad Khan. All his forts and property were confiscated. To keep him away from Ruhelkhand, he was sent as *faujdar* of Sirhind in Panjab. Safdar Jang took an active part in these battles in Ruhelkhand and made his presence felt in the corridors of power in the Mughal court.

Like Awadh, hereditary succession to the *suba* of Bengal, Bihar and Orissa had passed on to Alivardi Khan in 1740. In 1742, Bhaskar Pant, commander-in-chief of Raghoji Bhonsle of Nagpur, invaded Bengal at the instigation of some disgruntled officers of Alivardi Khan. Alivardi Khan sought the help of the Mughal emperor, Muhammad Shah, who directed Safdar Jang to march to his aid. The politics of the country was in bad shape all over. Like the courtiers of the Mughal emperor, the Marathas were also internally divided and the various *sardars* were extending their respective areas of influence and collecting *chauth*. When Bhaskar Pant went to Bengal, the Peshwa sent his forces against him. The Maratha attack on Bengal lost its vigour, but in the name of helping Alivardi Khan, Safdar Jang obtained the grant of Chunar and Rohtas forts from the Mughal emperor, which he and his son retained till the East India Company took them away in 1772. This was the first movement of Safdar Jang outside the *suba* of Awadh with his forces. In future also he was destined to play an important role in the affairs of the declining Mughal empire.

The Mughal court was full of intrigues between the Irani and Turani nobles. The emperor was also playing one group against the other. As an encouragement to the Irani nobles Safdar Jang was appointed *mir atish* on 21 March 1744, his duty being to protect the emperor and his family. He took his position in the fort of Delhi and organised its defences in a very skillful manner. Safdar Jang gained further ascendancy at the Mughal court when the marriage of his son Jalal-ud-din Haidar (the later Shuja-ul-daula) took place in 1745 with great pomp and show with Ummat-uz-zohra (popularly known as Bahu Begam), sister of Najm-ud-daula and adopted daughter of emperor Muhammad Shah. Safdar Jang won so much confidence and favour of the emperor that even the critical diplomatic relations with the Marathas began to be carried out through him

Raids of Ahmad Shah Abdali

Nadir Shah, after he occupied Qandhar, in 1738 had enrolled a brilliant young man Ahmad Khan, an Afghan of Abdali clan, on his personal staff. Ahmad Khan soon rose to be a commandant of the Abdali regiment. Impressed with his services, Nadir Shah conferred on him the office of the *bakshi* or the treasury officer. He became a great favourite of Nadir Shah and was considered to be his foremost lieutenant. After the murder of Nadir Shah in June 1747 in Persia, he fled to Qandhar, where the Afghans elected him their leader. Later he proclaimed himself king. He renamed his tribe as Durrani, himself assumed the tile of *Durr-i-Durran* (the Pearl of Pearls). He soon occupied the entire Afghanistan and extended his rule as far as Peshawar.

Safdar Jang as *Nawab-Wazir*

In 1748 Ahmad Shah Durrani made repeated attempts to seize Lahore and Panjab, but was defeated by the Mughals under the overall command of Prince Ahmad. Safdar Jang played an important role in this series of battles. As chance would have it, emperor Mohammad Shah died at this point of time on the night of 25 April 1748, in Delhi. The news reached Prince Ahmad at Panipat on 28 April, where Safdar Jang was camping with him. Safdar Jang advised Prince Ahmad to proclaim himself the emperor immediately. The advice was promptly accepted and the ceremony took place under a make-shift canopy on the battlefield. Safdar Jang was promised *wizarat*. The office of the *wazir* was formally conferred on Safdar Jang on 29 June 1748, after the death of the *nizam* on 31 May 1748. Safdar Jang was also given a *mansab* of 8,000 *zat* and 8,000 *sawar* and the title of 'Jumdat-ul-mulk Madar-ul-Muham Wazir-ul-Mamalik Burhan-ul-mulk Abu-ul-Mansur Khan Safdar Jang Sipahsalar', and appointed superintendent of the private chamber of the emperor. On 16 July, he was made the governor of Ajmer and *faujdar* of Narnaul, and his son Jalal-ud-din Haidar was given the title of Shuja-ud-daula Bahadur and made *mir atish*. Safdar Jang exchanged the *suba* of Ajmer with Allahabad. The *subas* of Awadh and Allahabad were consolidated and so was the power and influence of Safdar Jang.

The *wizarat* was not a bed of roses for Safdar Jang. The prestige of the Mughal emperor was sinking and the territories of the empire were fast breaking away. Bengal, Bihar and Orissa under Alivardi Khan, and Farrukhabad under the Bangash Afghans, owed merely a nominal allegiance to the Mughal emperor. Ruhelkhand had again passed into the hands of Ali Muhammad Khan and his successors. Suraj Mal of Bharatpur had established his sway over a major portion of Agra province and some parts of the province of Delhi as far north as Faridabad. Rajputana, including Ajmer, was under the Rajputs. The Marathas had wrested Bundelkhand and Malwa from the empire and had established their authority in Gujarat. The raids of Bhonsle of Nagpur on Bengal had led to the loss of the annual flow of the revenues to the Mughal emperor from there. Ahmad Shah Durrani was again hovering on the boundaries of Panjab.

Regardless of all the dangers, the Mughal court was full of intrigues. The *nizam* of Hyderabad had not forgotten that he was cheated out of his customary appointment as the *wazir* and the efforts were on to edge out Safdar Jang. But he held on. The uninterrupted squabbles between Turani and Irani nobles greatly weakened the defences of the north-west frontier and Panjab and encouraged repeated invasions of Ahmad Shah Abdali. In 1749, Chahar Mahal (Sialkot, Aurangabad, Pasrur and Gujarat) were ceded to him on the behest of Safdar Jang, more to weaken his rival court party.

Safdar Jang and Ruhelas

Safdar Jang considered the Ruhela Afghans as 'serpents infesting his road to Delhi'. Between 1750 and 1752 he was involved in a very intense warfare with the Ruhelas. In one of the battles, Newal Rai, the *naib-subedar* of Awadh, was killed. Safdar Jang made furious preparations for war but again lost miserably in the battle of Ram Chatauni in 1752. This battle nearly cost him his *wizarat* but he survived with the help of the Irani party at the Mughal court. He again waged a series of the battles against the Ruhelas with the help of Marathas. Having contained them he made peace with them in the same year. Safdar Jang then turned his attention back to Awadh. The *rajas* of Benares and Pratapgarh were brought under his discipline once again.

Between 1752 and 1754 the Mughal court was involved in an intensely suicidal war. The emperor had appointed Safdar Jang as *wazir* to strengthen the Irani party. But Turanis under the leadership of Imad-ul-mulk kept up their pressure. Both sides sought or bought help at different times from the Marathas, Jats, Rajputs and Ruhelas. There was even a long drawn fight in and around Delhi, in which the leading lights were Safdar Jang on the one side and Imad-ul-Mulk on the other. Ultimately Imad-ul-Mulk came out victorious and replaced Safdar Jang as the *wazir*. Emperor Ahmad Shah was taken captive, blinded and deposed. He was replaced by Prince Aziz-ud-din as Alamgir II. However, Safdar Jang was able to retain his *subedari* with the help of Intizam-ud-daula the *mir atish*. On his return journey to Awadh, he died a broken man at Paparghat in Sultanpur district on 5 October 1754. He was succeeded by his only son Shuja-ud-daula.

SHUJA-UD-DAULA (1754-75)

Shuja-ud-daula succeeded his father Safdar Jang as the *subedar* of Awadh without a dispute. He remained the *subedar* of Awadh from 1754 to 1775, a period of about twenty-one years. This was the most momentous period in the history of the *nawabs* of Awadh. This was also a time, when the three streams of history—the decaying Mughals, the ravaging Englishmen and the native strength of the people of this area came into a complex interplay. Mirza Jalal-ud-din Shuja-ud-daula,[1] the only son of Safdar Jang, was the third in the family to succeed as *subedar*. By now, the *subedari* of Awadh had come to be regarded as hereditary. He raised the Awadh dynasty's military power and political role in the affairs of the country to a great height. He inherited courage, ambition and cleverness from his grandfather and father, and diligence and tenacity of purpose from his mother. He was strong and extremely handsome according to the descriptions of contemporary writers, Company officials and travellers.[2] Steeped in the traditions of his father, Shuja-ud-daula immediately stepped in to take over Safdar Jang's place in Awadh and in the empire.

Shuja-ud-daula had a strong influence of his mother, Sadri Jahan Begum, on his personality. Sadri Jahan was an outstanding lady and was known for her piety, culture, family devotion and sense of justice. Along with all these qualities, she was endowed with a degree of courage wholly unusual among women of her time and may have put many men of her day to shame.[3] Har Charan, a contemporary of the *begum*, writes about her generous disposition. She aided the needy with discretion.[4]

A very interesting account about Sadri Jahan's strictness and disapproval of the irresponsible act of the young prince is mentioned in *Seir-ul-Muntakhirin*.[5] It so happened that one night, the young prince was caught red-handed trying to climb into the room of a young girl for whom he had taken fancy. Later, the matter was reported to the *kotwal* by the girl's guardians. The *kotwal* not knowing what to do with his noble prisoner, approached the *nawab*. Safdar Jang ordered that he should be put behind the bars. At this juncture, Shuja-ud-daula appealed to his mother for intervention. But as a strict and disciplined person, Sadri Jahan, paid no heed to her son's request. The prince was forced to remain in prison for a week.[6]

Soon after his accession to the *masnad* and feeling free from his mother's surveillance. Shuja-ud-daula indulged in a certain degree of moral laxity as was the wont for the people in his position at that time. Attracted by the charms of an 18-year-old Khatri girl at Ayodhya, he forcibly abducted her one night. In this act, he was assisted by the Naga brothers—Umrao Giri and Himmat Bahadur. The repercussions of this incident assumed very wide proportions. Some Mughal officers decided to invite Muhammad Quli Khan from Allahabad to occupy the *masnad* and banish the *nawab* to a distant *jagir*. Hence a crisis loomed large on the family of Saadat Khan. At this point, Sadri Jahan Begum came to the rescue of Shuja-ud-daula. She called *raja* Ram Narayan and expressed surprise that the high officials of the state were creating such an ado over an insignificant 'unclean' Hindu. She appealed to their sense of loyalty to their late master and his heir. Her words had the desired effect on the *diwan*, who promised to take care of the matter. He advised her to speak to Ismail Beg and other Mughal officers to pacify them. She invited them all and warned them of the consequences of their evil designs.[7] The nobles made an abject surrender before the *begum* and withdrew their opposition to the young *nawab*. This time Bahu Begum's stand was very different from what she did to Shuja-ud-daula in his younger days. The lady knew when to do what!

The vision of Bahu Begum was not confined to Awadh. She kept a watch on the events and movements in adjoining areas. It is reported that she helped Chait Singh of Benares. The evidence and depositions undertaken by Sir Eliziah Impey, in connection with the rebellion of Chait Singh, revealed that all the *khwaja-sera* who were said to have defied the English armies belonged to Bahu Begum.[8] That may have been the reason for the very cruel and even unethical behaviour of Warren Hastings towards the *begums* of Awadh. On the other hand, some historians say that such charges were only trumped up against the *begum* for ulterior motives.

Shuja-ud-daula ascended the *masnad* on 6 October 1754, at Faizabad. His mother, a very intelligent lady, announced the death of Safdar Jang only after the accession of Shuja-ud-daula had taken place. Safdar Jang, it may be recalled, had died en route from Delhi at Paparghat in Sultanpur district. His body was brought to Faizabad. It was later buried in Delhi in his famous mausoleum. Ismail Khan Kabuli was appointed the *naib* of the new *nawab*. Ram Narayan, eldest son of Atmaram, was appointed his *diwan*. His younger brother Maha Narayan was appointed an advisor.

When Shuja-ud-daula sat on the *masnad*, Awadh was going through a very difficult time. The Mughal throne was still the most important factor in determining the rulership of Awadh. Safdar Jang had barely managed to retain his *subedari*, but his *wizarat* had already been taken away. Imad-ul-mulk, son of Nizam-ul-mulk, had taken over as *wazir* and had become almost a dictator. In June 1754 he had deposed emperor Ahmad Shah from the Mughal throne and made Alamgir the puppet emperor. Shuja-ud-daula had to protect himself from Delhi as well as the Ruhelas and Bangash Afghans on the west of Awadh. Very diplomatically, he sought peace with the Ruhela chief, Saad-ul-lah Khan, and proclaimed with a lot of fanfare a lasting friendship with him. He kept it till it suited his convenience. Towards the end of his career as *nawab-wazir*, Shuja-ud-daula invaded the Ruhela territory with the help of the East India Company and subjugated the Ruhelas.

In 1752, the Mughal emperor Ahmad Shah bought peace with Ahmad Shah Abdali by ceding the provinces of Panjab, Sindh and Multan to him. Abdali had appointed Mir Mannu as the *subedar* of Panjab. After Imad-ul-mulk had become all-powerful in Delhi, he reclaimed Panjab from the successor of Mir Mannu. Abdali swooped on Delhi in 1757. Imad-ul-mulk submitted to his prowess and made peace with him. Abdali remained in Delhi for a brief period. During his stay and with his help Imad-ul-mulk planned to checkmate his two main enemies, Suraj Mal and Shuja-ud-daula. One army was sent to Agra and Bharatpur, where it plundered the entire area and collected a lot of booty. In the second move, Imad-ud-mulk sent the two princes Hidayat Baksh and Mirza Baba towards Awadh. Hidayat Baksh was invested with the *subedari* of Bihar and Bengal, and Mirza Baba with that of Awadh. Shuja-ud-daula sought the intercession of Ruhela *sardar* Saad-ul-lah Khan and ultimately peace was concluded between the *nawab* of Awadh and the *wazir* of the Mughal court. Shuja-ud-daula came back to Lucknow and adopted this town the seat of his government. When Abdali decided to leave Delhi, emperor Alamgir met him and complained to him about the behaviour of Imad-ul-mulk. Abdali appointed Najib-ud-daula as *mir-bakshi* to protect the person of the emperor. The emperor gave away the administration of Delhi and the area around it to Najib-ud-daula. Najib-ud-daula was an upstart and rather than protecting the person and the family of the emperor he himself started on a course of extreme disrespect to the emperor. Imad-ul-mulk again took over Delhi with the help of the Marathas in August 1757 and banished Najib-ud-daula. The Marathas were in control of Delhi once again, but Imad-ud-mulk came into his element once again. He wanted to take custody of Prince Ali Gauhar, but the young man proved smart and escaped to Awadh, where he was received by Shuja-ud-daula. From that point of time started the fateful friendship between Shuja-ud-daula and Ali Gauhar, who later became the Mughal emperor and fought in the battle of Buxar with him.

In 1758, Shuja-ud-daula had to deal with *raja* Balwant Singh of Benares. During the time when Shuja-ud-daula was busy protecting his western front, the *raja* of Benares had conquered the forts of Vijaygarh, Angori and Lateefpur. He was preparing to take over the fort of Chunar also. When Shuja-ud-daula marched towards Benares, Balwant Singh meekly sought his pardon. It was granted to him on an increased payment of five lakhs of rupees towards the revenues of the state.

Meanwhile Imad-ul-mulk was not sitting quiet in Delhi. He wanted to punish Najib-ud-daula and with the help of the Marathas mounted an attack on him. Najib-ud-daula sought the help of Saad-ul-lah Khan, the Ruhela chieftain. Saad-ul-lah Khan invited Shuja-ud-daula for help. The combined forces of the Afghans and the *nawab* of Awadh faced the armies of the Mughals and Marathas, but the rains intervened, and the two parties disengaged and there was a temporary peace.

Imad-ul-mulk persisted with his intrigues. The new emperor Alamgir got so frustrated with him that he secretly helped Najib-ud-daula and also invited Ahmad Shah Abdali. Abdali once again moved towards Delhi with his armies. Imad-ul-mulk sensing the involvement of the emperor in this invitation to Abdali, had him killed him in a most horrendous manner. On the fateful day, the emperor went to a *darvesh* in Ferozshah Koṭla. The *darvesh* in reality was an Uzbeg conspirator. The old and infirm person of Alamgir fell an easy prey. His head was chopped off and the headless body of the Emperor lay unattended on the ground outside till it was removed on the orders of the *wazir*. He also got the *mir-bakshi* of the Mughal court—Intazam-ud-daula killed one day before this ugly incident. A weak royal family member, the grandson of Aurangzeb's son Kaam Baksh was placed on the throne with the title 'Shah Jahan II'.

Next, Imad-ul-mulk went after Najib-ud-daula with the help of the Maratha army under Dattaji Scindhia and laid siege against him in Shukratal area of Saharanpur. The allies, however, retreated towards Delhi on receipt of news of the impending invasion of Ahmad Shah Abdali.

When Prince Ali Gauhar came to know about the murder of his father, he proclaimed himself emperor under the title of 'Shah Alam' at Nazimabad (Bihar). Shuja-ud-daula was appointed *wazir*, since he was constantly helping him. The *wizarat* of the Mughal court which had been taken away from Safdar Jang by the emperor Ahmad Shah after the abortive battle in 1753 was regained by Shuja-ud-daula from an emperor who was far away from Delhi and was almost under the tutelage of the *nawab* himself.

In 1759, when Ahmad Shah Abdali proceeded towards India for his last invasion, the Mughal throne in Delhi was under a puppet occupant. The court was under Imad-ul-mulk and the Marathas were his allies. Shuja-ud-daula had retreated to Awadh. Ahmad Shah Abdali skirted around Panjab and joined the forces of Ruhela and Bangash Afghans at Kunjpura in Haryana in the first week of December 1759. In January 1760, he entered Delhi and on the advice of Najib-ud-daula, dethroned Shah Jahan II. The Ruhelas and Abdali troops plundered the city of Delhi for three days. The Mughal throne remained vacant since Shah Alam was away in the east. The Mughal court was put under the command of various Afghan chieftains, one after the other, at the pleasure of Ahmad Shah Abdali. Between January and October 1760, the Afghans and Marathas fought many battles from Doab to the plains of Haryana. A large Maratha army proceeded towards north under the command of Sadashiv Bhau, a veteran commander. The Peshwa's son Vishwasji Rao also accompanied the great Maratha army. The rival armies occupied the great plain of Panipat in October 1760.

It was surprising that Shuja-ud-daula joined Ahmad Shah Abdali in the battle of Panipat. It was barely 18 months earlier in June 1758, that the confederate armies of the Afghans and the Mughals at the behest of Ahmad Shah Abdali and Imad-ul-mulk had taken the field against him. When the battle lines were being drawn between the Marathas and Ahmad Shah Abdali, Shadashiv Bhau despatched his envoy to Shuja-ud-daula. Bhau reminded Shuja-ud-daula that the Afghans had a long and established hostility against the State of Awadh. Shuja-ud-daula's father, Safdar Jang, had almost lost his life fighting against the Afghans and the *wizarat* of the Mughal empire had been taken away from him. He also asserted that the Afghans hated the Indian Muslim more than the Hindus. At this point of time Abdali took the extraordinary step of sending Malika-e-Zamani, the widow of emperor Muhammad Shah to Lucknow to persuade Shuja-ud-daula. There was also an appeal to Islam and Abdali made it look like a *jihad* against the infidel Marathas. Shuja-ud-daula made the gravest mistake of his career and joined Abdali. The events of the battle of Panipat (1761) are too well-known to be narrated here. No doubt, in the battle of Panipat he was on the winning side, but his losses were great. It was Shuja-ud-daula's forces which bore the brunt of Maratha attack and suffered most. When these forces had pulverized each other, Abdali came in, poured his fire and destroyed the Maratha army. Shuja-ud-daula's army was so greatly weakened that it was not able to regain strength when need arose to fight another war against the British. Besides, he lost the goodwill of the Marathas for ever. At this point, it was a foreign invader who had won and the Indian side had lost. The same story was going to be repeated very soon in another theatre of war in the east of Awadh, Shuja-ud-daula now coming on the losing side. For him these two wars—the battle of Panipat and the battle of Buxar proved suicidal. After the first battle, he had become infirm. After the second battle, he was made subservient. A new post of British Resident was created to oversee the rule and the government of the *nawab* of Awadh.

Battle of Buxar

The battle of Buxar (1764) was the most important event in the life of Shuja-ud-daula. The East India Company having found a foothold in Bengal, after the battle of Plassey (1757) wanted to extend its trade and establish its dominance in Awadh on the same lines as in Bengal. Shuja-ud-daula as *wazir* of the Mughal emperor, warned Englishmen against any such moves. The battle lines were being drawn and were accelerated by the events in Bengal. Mir Jafar was put up as the *nawab* after deposing Siraj-ud-daula, but he could not accommodate the constant demands of the East India Company and its avaricious officials and was soon disillusioned. He was removed and Mir Qasim, his son-in-law, was made the *naib-nazim*, but with full powers of the *nazim*. Soon Mir Qasim was also driven to unhappy situation and revolted against the English. He was deposed and Mir Jafar was reinstated on the *gaddi* of Bengal. Mir Qasim came to Bihar, sought help of Prince Ali Gauhar and together they attacked Patna. Shuja-ud-daula also helped them in this venture. As a help to Mir Jafar, the English forces repulsed the attack. After some time Ali Gauhar who had proclaimed himself as emperor Shah Alam, again attacked Patna with his forces, but was repulsed again. The English forces followed Mir Qasim and chased him out of Bihar. Mir Qasim came to Awadh and sought help and patronage of Shuja-ud-daula.

In 1764 Shuja-ud-daula led the combined forces of Shah Alam, Mir Qasim and his own against the British. The idea of this battle was to regain for Mir Qasim the *nawabi* of Bengal, Bihar and Orissa. Mir Qasim pledged to pay Shuja-ud-daula eleven lakhs a month. The intrigues in the war camps helped the British forces to find a hole in the defences of the joint command of the Indian armies. *Raja* Beni Bahadur who was the *naib* of Shuja-ud-daula, ditched his own ruler and proved treacherous. The Indian forces lost a decisive battle against a better army. Shuja-ud-daula brought his forces back to Benares in an orderly retreat and camped there. Here again dissensions started. The English established contact with Shah Alam and those two entered into a treaty on 22 November 1764. According to this treaty, the British offered protection to Shah Alam and proffered him hope to recover his throne at Delhi. The land revenues of Ghazipur, Ballia and Benares were taken away from *raja* Balwant Singh and Shah Alam granted them to the East India Company. The British had their first experience of collecting land revenue directly in these districts on the Indian soil.

Shuja-ud-daula kept running around, sought help from the Ruhelas and the Bangash Afghans, but nobody came to his rescue. The punishment of Panipat was complete. In desperation, he once again turned to the Marathas, and with some detachments of the Marathas, engaged the British in the battlefield of Kara on 3 May 1765 and lost. The *nawab* having been refused help from all quarters, finally sought peace with the East India Company on the advice of Ahmad Khan Bangash of Farrukhabad. Ahmad Khan Bangash advised him that after he holds the reign of power again he should not depend on the Mughals and secondly, he should make Faizabad his capital. The treaty between Shuja-ud-daula and the East India Company was finally concluded on 16 August 1765. Clive, who had come back to India, arranged two separate treaties—one with the emperor Shah Alam and the other with Shuja-ud-daula. According to the first treaty on 9 August 1765, the emperor granted the *diwani* of Bengal, Bihar and Orissa to the East India Company. The *nawabs* of Bengal became titular rulers and the dual government began in Bengal. In lieu of this 'favour' the emperor was offered a *nazar* of twenty-six lakh rupees by the Company. According to the second treaty, the *nawabi* of Awadh was restored to Shuja-ud-daula, who agreed to pay fifty lakh rupees as compensation to the East India Company. The districts of Allahabad and Kara were given to Shah Alam, who chose to live in Allahabad Fort. A British Resident was posted at the court of the *nawab* as observer, but was not supposed to interfere in the administration of the state. *Raja* Balwant Singh was again accepted as the zamindar of Benares. Ballia and Ghazipur remained with the Company for the recovery of the revenues. The two parties also agreed to regard the friends and foes with a common understanding. As one measure of his authority, the *nawab* did not agree to provide help and facilities to the English Company for extending their commercial activities in Awadh. Shuja-ud-daula was allowed to retain the *subedari* of Awadh more as a buffer between the East India Company and the Marathas and not because the *nawab* of Awadh was in a position to retain his position on the basis of his own strength. His forces at this point of time were no match to the well disciplined and well commanded troops of the Company.

After the battle of Panipat in 1761, Abdali stayed in Delhi for more than one year. Najib-ud-daula was made *mir-bakshi* with the title 'Amir-ul-Umara'. In a surprising development, Imad-ul-mulk was recalled to the *wizarat*. Ahmad Shah Abdali probably hoped to keep Najib-ud-daula in check and prevent him from carrying out any ambitious plan on his own in India. Shah Alam was proclaimed emperor in absentia by Ahmad Shah Abdali and Prince Jahan Bakht was appointed Regent. But as a matter of abundant caution, Shah Alam desisted from going to Delhi due to prevailing uncertainty. It was only in 1772 that the Maratha chief Mahadji Scindhia persuaded Shah Alam to come to Delhi under his protection and provide respectability to Maratha power by his presence. Allahabad and Kara districts were again thrown open for negotiations. Shuja-ud-daula bought them from the East India Company on payment of twenty-five lakh rupees in 1773. He also concluded an agreement to seek help of the British arms for the protection of Awadh. By a clever interpretation of these terms of agreement, Shuja-ud-daula persuaded the East India Company to provide him help with its forces to invade the Ruhelas on the alleged pretext of unfriendly acts perpetuated by them. Ruhela country was conquered and annexed to the *nawabi* of Awadh in 1774. The Bangash Afghans also became weak because of their internal conflicts and Shuja-ud-daula came to acquire a control over Farrukhabad also. The ambition of Shuja-ud-daula was fulfilled. His father had died a broken man. But the Company's Resident had taken his position in the court of Awadh by the treaty of 1765. This post evolved as a parallel and then dominant centre of power till the deposition of the last ruler of Awadh in 1856.

Growth of Composite Culture in Awadh

Composite culture evolved in Awadh as a social phenomenon because certain political and ideological conditions prevailed under the *nawabs*. The broad-mindedness of Shuja-ud-daula is clearly evident from his tolerant and liberal religious policy which promoted communal harmony in Awadh.

Shuja-ud-daula was anointed on the *masnad* of Awadh, in Faizabad, in 1754, where he started his life as a ruler. He was a man instinctively given to physical pleasures. His *naib* Ismail Khan Kabuli encouraged him in this direction so that he could assume the real power of administration. Luckily for Awadh, Kabuli died after 8 months and Tamkeen Khan was appointed as the next *naib*. Shuja-ud-daula's mother intervened and encouraged her son to take over the reins of administration in his own hands and control the rebellious elements in the state. From 1754 to 1757, he remained busy on the western front because of the dubious policies of Imad-ul-mulk, the *wazir* of the Mughal court. We have mentioned earlier the episode of the two Mughal princes coming towards Awadh, but with the intervention of Ruhela chieftain—Saad-ul-lah Khan. Shuja-ud-daula came to terms with Imad-ul-mulk. To keep a close watch on the situation he adopted Lucknow as his capital in 1757. From 1757 to 1765 he was involved in various military campaigns, leading to Panipat and Buxar. After the battle of Buxar he concluded a treaty with the East India Company in 1765. He was advised by the Bangash chief to make Faizabad his capital. He took that advice and remained in Faizabad till the end of his life in 1775. During his lifetime Faizabad and Lucknow had a parallel growth—Faizabad as the capital town, and Lucknow as the centre of commercial activities, arts, culture and learning. Geographically Lucknow was the centre for trade between the Doab and the area east of Gomti. Here geography and history came together and in that fusion evolved a new culture which may justly be called the *Ganga-Jamuni Tahzib*. With the decline of Delhi, Lucknow rose in eminence in all fields of activity.

As soon as it was known that Shuja-ud-daula had decided to make Faizabad his headquarters, crowds flocked to that town and thousands of people came and settled there. In no time people of every race and creed, individuals of every rank and class gathered there. During the reign of Shuja-ud-daula, the *madarsas* of Faizabad had come to acquire great fame and attracted a very large number of students from Bengal, Gujarat, Malwa, Hyderabad, Shahjahanabad, Lahore, Peshawar, Kabul, Kashmir and Multan.[9]

Several members of the Mughal administrative service in the executive branch who joined Saadat Khan's staff early in his career achieved success as he did. Newal Rai, a Saksena Kayastha, was the son of a poor clerk from Doab, a region adjacent to Awadh. After joining service under Saadat Khan, he rose rapidly and reached the office of provincial *bakshi* or paymaster. When Safdar Jang succeeded Saadat Khan, Newal Rai was promoted to the rank of *maharaja* and *naib* of Awadh. He died in harness leading the Awadh army in the battle against Ruhela Afghans in the year 1750.[10]

After the death of Newal Rai, the post of *naib* was given to Ismail Khan by Safdar Jang.[11] He was neither a member of the Awadh's ruling families nor part of any established administrative house.

The efflorescence of Awadh's composite culture under the *nawabs* emanated because there were deep roots of mutual understanding among various communities in this region during ancient and medieval periods. Some facts speak for themselves. Suraj Kund, located on the bank of river Gomti, had enjoyed the status of being among the holiest places in the country. The *Ain-e-Akbari* explicitly refers to it as a place of religious significance, where pilgrims belonging to all communities from far and remote places congregated for taking bath and offering oblation.[12] Lucknow being the original abode of Pratiharas, Bhars, Nagas, and Rajputs, abounds in ancient *devi* temples. These temples faced continuous onslaughts of marauders throughout the middle age. During the reign of the *nawabs*, however, the *devi* temples enjoyed special protection. *Devi* is the consort of Lord Shiva and in temples devoted to her worship—*yantras* or *pindas* also had a religious sanction. Oblations continued to be offered to the broken idols and such idols were reconsecrated alongside the new *devi* idols.[13] These temples had a non-descript architectural style. Other than these temples, during the reign of the Mughal emperor Akbar quite a few large Jain temples were built at Lucknow. The middle of seventeenth century witnessed the construction of temples of Shantinathji and Rishabhnathji Digambar in the Mina Bazar, Chowk area of Lucknow.[14]

In the area of revenue administration, that is, *diwani*, the house of Atmaram, a Khatri, played a dominant role from the beginning. Atmaram was the *diwan* of Burhan-ul-mulk. In the time of Safdar Jang, his son Ram Narayan succeeded him. He held this post throughout the reign of Safdar Jang. In Shuja-ud-daula's time also, Ram Narayan continued as *diwan*. His son Maha Narayan was appointed as *itlaq navees*. During the reign of Shuja-ud-daula, two other persons belonging to the same family played an important role—Surat Singh and Beni Bahadur. Beni Bahadur rose rapidly during the reign of Shuja-ud-daula and was also given military responsibilities. He fought along the *nawab* in the battle of Buxar, but his loyalty came under a cloud. The English broke through the army lines of the *nawab* where Beni Bahadur was in command. After the battle of Buxar, the *nawab* dismissed Beni Bahadur, blinded him and put him into jail where he died.

Surat Singh carried on with his duties in the *diwani*. His son *raja* Jaggan Nath followed him and eventually became *diwan*. *Diwani* had a stable administration under the house of Atmaram for four generations, which contributed to a great extent to the financial prosperity of the state.

The office of the head of the political executive known as *naib* or the Vice-Regent was subject to greater pressures from conflicting interests and therefore proved very unstable. One historian has observed that this office

> ... explicitly perceived by the *nawabs* of Awadh as the proper domain of Muslims, none of the Hindu houses was able to secure the same strong dominance over the executive branch as they had over the financial branch.[15]

This does not seem to be correct because during the reign of Safdar Jang, Newal Rai was the *naib*. In his own time, Shuja-ud-daula brought Beni Bahadur almost to the same level. In the time of Asaf-ud-daula, Tikait Rai and Jhao Lal, were given the office of *naib*. It was only during the time of later *nawabs* in the nineteenth century that the Hindus could not make it to the top post of the political executives. That exclusion also applied to the Sunnis. The domain became confined to Shias of proven loyalty to the *nawabs* and later the Kings of Awadh.

The Army and Court

Shuja-ud-daula paid great attention towards improving his army, which was itself a fine example of composite culture. The highest cavalry leaders were *nawab* Murtaza Khan Bareech and two Brahmins named Himmat Bahadur and Umrao Giri. Moreover

Raghunath Singh and Parshad Singh each had three hundred cavalry and four battalions of infantry under their command.[16]

During the *nawabi* period, Persian was the court language and the people of India had adopted many Persian social customs. In the time of the Safavid dynasty, the main faith in Iran was Shiaism. Even though the ruling family in India, the Mughals, were Chaghatai Sunnis, Persian influence on society was such that in spite of religious differences, whenever a Persian came to the country, he was treated with respect.[17]

Shuja-ud-daula started the fashion of not keeping a beard. Following him all the *nawabs* and later the kings of Lucknow kept only moustaches. The inevitable result was that most Shias abandoned the custom of wearing beards. Later on, many Sunnis also adopted the same style.[18]

The reign of Shuja-ud-daula was the watershed in the history of Awadh. Perhaps, the whole of India. He was the only ruling prince who took part in two wars in which two foreign powers were arraigned. The power finally passed into the hands of the East India Company. Shuja-ud-daula ruled from Faizabad when the Mughal emperor Shah Alam was stationed at Allahabad. The relations between the two were at best formal and Shuja-ud-daula always kept the emperor at a safe distance. Between the emperor and the *nawab-wazir*, the *nawab-wazir* was on a stronger wicket. His strength was the support of the East India Company, his own army and the revenues of his state. This was reflected in the court culture and the social life of the people. The revenue system was going through a transition from *jagirdari* to zamindari and *taluqdari*. The consolidation of administration in the hinterland of Awadh gave the landed interests, time and atmosphere to live in peace and bring about prosperity in agriculture, trade and commerce. Before Shuja-ud-daula died he had been able to realise the ambition of his life by conquering Ruhela country with the help of British arms. The expenses of the Company's troops were borne by the people of Awadh by sharing the profits of their prosperity with the state of Awadh. The lesson was not lost on the court of Awadh and there was a growing realisation that the countryside had a role to play in the strength of the state. After Shah Alam departed from Allahabad the districts of Kara and Allahabad were purchased on payment from the State Treasury. For Awadh, the break from the Mughals was complete. Hereafter during the reign of two succeeding *nawab-wazirs* the relationship was at best perfunctory. It was not surprising that the *nawab* depended more and more on the people of Awadh. The attitude based on the traditions prevailing in this part of the country and the legends of Ayodhya continued to become stronger as time passed.

NOTES

1. M.H. Fisher, *A Clash of Cultures: Awadh, the British, and the Mughals*, Delhi, 1987, p. 24.
2. Sultan Ali Safauvi, *Maadan-us-Saadat*, Chap. IV, p. 285, quoted by A.L. Srivastava in *Shuja-ud-daula*, Vol. I, pp. 56-7; See also Alexander Dow, *History of Hindustan*, London, 1868, Vol. II, p. 92, see also George Forester, *A Journey from Bengal to England through the Northern part of India, Kashmir etc.*, London, 1798, Vol. I, p. 184.
3. W. Hoey (tr.), *Memoirs of Delhi & Faizabad*, Vol. II, p. 246.
4. M.H. Fisher, op. cit., p. 34.
5. Ghulam Hussain Khan, *Seir-ul-Muntakhirin*, Vol. IV, pp. 65-6.
6. Ibid., pp. 66-7.
7. E.S. Harcourt & Fakir Hussain (tr.), *Lucknow: The Last Phase of an Oriental Culture*, London, 1975, p. 30.
8. Jagdish Sahai, *Awadh Mein Nawabi Shasan Ka Ithihas* (Hindi), Faizabad, n.y., p. 65.
9. W. Hoey, *Memoirs of Faizabad*, Vol. I, p. 67.
10. K.S. Santha, *Begums of Awadh*, Varanasi, n.y., pp. 48-50.
11. Bahadur Singh, *Yadgar-i-Bahaduri*, Partly translated by Munshi Sadasukh Lal. MS Add. 30,786, British Library, London, fol. 116.
12. H.S. Jarrett & Sir J. Sarkar (tr.), *Ain-i-Akbari*, Calcutta, 1942, 2nd edn., Vol. II, pp. 56-7.
13. Sidney Hay, *Historic Lucknow*, Lucknow, 1937, pp. 78-85.
14. H.S. Jarrett & Sir J. Sarkar, op. cit., Vol. II, pp. 64-5.
15. Michael H. Fisher, op. cit., p. 57
16. E.S. Harcourt & Fakir Hussain (tr.), *Lucknow, The Last Phase of an Oriental Culture*, London, 1975, pp. 32, 35.
17. Ibid., p. 77.
18. Ibid., p. 190.

CHAPTER III

The Noon Time (1775-98)

In 1775 Asaf-ud-daula took over as *nawab* of Awadh. He was the eldest son of Shuja-ud-daula and was declared heir apparent during the lifetime of his father.[1] Even then the succession was approved more by the East India Company than by the will of the old *nawab*. The Mughal emperor ceased to be the deciding factor. After the battle of Buxar, the Mughal emperor stayed at Allahabad due to the patronage of the East India Company because by the Treaty of 1765 he had performed the formal act of granting the *diwani* rights of Bengal, Bihar and Orissa to the Company. He remained there till 1772 and then was brought to Delhi under the umbrella of Mahadji Scindhia. Subsequent to this treaty with the Mughal emperor, Shuja-ud-daula had entered into another treaty almost one year after the battle of Buxar on 16 August 1765. This treaty initiated the process of dismemberment of the state of Awadh. The Company obtained the overriding powers on the state of Awadh. A Resident was appointed in the court of the *nawab*. In course of time this subterfuge of the Resident became the channel through which pressure was put on the *nawab* and ultimately all his powers were sucked out of him.

Accession of Asaf-ud-Daula

Soon after Asaf-ud-daula's accession there was a marked change in the attitude of East India Company. It was conveyed to him that the treaty with the old *nawab* Shuja-ud-daula was done on a personal basis and that he should enter into a fresh treaty with the East India Company. The new treaty was concluded on 21 May 1775 at Faizabad.[2] It added more burden on the finances of Awadh and took away some more powers from the administration of the *nawab*. In October 1775, Asaf-ud-daula requested his mother and grandmother, the Nawab Begum and Bahu Begum, to give back the treasure of the late *nawab* to the state treasury. After some consternation, the *begums* gave a sum of twenty-six lakh rupees to him. The reported amount in the treasury was about rupees two crores. At one point of time the matters took an ugly turn and the *nawab* prepared to march his forces on to the palace. But the troops of the *begums* were soon arraigned against him. The British Resident intervened and the *nawab* came to an agreement with the *begums* and had to satisfy himself with the receipt of an additional sum of rupees thirty lakhs.[3] Soon thereafter the capital was shifted to Lucknow and this town became still more important in the history of Awadh.[4] Having learnt the lessons in the battles of Buxar and Panipat and subsequent patterns of behaviour of the Company officials it must have devolved upon the new *nawab* that he could rule only with the help of the local population and the native ethos. The growth of understanding between the Hindus and Muslims during this time was a natural corollary to this. The life and time of Asaf-ud-daula represents the great transition of the State of Awadh after the breakdown of the Mughal empire. The East India Company increasingly took over the reins of power sometimes surreptitiously but mostly in a blatant manner. The East India Company began making further ingress into all aspects of Awadh rule and administration by the treaty of 1775. Soon after the accession of Asaf-ud-daula, the Company had increased the subsidy for their forces from the new *nawab*. Within six months of the treaty the *nawab* was forced to cede the areas of Benares, Jaunpur and Ghazipur to the Company, something which Shuja-ud-daula had been able to avoid diplomatically till the very end.[5] By 1779 the annual payments to the Company increased to almost a crore of rupees. Asaf-ud-daula retained Ruhelkhand as a reward for his loyalty and friendship towards the British. Moreover Asaf had solicited British help in robbing his mother and grandmother for which they very generously gave him their moral support.

Asaf-ud-daula never broke his ties with the Mughal emperor — that remained for his nephew Ghazi-ud-din Haider to do. He did not observe more than the minimum symbolic and financial requirements, necessary to obtain the title and then retain his authority within the empire as *nawab-wazir*. From the beginning of his reign Asaf-ud-daula had to admit and adjust himself to *de facto* dependence on the East India Company.[6] In spite of this, during his rule it was hardly perceptible to the people of Lucknow that an external power was increasingly interfering in their internal affairs. The principal reason for this was that Asaf-ud-daula's public munificence and love of luxury encouraged everyone to lead a life of self-indulgence. No one considered it necessary to give a thought to the outcome of this mode of living.

The treaties of 1775 and then 1776 put pressure on the *nawab* to reduce his own forces and to meet the increased financial burden of maintenance of the Company's forces. The Gusain generals who had fought bravely for Shuja-ud-daula at Allahabad were cashiered and were asked to leave. There was a general dissatisfaction in the ranks where rebellious tendencies began to be exhibited.[7] In a queer turn of events, *raja* Jhao Lal,[8] Basant Ali and Thapar Chand came together. A situation was created in which the forces of the *nawab* came in conflict with the Company's forces.[9] The situation was so thoroughly confusing that nobody knew as to what actually happened. Muktar-ud-daula, the *wazir* was killed in action,[10] Jhao Lal, Basant Ali and Thapar Chand were put under arrest.[11] Saadat Ali Khan, the younger half brother of the *nawab*, was also camping in the area and an attempt was made on the life of *nawab* himself.[12] At long last on the personal intervention of the *nawab*, the matters were brought under control. These conspiracies exposed the slender loyalties of the various nobles in the *suba*. The *nawab* thereafter handled the situation very well, always juxtaposing one set of officers against the other. His life remained secured and there were no further attempts on his life and security. Saadat Ali Khan was sent out of Awadh and he settled in Benares on a pension of rupees three lakhs granted by the *nawab-wazir*. He remained there till the death of Asaf-ud-daula and his successor Wazir Ali.[13] He was later recalled to the *nawabi* of Awadh in 1798.

Haider Ali, Marathas and Awadh

When the Mughal emperor Shah Alam shifted from Allahabad to Delhi under the cover and patronage of Mahadji Scindhia, the eclipse of Mughal empire was complete. The Marathas ruled over almost the entire western India from the northern boundaries of Karnatak (Mysore) to the banks of Sutlej. In the south, Haider Ali had taken over the reins of power from the Hindu King of Mysore.

Arcot was being ruled by a Muslim *nawab*. The Nizam had his seat of power in Hyderabad and the original viceroyalty of the Deccan had now contracted to areas around Hyderabad and Aurangabad. He had the legend of a high office in Mughal empire behind him, but none of the power, purpose and determination of the great position, the first Nizam-ul-mulk once held. The British had established their seat in Calcutta and with the grant of the *diwani* of Bengal, Bihar and Orissa, they had established themselves as a territorial power, even though they were merely a trading company by their Charter. The period between 1775 and 1799 which started with the First Mysore War and ended with the Fourth decided the fate of India for good. The Marathas, the Nizam and the Mysore rulers fought against each other and the East India Company took due advantage of it. The Indian rulers fought for themselves and the East India Company fought for England. The First Mysore War raged for three years between 1766 and 1769. The Marathas, Nizam and East India Company formed a coalition against Haider Ali. As a shrewd ruler Haider Ali bought off the Marathas by ceding some territory to them. He allied with the Nizam and fought against the British. After the first few defeats at the hands of the company, the Nizam lost nerve and withdrew. Left alone, Haider Ali continued his fight and defeated the Company's forces near Madras. After this, Haider and the East India Company came to terms in 1769. The peace agreement at the end of the First Mysore War (1766-9) provided for mutual restitution of conquests and reciprocal assistance in defensive wars. The last clause involved the English in future difficulties.

In the following years, Maratha affairs took an unhappy turn. In 1772 Peshwa Madhav Rao I died and was succeeded by his brother Narayan Rao. In an internal struggle among the Marathas Narayan Rao was killed and the *peshwai* was taken over by his half-brother Raghunath Rao (Raghoba). The other party soon formed a Regency and challenged the authority of Raghoba. As a matter of extreme degradation, Raghoba sought the help of the East India Company at Bombay and granted them substantial concessions by the Treaty of Surat in 1775. But this treaty was annulled by the Governor General's Council at Calcutta and another treaty was signed with the rival group of the Maratha Regency in 1775 at Purandhar. By this agreement the British surrendered most of the gains made by the Treaty of Surat and the cause of Raghoba was abandoned. But the uneasy situation continued, since this treaty was also disowned by the Calcutta authorities. The British and Maratha forces engaged each other at Wadgaon, Ahmadnagar, Poona and Gwalior. Ultimately on the initiative of Mahadji Scindhia the British came to an understanding with Marathas and signed the Treaty of Salbai in 1782. It was approved by the Peshwa and Nana Phadnavis only one year later in 1783. The treaty provided peace between the British and the Marathas for the next twenty years. The British were then left free to deal with Haider Ali. When they finished with him and his successor Tipu, they turned to the Marathas and subjugated them. But in 1782, Marathas could not look beyond their own interest and left the field clear for the British to let them consolidate their position.

The Second Mysore War (1780-4) started, when the French joined the struggle for power in India after the revolt of the American Colonies in 1776. They formed a coalition with Haider Ali and the Nizam of Hyderabad and fought against the British. In 1782 Haider Ali died but he was succeeded by his equally able son Tipu. The sea-saw struggle continued for four years. One by one, Tipu's allies fell apart. Warren Hastings persuaded Nizam to withdraw. The French concluded peace in Europe with England in 1783 by the Treaty of Versailles and deserted the Indian coalition. Tipu was left alone. After a few brilliant victories, he concluded peace with the British in 1784 by the Treaty of Bangalore. Both sides agreed to give back the areas they had conquered. There was exchange of prisoners also.

The conflicts of East India Company with Haider Ali, the Nizam and Marathas put a tremendous strain on the finances of the trading Company. Warren Hastings, who had been made the Governor-General by the Regulating Act of 1773, had only Awadh to look forward to as the milching cow. He first put pressure on Chait Singh of Benares to make a special contribution of rupees five lakhs over and above the treaty obligations of 1778.[14] The demand was repeated 1779 and 1780. Ultimately he revolted and had to flee Benares in 1780. He was deposed and was succeeded by his nephew but the Company failed to get the requisite money. Chait Singh took refuge with the Scindhia and died in Gwalior in 1810.[15] This gave the Company and Warren Hastings a bad name. But money had to found, and so Warren Hastings next turned to the *begums* of Awadh. They were charged with helping Chait Singh and were put under great humiliation and were made to give up almost their entire treasury. Asaf-ud-daula was also made a party to this extremely disconcerting series of events. Ultimately a sum of rupees one crore and twenty lakhs was extorted from the *begums*.[16] This money helped the East India Company to fight their wars in the south. It may appear ironical to say so but the fact remains that the conquest of south and the Marathas by the East India Company was financed by the wealth plundered from the *begums* and the *nawabs* of Awadh.

GROWTH OF LUCKNOW

In 1783, the finances of the State of Awadh had become very weak. As an act of kindness, after the loot of the *begums*, the establishment of the Residency had been withdrawn at the end of 1783 on the request of the *nawab*.[17] In the year that followed, there was a severe drought in Awadh. Asaf-ud-daula began the construction of Bara Imambara as a relief measure to the distraught population of Awadh.[18] Rich and poor received the succour and survived. In 1785, Warren Hastings was recalled. His successors Macpherson and Cornwallis provided relief to the *nawab*.[19] The number of British forces was reduced and the maximum payment by the *nawab* was fixed at rupees fifty lakhs.[20] After this Lucknow started on its path to glory. Many new buildings were constructed. The heartland of Awadh responded magnificently and created prosperity in the field of agriculture and trade. There was general peace and prosperity in the times of Asaf-ud-daula. The second run of devastating impact of British extortionist designs started only after the end of his rule in 1796.

The transfer of capital from Faizabad to Lucknow brought about a sea change in the atmosphere of Lucknow. Lucknow, as the nucleus of Awadh, underwent a dramatic transformation during the regime of Asaf-ud-daula. He developed around him a centre of composite culture that surpassed all others of his day. He wished to make his court a distinctive cultural centre on a continental or even world scale.[21]

It would certainly be wrong to assume as some writers have done that Lucknow was merely a cluster of villages along the southern bank of river Gomti. Lucknow was already a rapidly growing commercial town and was the centre of trade between Doab on the west and Saryu and Rapti on the east.[22] Akbar started the settlement of this town and built a gate, which even today carries the name Akbari Gate. Jehangir established the *taksal* or mint in Lucknow.[23] Lucknow was also the seat of learning. Firangi Mahal,[24] known after the abandoned Dutch factory in which the theological family was established in the reign of Aurangzeb, became a major seat of learning. The syllabus of training in this institute acquired great fame in the entire Muslim world.

During the time of Lord Cornwallis when Asaf-ud-daula had some relief from the pressures of the East India Company, he gave his full attention to glorify his *darbar* and the court. Construction activity began on a large scale in 1784, when the foundations of Bara Imambara were laid.[25] This, as has been mentioned above, was started as a relief measure during the famine of 1784. The Imambara, the Asafi Masjid and the Roomi Darwaza were completed in 1790. Roomi Darwaza remains the signature building of Lucknow even to this day. An erroneous impression has been created that the Roomi Darwaza carries its name from Rome and has the impress of Italian buildings. 'Rum' in Persian usage had come to mean Turkey, or the Ottoman empire by this time. The literal meaning of the word is big. Roomi Darwaza is the big gate, a grand entrance to the Imambara, Asafi Masjid and *Naubat Khana,* created as one single complex. The architecture of Roomi Darwaza presents a unique combination of Hindu and Muslim styles.[26] It has adopted the shape of Buland Darwaza of Fatehpur Sikri, near Agra, but its *mehrabs* are decorated with figures which look like serpent heads but are in reality shaped like lotus flowers. These two symbols are the traditional cultural insignia of ancient Awadh.

After Lucknow became the capital, the business of dealing with revenue and tax collections from all over the province centred on this town. The main treasury was here. So were the judicial courts; and prisoners were sent for trial to Lucknow. The business of government took place here, the ambassadors and notables from foreign countries were presented in Lucknow to the *nawab*. The headquarters of the army were shifted to Lucknow and all the high ranking army commanders were staying here. New palace complexes grew up, each comprising of a large number of servants, skilled craftsmen and gardeners. There were servants who ministered to the paraphernalia of the state, the royal coachmen and the personal bodyguards in their colourful attires.[27] The *nawab* had built a palace for himself near Macchi Mahal and the Imambara. Bibiapur Palace was built on the outskirts of the town, by the Gomti, for his pleasure hunt. Another residence had came up in Chinhat about 8 miles from Lucknow. Shopping centres were built in Charbagh.[28] This tradition was followed in the times of the succeeding *nawabs* and by 1837, a large number of buildings carrying Shia motifs and names were built in Lucknow. Lucknow had become a place of pilgrimage for the Shia faith all over the world. When Muhammad Ali Shah completed his Imambara and Jama Masjid and a pair of miniature gates on the lines of Roomi Darwaza, Lucknow had been given the name of *Babylon of India.* In the words of Abdul Halim Sharar,

> Asaf-ud-daula's buildings are in no way influenced by European architecture. In style, they are purely Asiatic, without ostentation, but with genuine splendour and dignity.[29]

Asaf-ud-daula had become renowned for his munificence. His generosity was a subject of popular lore in the entire state of Awadh. The general phrase was *'jisko na de maula, usko de asafuddaula'*[30] (To those whom even God denieth, Asaf-ud-daula giveth).

Asaf-ud-Daula as a Ruler

The beginning of Asaf-ud-daula's rule was the beginning of the new state of Awadh. The *nawab* was coming out of the shadow of the Mughal emperor. He was *nawab-wazir* in name but did not pay court to the nominal emperor at Delhi. He never even visited Delhi during his reign. In 1784, second son of Shah Alam—Prince Jawan Bakt visited Lucknow and was welcomed with a lot of accolade. He stayed in Lucknow for some time and was awarded an honorarium of rupees three lakhs per annum. The Mughal prince got married here in Lucknow and then went away to Benares for good.[31] That was the only link that Awadh had with the Mughal family. Asaf-ud-daula started organising his own administration. He appointed Murtuza Khan as his *wazir*, under the title of Mukhtar-ud-daula.[32] Iraj Khan *alias* Ilich Khan, who was *naib-wazir* in the time of Shuja-ud-daula, went away to Delhi on the pretext of getting the recognition of *wizarat* for the new *nawab* from the Mughal emperor, but stayed on in Delhi and got a job under Najaf Khan, *wazir* of the Delhi court.[33] *Raja* Maha Narayan was appointed *itlaq-nawis*.[34] Basant Ali was made the *bakshi*, in charge of the infantry.[35] Almas Khan[36] and Haider Beg[37] were given the responsibility of financial matters. *Raja* Jaggan Nath was made the *diwan*.[38]

After Mukhtar-ud-daula was killed in an initial conflict of a small army uprising following reduction of numbers of native detachments, the *nawab* thought it fit to recall Iraj Khan and made him the *wazir*. He died within a year of his appointment and Haider Beg Khan succeeded him in 1776. Haider Beg took upon himself the responsibility of the major part of administration and effectively controlled affairs. He remained *wazir* till 1791, a period of sixteen years.[39] He was a worried man, constantly afraid of conspiracies around him and was ruthless against his opponents. He always kept an eye on his relations with the East India Company. The loot of the *begums* of Awadh was conducted during his time.[40] Although he was greatly indebted to the *begums*, yet at this moment of crisis, he did nothing to save their honour.[41] On that occasion, it appears that everybody, the *nawab* and the *wazir*, succumbed to the overweening pressure of the East India Company. He also made changes in the financial administration, having removed Surat Singh from Bareilly[42] and giving charge to Thapar Chand. Thapar Chand was also removed after some time.[43] Later Tikait Rai found favour and moved up the ladder of power. On the death of Haider Beg in 1792, *raja* Tikait Rai, a Srivastava Kayastha, succeeded him as *wazir*.[44] In 1795 Tikait Rai was removed from the *wizarat* on the insistence of the East India Company[45] and Jhao Lal was appointed *wazir*. In 1797 the East India Company forced an additional expenditure of rupees five lakhs per annum for an army detachment in Awadh. The *nawab* resisted it reminding the Company of its earlier commitments. The Company thought that Jhao Lal was behind this resistance of the *nawab* and he was forced out of the *wizarat* and banished out of Awadh.[46] The *nawab* was greatly disturbed by the treatment meted out to Jhao Lal and this possibly hastened his end: The *nawab* died in September 1797.[47]

The above narrative reflects the administrative thinking and constant restructuring of administration. *Diwani* and the land revenue system remained with the Hindus all along. In the initial stages, it was the Khatris who were in the forefront.[48] Some time later after the removal of Surat Singh from power, Kayastha families of Tikait Rai and Jhao Lal took over and remained in control. Both Tikait Rai and Jhao Lal rose to become *wazirs* and enjoyed political power and also proved their loyalty till the very end. After the unceremonious removal of Jhao Lal, Almas Khan was made *wazir*.[49] The period is replete with the efforts of different families trying to gain favour and edging out the others. The East India Company had started playing the game of interference in the administration of Awadh, every time trying to extract more and more money from its treasury. The East India Company was busy fighting its battles with Haider Ali, Tipu, Nizam and Marathas. Awadh was the only place from where the Company replenished its resources to fight the various conflicts. The officials of the *nawabs* had to seek favours from the court and also obtain patronage from the Resident. This set a pattern which continued till the last days of Awadh administration. Since the loyalties of the officers were always divided, the *nawab* was always under conflicting pressures from various groups.

Evolution of Shia Identity

The *nawabs* of Awadh derived their lineage from the Imams and considered themselves the patrons of Shia thought and philosophy. They also considered themselves the religious successors of the defunct Safavid dynasty of Iran. In the initial stages the court of Awadh was fumbling with different ideas. At Faizabad a large number of Shia Ulema had assembled who came from the background of Unani physicians.[50] Since they were subordinate to Sunni ecclesiasts at the Mughal court their open or public allegiance to Shia theology was rather slow in coming. The first initiation for an independent Shia school of philosophy came from an outstanding scholar settled in Benares (Varanasi), Maulana Shaikh Ali Hazim.[51] Sheikh Ali Hazim was a man of erudition. He was a master of various secular and religious sciences such as logic, philosophy, mathematics, Koranic exegesis, Muslim jurisprudence and theology. He was born in Isfahan on 7 January 1692.[52] From early childhood he showed signs of brilliance. He learnt Arabic and Persian and earned recognition from the recognised divines of the Shia sect. Shah Abbas II of the Safavid dynasty in Persia appointed Sheikh Ali Hazim as the teacher of his son Tahmas.[53] At that time Nadir Shah was an ordinary soldier in the royal army and was deputed to serve in the palace. The manners of Nadir Shah offended the great scholar Sheikh Ali Hazim and he censured him. Nadir Shah did not appear before the Sheikh any more. Later, when the Safavid dynasty was overthrown, Nadir Shah took over the reins of power. His invasion of India and sack of Delhi are well-known. During this time Sheikh Ali Hazim emigrated from Iran, and lived in Delhi briefly when Mohammad Shah was on the Mughal throne. On the news of Nadir's coming to India, Sheikh moved out of Delhi and went to Benares via Agra and Lucknow. He was offered protection and patronage by Maharaja Balwant Singh of Benares.[54] There he pursued his scholarly vocation. He has to his credit a large number of works showing prolific learning.[55] His writings were the first which gave some guidance to the Shia scholars in the new state of Awadh.

The other leading light of Shia thought in the early stages of Awadh was Mir Tafazzul Hussain Khan Kashmiri.[56] He was sent to Iran and studied in Najaf. On his return he came to be known as *khan-e-allama* ('the Scholarly Khan'). The real genius behind the concept of a Shia state was Sayyad Dildar Ali. He was a student of Firangi Mahal,[57] went to Iraq, studied there for two years and then came back to Lucknow.[58] In 1781 he started his scholarly diction on the basic theoretical Shia tenets. In course of time he was given the title *gufran maab*, meaning that all his sins had been pardoned in his lifetime and he would have an angelic existence in heaven. He and his sons Maulana Sayyad Hussain and Sayyad Mohammad formed the trilogy on which revolved much of the Shia thought and philosophy in Awadh.

Over a period of time this tendency of narrow and assertive Shiaism led to some ill-will against other communities, but the only *nawab* who strongly supported a purely sectarian attitude was Amjad Ali Shah. Others kept themselves above such a limited approach and always looked to the general good of the people of Awadh.

Another prominent figure from the Shia community was Murtaza Khan. He was employed by Asaf-ud-daula to look after his *jagirs*. The two were distantly related by marriage. Murtaza Khan was descended from a Persian Shia family, and he and his family had served the Mughal and Awadh administration for a very long time.[59]

The Shia faith is based on two basic tenets. The first is the belief in the Prophet, the special sanctity of his descendants, notably the main line of Imams beginning with the Prophets cousin and son-in-law Ali, whose son and third Imam, Hussain, was martyred at Kerbala. Secondly the first three Caliphs are regarded as usurpers and as such supposed enemies of the genuine Imams and so are objects of condemnation.[60] The killing of Hussain at Kerbala by the Umayyad Caliph Yazid makes the condemnation very intense. A Shia shows his love for the Prophet and the Imam in the form of *tawalla* meaning affection. His animosity to the usurpers is expressed as *tabarra* meaning condemnation and unforgivableness.[61] The Sunnis on the other hand believe, that the first three Caliphs are also true and genuine successors of the Prophet, along with Ali, the fourth Caliph. Hence *tabarra* for them is bad in faith and is itself condemnable. These prejudices are so deeply ingrained in the Shia and Sunni psyche that they nurture an undying schism between them.

The two novel aspects of Shia practice in Lucknow were the Friday prayers and the public celebrations of Moharram. The Friday Prayers at Asafi Masjid were led by Sayyad Dildar Ali.[62] In the Islamic state after the public prayers, *khutba* is read in the name of the rulers. The *nawabs* replaced the Mughal emperors in the *khutba* in course of time.[63] Public mourning of the Kerbala tragedy during Moharram was something specific to Lucknow. In these celebrations the amount of expenditure involved remained far from inconsiderable. Emma Roberts remarked that 'it was accompanied by so much pomp and splendour that strangers are at some loss to distinguish it from the festivals of pure rejoicing.'[64]

The religious doctrines of Shiaism pervaded the entire tenor of poetry in Lucknow. *Tawalla* or the affection for Imam, and the martyrdom led to the writing of *marsias* or elegies. The sense of sorrow at the tragedy of Kerbala and consciousness of the fortitude and the sense of self-sacrifice displayed by Imam Hussain, his lieutenant Abbas and other warriors, was heightened as it was narrated in plaintive tones and evolved as an art form of the highest degree. Asaf-ud-daula's court attracted many *marsiya-khwans* or elegy reciters. These *marsiya-khwans* had a very important place in the public life also. During the time of Asaf-ud-daula, Mirza Muhammad Raza was regarded as the greatest *marsiya* reciter of the day. Muhammad Shustri and Shah Husayn Vilayat came from Iran and got a great patronage in the court of Asaf-ud-daula.[65] As a result, poets like Sikandar, Gada, Maskin and Afsurdah began to specialise in composing *marsiyas*. In the mid-eighteenth century a change was marked in the style of *marsiyas*. The *marsiyas* which used to be of four lines earlier, were expanded to six lines.[66]

During the time of Wajid Ali Shah, Mir Babar Ali Anees (1802-74) and Salamat Ali Dabir (1803-75) were regarded as the most distinguished writers of this art.[67] The celebrations of Moharram became occasions of great public exhibition of mourning because of the recitation of these *marsiyas*. The *marsiya* and the public celebration of Moharram became complementary as a characteristic of Lucknow social life. *Tabarra*, with its object of condemning the usurpers adopted different forms. That tenor of poetry is known as *harzia* in which satire and outright name-calling is resorted to. At a lower level it was used for immodest utterances and even obscenity. Similarly *soz-khwani* became another art form in which the sense of the funerals was expressed. The art of *soz-khwani* was developed by Khwaja Hasan Maududi—a Sunni Muslim.[68] The fervour created by *marsiya, harzia* and *soz-khwani* added many dimensions in the field of poetry designed to appeal to Shia sentiments. In later years Anees took it to the level of excellence by adopting native thoughts and expressions. He remains to this day the king of *marsiya* writers. It is worthy of attention that Anees and Dabir wrote their *marsiyas* in Urdu.

Urdu Comes into its Own

Lucknow was enriched in the field of Urdu poetry initially by the inflow of a very large number of poets from the decaying city of Delhi and many other places in India. It is said that Ghalib also made an unsuccessful attempt to come to Lucknow. He had to stay back in Delhi, since he failed to get an appointment with the *naib-wazir* on his visit to Lucknow. Bad luck for Lucknow. But his *diwan* was later published by Newal Kishore in his printing press. Urdu poetry was undergoing a metamorphosis at that time. It was trying to find an identity against the dominance of Persian. 'Mir' and 'Ghalib' together represent the epitome of that transition. Similarly, in Lucknow Urdu prose rose in strength and calibre against Persian and it was slowly adopted as the court language. Urdu prose evolved as a powerful expression of the identity of Lucknow culture. What distinguished the Urdu of Lucknow from its counterpart in

Delhi was its urbanity and its sophistication. Nasikh, the native Urdu poet, contributed a great deal in providing grammatical purity to Urdu expressions. In the literary life of Lucknow, *mushaira* or recitations of their verses by poets played a very important role. During *mushairas*, the literary rivalry use to be given an open vent—much to the entertainment of the people of Lucknow.

As against the areas of art and music in which Shia theology played an important role, Sunni scholars concentrated on one particular institution, the Firangi Mahal. Firangi Mahal acquired great fame in the field of traditional Islamic learning. Its special pursuit was Islamic jurisprudence based on Koran and *kalam*. Even for the study of Arabic and Persian literature, the school was able to assemble a very large number of scholars, who contributed mainly to grammar and critical literary studies. The school also contributed to the Sunni version of Islamic concepts. The public debate between Shia and Sunni scholars became highly charged, in which religion and prejudices played an equally important role. These public debates were called *munazirah*.

Another significant literary development in Lucknow was the revival of interest in the genre of poetry known as *masnavi*. The *masnavi* or long narrative poem had its origin in Persian, and was then transmitted to Urdu. In Lucknow it was given special prominence by Mir Ghulam Hassan and Pandit Dayashankar Nasim. Mir Ghulam Hassan's *Shir-ul-Bayan* (The Secret of Narration) and Pandit Dayashankar Nasim's *Gulzar-e-Nasim* (The Garden of Nasim) are diametrically opposite in their narrative style. The former is simple and direct while the latter is full of artifice, but their contribution has a lasting fame. The third great master of *masnavi* was Tasadduq Hussain 'Shauk'. His book *Zahre-Ishq* (Poison of Love) has an ever-lasting fame.[69] Contributions to Urdu came both from Hindus and Muslim poets.

Another major development in the Urdu literature was a style of poetry which came to be known as *rekhti*. The word *rekhti* is the Hindi feminine of the Persian word *rekhta* (lit. 'fallen'), a colloquial term for the language that was evolving in the cantonments. It had the grammar and syntax of Hindi but a large number of words were absorbed from Persian, Arabic and other languages which had come with people immigrating from across the Indus. Amir Khusro was reputedly the first great writer to adopt and adapt this language and give it a literary form. In Persian verbs are unaffected by gender, so that the sex of the beloved is not immediately clear. In Urdu the beloved is a male. Perhaps the idea is derived from Hindu philosophy where God is *purush* and *prakriti* is the female existence. The idea of all love is to reach God. In Urdu as well as in Hindi the verb has a gender. Pronouns have no gender. In *rekhti* the verses were composed by men employing a feminine voice dealing with household and sex matters that exclusively concerned women. *Rekhti* was not poetry by women; it was poetry about women. The original idea was floated by Saadat Yaar Khan 'Rangeen'. He was a friend and companion of Prince Suleman Shikoh who had made Lucknow his abode. 'Rangeen's poetry was aimed at entertaining its male audience by making gross fun of women, its enhanced appeal lying in the fact that it also pretended to be a view from inside. 'Rangeen's close friend Inshah also wrote some of his poems in *rekhti*. The most famous poet who followed the lead was Jaan Sahib. Over a period of time the salacious elements in *rekhti* were brought down and a genuine concern for women confined to the domestic sphere found a sincere expression. One could say it was a forerunner of feminism.[70]

Contribution of Hindi Literature

An even greater contribution to the composite culture of Awadh came from Hindi poetry. The area of Bilgram in Hardoi district of Awadh produced a number of Muslim poets who wrote in Hindi. They adopted Hindi expressions and gave a new meaning to Islamic ideas. They also adopted some elements of Hindu philosophy and the legend of Krishna to give a more meaningful concept to the society at large. The names of the poets who made very purposive contribution to social ethos of the time were Sayyad Mubarak (1583-1687), Sayyad Nizamuddin Madhnayak (1561-1687), Sayyad Rahamat Ullah 'Rahmat' (1650-1706), Mir Abdul Jalil (1660-1725), Sayyad Barkat Ullah 'Premi' (1660-1729), Mir Gulam Nabi 'Rasleen' (1699-1750), Sayyad Mohammad Arif 'Jan' (1710-75). They were poets of culture and religion. None of them sought appointment or remained a court poet. Even though Rasleen was a soldier in the time of Safdar Jang and fought in the battle of Ramchutani in 1752, he never wrote any poem to eulogize the *nawab-wazir*.

This was a time of great creativity in Hindi literature. The period is known as *riti kaal*, when poetry of love and *shringar* (idyllic romance) was the idiom of the day. Another school of poets, led by Padmakar Bhatt, was writing poetry of *veer ras* (valour). He was himself a soldier and served under Himmat Bahadur, the cavalry leader of the *nawab* of Awadh. In his poetry there was a streak of nationalism also, where a call was made to fight the British and throw them out of Calcutta.[71]

Construction of Temples in Lucknow and Patronage of Culture

During the reign of Asaf-ud-daula, the construction of Hindu temples took place on a large scale. The most famous was the Hanuman temple in Lucknow built by Lala Jatmal in 1783. In the *sanctum sanctorum* of the temple there is an idol of Hanuman. It is said that the idol was unearthed by Lala Jatmal following divine guidance received in a dream. An ancient *pushkarini* near the temple establishes its antiquity as a place of worship. This temple was built at the request of Mahant Khasa Ram.[72]

Raja Tikait Rai, who was famous for his strong religious leanings, built a magnificent tank beside the Shitla Devi temple at Tikaitganj Kadim.[73] Similarly a rectangular tank in the Sheesh Mahal of Daulatkhana area was built by *nawab* Asaf-ud-daula, but with the objective of cooling the palace during summers.[74]

During the reign of Asaf-ud-daula, a number of Jain temples were built in Lucknow, at Saadatganj, Tatpatti and Raja Bazar. At Charbagh a Jain temple was built in the Munne Lal Kazi's Dharamshala and is popularly known as the 'Shikarband Digambar'. Another Jain temple was built at Jain Bagh of Daliganj area (Lucknow), which provided a venue for numerous festivals, meetings and celebrations.[75]

The history of some temples at Lucknow, is mingled with interesting folklore. In 1775, when Asaf-ud-daula became the ruler of Awadh, his most favourite attendant was Bhawani Mahra, a Kahar by caste. It was also said of him that he was the unofficial treasurer of the *nawab*, and was nicknamed 'Raja Mahra' by his companions. The present Bhawani Ganj Mohalla is named after him. The history of Kalyangiri temples is associated with Baba Kalyangiri, who chose Lucknow as his favourite abode, after abandoning his earlier hermitage on the bank of river Ganges at Haridvar. On his arrival; he was given a warm welcome by the *nawab*. During the reign of Asaf-ud-daula, two other famous saints Baba Hazra and Baba Gomti Das also visited Lucknow and were warmly received.[76]

Another Hindu temple built by *nawab* Asaf-ud-daula was the famous Jagannath Temple. The temple covered a large area and was nine metres in height. It is quite interesting to note that the spire of the temple had a crescent moon emblem, bearing testimony to its builder.[77]

The old Sangat temple of Lucknow dates if not to the Mughal period, certainly to the eighteenth century. It was during the reign of Asaf-ud-daula that the famous Saint Baba Fatehchandji, the *acharya* of the *udasi* sect visited Lucknow. He got a very warm welcome from the *nawab*. Later a *maulvi* tried to create friction between the *nawab* and the Baba. But it proved futile. The *nawab* was impressed with supernatural powers of the saint and a number of *jagirs* were assigned to his service. Income from these *jagirs* was used to finance the construction of the Udasi Panth Gurudwara at the place now known as the Purana Bansmandi, Lucknow.[78]

An important incident of Asaf-ud-daula's reign was the advent of Sant Waldi Saheb, eleventh descendant in succession to the great Sant Kabir, in Lucknow. He was a follower of the Kabir Chaurahas of Kashi, and migrated to the outskirts of Lucknow. The philosophy of this Saint deeply impressed the *nawab*, and he immediately offered the part of land, where the Saint was staying, for construction of a temple. An income from eighty-four villages was also offered by Asaf-ud-daula to the Saint for such a noble cause. But Saint being a true follower of Sant Kabir, refused the offer. But the *nawab* arranged for the construction of a boundary wall around the land, the ruins of which are still to be seen at the place.[79]

The *nawab* never discriminated among his subjects on grounds of caste or creed. It is worthwhile to note that the palanquin-bearers of the *nawab* too had the permission to attend the court. Amongst these, special status was offered to Moti Singh, Maiku Singh, Shobha Singh and Bhola Singh. As mentioned earlier, Bhawani Singh or *Raja* Mahra was the favourite palanquin-bearer of the *nawab*. He trained the *tawaifs* (dancing girls) of the city in *kahra* dance, an exclusive folk dance of the 'Kahars'. During the Holi festival such dances were performed before the *nawab*, who had taken special measures to promote folk music, dance and old traditions. The performers were given substantial financial rewards by Asaf-ud-daula. During Asaf-ud-daula's reign Holi, Basant, Shravan and Moharram were celebrated with equal enthusiasm, and such celebrations cost lakhs of rupees to the state treasury.[80]

Kathak style of dancing received special patronage during the reign of Shuja-ud-daula and Asaf-ud-daula. Khushi Maharaj, who was regarded a great exponent of this style, flourished during the reign of Asaf-ud-daula.[81]

OTHER BUILDINGS

Asaf-ud-daula and his courtiers were famous for their philanthropic nature. *Raja* Tikait Rai was compared for his munificent nature with Karna the epic hero of *Mahabharat*. It is said that when King George-III was seriously ill, Asaf-ud-daula sent a *hakim* and rupees 25,000 for his treatment! The *nawab* also helped the people of Najaf Ashraf in Iraq. He sent Haji Mohammad Tehrani to Iran with a financial grant of rupees seven lakhs for the construction of a canal known as *nahr-e-aasifa* at Mashahad Shareef.[82]

The foundations of the famous Residency in Lucknow were laid during the reign of Asaf-ud-daula in Lucknow. Its construction was completed in the year 1800, that is during the reign of *nawab* Saadat Ali Khan. The complex was mainly meant for the residence of various British officers, posted from time to time by the East India Company at Lucknow. It was built as an exclusive European settlement within a circumference of 1 mile, 3 furlongs and 433 feet.[83]

The large-heartedness of Asaf-ud-daula was not confined to his encouragement of his own people. It went beyond. Two Europeans who made significant contributions to the buildings and living style of Lucknow are worthy of mention—Claude Martin and Maj. Antoine Polier. Claude Martin was a French soldier of fortune.[84] Reportedly he joined the army of the East India Company as a common soldier towards the end of seventeenth century, and rose from the ranks.[85] He was next heard of as a senior officer in the army of Shuja-ud-daula. He lived in Faizabad in great style. He was a collector of the works of art and also encouraged local craftsmen. After his army career, he engaged himself in trade and made fabulous amount of money. He was a builder and constructed the famous building of Lucknow named after his late wife *Constantina*.[86] The building exhibits a confluence of French and Indian styles. He also helped Asaf-ud-daula to construct Musabagh on the banks of Gomti which was a pleasure hut. That building now lies in a forlorn state but its structure bears the imprint of European influence.[87] Kothi Farahbaksh was also constructed by him, but it was purchased by the *nawab*.[88] Claude Martin wanted to avoid any such possibility for *Constantina*, and so he wrote a *Will* to be buried there, claiming possession and attachment with the building in perpetuity. Martin created a Trust consecrating this building as a school under the name La Martinere. This Trust also controls two other schools in Calcutta and Lyons in France carrying the same name—La Martinere. There may be few examples in the world of granting so much importance and patronage by a native ruler to a foreign national. But that was the *darya-dili*—the large heartedness of Awadh as created by Asaf-ud-daula.

The other case is of a European engineer Antoine Polier.[89] He worked as chief engineer with East India Company and was posted in Fort William at Calcutta. Later he joined Shuja-ud-daula at Faizabad and then moved on to Lucknow and lived there till 1788. He was a friend of Martin and was engaged in producing perfume from roses.

Asaf-ud-daula created a new world in Lucknow. The Mughal empire had vanished, all but in name. New provincial states were coming up. Asaf-ud-daula's time saw the rise and fall of the Mysore of Haider Ali and Tipu Sultan; the glow of Maratha power and its slow decline, the reduction of Nizam to the status of a subsidiary power; Panjab slogged under the uncertainties of its power equations among the various warring factions after Ranjit Singh; it was Asaf-ud-daula alone who survived and even financed the wars of East India Company. He created an administration which had equal participation of all communities. The revenue administration during Asaf-ud-daula's reign was dealt with by Hindu *diwans*. Two *diwans* graduated to political leadership as *naib-wazirs* namely Tikait Rai and Jhao Lal. The continuous strain of the Company's demand had its repercussions on the administration, undoubtedly and the officials had to be on the right side of both the *nawab* and the Company. The ambivalence was there for all to see. Shia ideology was beginning to rise and a theoretical framework of the Shia state was making its appearance. A separate Shia congregation had started to assemble at the Asafi Masjid for its Friday prayers. The *khutba* was being read in the name of the *nawab*. But Awadh was not a Shia state: Hindus did reach the highest executive posts in the administration of Awadh. A new and urbane language was coming up breaking the hegemony of Persian. It was Urdu which adopted the grammar and syntax of Hindi. The themes of Hindu mythology were being adopted by Muslim poets writing in Hindi at Bilgram, the Kashi of Awadh. The court of Asaf-ud-daula was glittering with the jewels of poetry and learning. Some were of native growth others came from Delhi and other places to lend their glow and brilliance to the culture of Awadh. It was truly the noon time of the Awadh dynasty which carried with it the *Ambience of Awadh*.

NOTES

1. W. Hoey (tr.), *History of Asaf-ud-daula: Nawab Wazir of Oudh*, Lucknow, 1971, p. 4.
2. H.C. Irwin, *The Garden of India*, Lucknow, 1974, p. 76.
3. W. Hoey, op. cit., p. 8.
4. In this context there are various versions. Some historians regarded it was a strained relations of mother and son which became the immediate cause of the transfer of capital—see *Faizabad Gazetteer*, p. 60. According to Yogesh Praveen, in one of his articles, as *nawab* Asaf-ud-daula changed the capital according to his own wishes, her widow mother, Bahu Begum, got annoyed with him—Yogesh Praveen, 'Nawabene Awadh', *Dharamyug*, 20 May, 1979.
5. H.C. Irwin, op. cit., p. 76.
6. M.H. Fisher, *A Clash of Cultures: Awadh, the British and the Mughals*, Delhi, 1987, pp. 72-3.
7. Jagdish Sahai, *Awadh Mein Nawabi Shasan Ka Itihas*, Faizabad, n.d., pp. 88-9.
8. It has been said of *raja* Jhao Lal by the contemporaries that he adopted Muslim customs, dress and religious duties such as the *Ramzan* fast—Bahadur Singh, Yadgar-i-Bahaduri, MS 255, Regional Archives, Allahabad, fol. 598. M.H. Fisher has stated in context of *raja* Jhao Lal's sincerity that he worked consequently for five days in monsoon rains to finish a bridge so that the *nawab* could comfortably continue a journey. For this he has cited Abu Talib, p. 37 (cited in his book on p. 69.) But Fisher is not accurate here in his quotation because the text tells us that Jhao Lal himself stood at the *ghat* of river Ghagara for five days in rains and superintended the transport of the troops and not the construction of a bridge. By 1796, he was assigned the duties of Commander-in-Chief, and Paymaster of the Army and various duties of the Financial Department—Akhbar of May, 1796, Munshi Sital Prasad,

Mirat al-Auza, Persian MS 2194, Raza Library, Rampur, fols. 209-10; Ratan Singh, Sultan al-Tawarikh, Persian MS, Lucknow University Library, Lucknow, fol. 242; Munshi Ram Sahai, *Ihsan al-Tawarikh*, Lucknow: Tamanni Press, 1876, pp. 126-7.

9. Jagdish Sahai, op. cit., p. 89.
10. W. Hoey, op. cit., pp. 15-17.
11. Ibid., p. 17.
12. Ibid., p. 16.
13. Jagdish Sahai, op. cit., p. 115; W. Hoey, op. cit., p. 16.
14. Moti Chand, *Kashi Ka Itihas*, Varanasi, 1985, p. 255; see also C.U. Aitchison, *A Collection of Treaties, Engagements, and Sunnads relating to India and Neighbouring Countries*, Vol. II, Calcutta, 1909, p. 72. By the Treaty of 1775 the sovereignty of the districts dependent on *raja* Chait Singh was ceded in perpetuity to the British Government. An agreement was made with the *raja* confirming him in his government, subject to a revenue of Rs. 22,66,180, and on condition of his adopting measures for the interest and security of the country and preservation of the peace—*Rajas and Nawabs of North-western Provinces*, Allahabad, 1877, p. 8.
15. *Rajas and Nawabs of North-Western Provinces*, op. cit., p. 8.
16. Muhammad Faiz Baksh, *Memoirs of Delhi and Faizabad, Being a Translation of 'Tarikh Faizbaksh'*, Vol. I, Tr. by W. Hoey, Allahabad, 1888-9, pp. 127-9.
17. R.W. Bird, *Dacoitee in Excelsis or, the Spoilation of Oude by the East India Company*, Reprint, Lucknow: Pustak Kendra, 1971, Chapter II.
18. Abdul Halim Sharar, *Guzishta Lakhnau Mashriqi Tammadun Ka Akhri Namona*, New Delhi, 1971, p. 26.
19. W. Hoey, op. cit., pp. 60-7; see also Jaggan Nath Mishra, *Adhunik Bharat Ka Itihas* (Hindi), p. 128.
20. Jaggan Nath Mishra, op. cit., p. 175.
21. M.H. Fisher, op. cit., pp. 61 & 87.
22. Sidney Hay, *Historic Lucknow*, Lucknow, 1939, p. 14.
23. Ibid., p. 15.
24. *Asiatic Annual Register*, Vol. IV, 1804, pp. 9-10. William Foster gives an interesting account of the Firangi Mahal in the pre-*nawabi* period which later flourished as a centre of learning. In the seventeenth century two employees or 'factors' were sent permanently to Lucknow in the Firangi Mahal area, which was situated in the eastern side of the Chowk. The main motive behind sending these two 'factors' was to buy bales of 'dereabauds' (a kind of muslin) which was manufactured in bulk in the Hassanganj area, situated on the northern side of river Gomti. The Firangi Mahal area was mainly used as bullion market which survived till 1665 — William Foster, *The English Factories in India*, Vols. 1637-41, 1646-50, 1651-54, Oxford, 1912, pp. 278, 140 & 122, 114, 148. During the reign of Aurangzeb, Firangi Mahal was given to Mullah Nazam Aladin Sahalvi—a religious leader. (Abdul Halim Sharar, op. cit., p. 59.) There is no reference about the British trade in this area in the latter part of the seventeenth century. It is curious enough to note that the latter Company officials who started making contacts with the *nawabs* were

completely unaware of the efforts of the early English traders and no further efforts were made to set up a British factory in the Firangi Mahal area.

25. Abdul Halim Sharar, op. cit., p. 16. It is said about Imambara that its construction cost about one lakh sterling or rupees ten lakhs. According to Charles Alfred Elliot, Asaf-ud-daula invited many architects from all over India and a contest was organised among them to draw a plan of the proposed construction—cited in Pawan Kumar Singh, *Shahar-e-Lucknow* (Hindi), Lucknow, 1990, p. 82. In this contest the winner was the famous architect Kifayatulla. Kishori Lal Goswami has mentioned that when the foundations of Imambara were being laid, the labourers found some hidden wealth. This wealth later came to be known as *Khazana-e-Ghaib*. It is said that *nawab* did not think it proper to utilise the whole wealth. He took only two crore rupees for the construction of Imambara and other buildings of Lucknow. The rest of the wealth was buried deep on which the foundations of Bara Imambara was laid—cited in Pawan Kumar Singh, *Shahar-e-Lucknow* (Hindi), Lucknow, 1990, pp. 82-3.
26. Yogesh Praveen, op. cit., pp. 46-7.
27. Rosie Llewellyn-Jones, *A Fatal Friendship, The Nawabs, the British and the City of Lucknow*, New Delhi: O.U.P., 1985, p. 15.
28. E.S. Harcourt & Fakir Hussain (trs.), *Lucknow: The Last Phase of an Oriental Culture*, London, 1975, p. 48.
29. Ibid., p. 47.
30. Ibid., p. 48.
31. In Abu Talib's *Tafazzul Ghaflin* we get this interesting account of Prince Jawan Bakht's visit to Lucknow—'During this period Prince Jawan Bakt fled from Shahjahanabad and came to Lucknow. The Governor and *wazir* wanted to receive him with usual ceremony. A pension of rupees three lakhs was assigned to him. As he had a political connection with the *wazir*, a close intimacy also sprang up between them, but this intimacy was destroyed by the prince's youthful follies, one of which was his marriage with the two women of the town, and so the prince elected to reside at Benares. But after the quarrel between Ismail Beg and Ghulam Qadir, and the departure of the Patel, the Prince came with Lord Cornwallis up to the suburbs of Lucknow and went towards Shahjahanabad without entering Lucknow.'—W. Hoey, op. cit., pp. 61-2.
32. Ratan Singh, op. cit., fol. 271; Bahadur Singh, op. cit., fol. 594.
33. Munshi Sital Prasad, op. cit., fol. 212; Shew Prasad, Tarikh-i-Faiz Baksh, Persian History 115, Salar Jang Museum Library, Hyderabad, fol. 194b; Resident to Governor-General, 10 June, 1776, Bengal Secret Consultations, National Archives of India, New Delhi, (from herein cited as N.A.I.) 8 July, 1776.
34. Bahadur Singh, op. cit., fols. 590b, 591; W. Hoey, op. cit., p. 2.
35. W. Hoey, op. cit., p. 12.
36. Bahadur Singh, op. cit., fol. 595b; Governor-General to Vice-President in Council, 5 April, 1797, Bengal Political and Secret Consultations, 10 April, 1797, N.A.I.
37. W. Hoey, op. cit., p. 25.

38. Harnam Singh, Tarikh-i-Saadat-i Jawid, Partly translated by Munshi Sadasukh Lal, MS Add. 30786, British Library, London, fols. 56b, 59b.
39. A wild account of Haider Beg's death is given in *Tafazzul Ghafflin*: 'In this year Haider Beg died, and Tikait Rai was appointed in his place. As already related, a vast number of women were gathered into Haider Beg's house in the famine year. Owing to this and to the old age of seventy years which he had reached, he became impotent, but his lust became more keen, and he asked Hakim Shifa'i Khan for some medicine. The Hakim told him to dip a shoot of grass in cinnamon 'itar and rub it on betel leaf, and eat once or twice a day. Haider Beg, finding this beneficial, began to use it freely without informing the hakim. The spirituous nature and the heating properties of cinnamon 'itar dried up the decreasing moisture of his system, and gave the mastery to the unnatural heat which was irritating his body because of some chronic fever. Haider Beg and his medical advisers did all they could, but it was no use, and he went to his reward.'—W. Hoey, op. cit., p. 77.
40. W. Hoey, op. cit., pp. 46-7.
41. Ibid., p. 47.
42. Abu Talib says, 'In this year Haider Beg Khan removed Surat Singh, who use to collect nearly 70 lakhs from the Bareli Division, and entrusted it to Kundal L'al and two or three Kayaths, who were *proteges* of the Rahela family and residents of that country. They remained in office two years, and during that time they sent numbers of cultivators from that district into Faizulla Khan's territory. To that period the beginning of the depopulation of Ruhelkhand is referred. The Kayaths were imprisoned for their embezzlements and died in confinement, and large sums which they owed to bankers and traders remained unpaid. The only cause for the removal of Surat Singh was the Naib's private greed.'— cited in W. Hoey, op. cit., pp. 23-4.
43. Thapar Chand was dismissed and imprisoned by Haider Beg Khan, subsequently the charge was handed over to Bijairaj—W. Hoey, op. cit., p. 53. Further, Jagdish Sahai in his book, while mentioning the atrocities and high-handedness of Haider Beg Khan, has also mentioned that the Governor-General got Col. Hannay hanged as he was unable to reach in time for help during the revolt of Chait Singh—Jagdish Sahai, op. cit., p. 27. This is incorrect as the source from where this information has been cited (W. Hoey, op. cit., p. 47) is misinterpreted by Dr. Sahai. Actually Col. Hannay was not hanged on the orders of the Governor-General, but after losing all hopes, he committed suicide by hanging himself.—W. Hoey, op. cit., p. 46.
44. Bahadur Singh, op. cit., fol. 595b; Munshi Ram Sahai, *Ihsan al-Tawarikh*, Lucknow, 1876, p. 130. We find a little contradiction regarding the caste of Tikait Rai. According to Purnendu Basu, Tikait Rai was a Saksena Kayastha —Purnendu Basu, *Oudh and the East India Company 1785-1801*, Lucknow, 1943, p. 17.
45. Resident to Governor-General, 13 October, 1796, Bengal Political Consultations, N.A.I., 29 October, 1796, No. 22.
46. Governor-General to Vice-President in Council, 5 April, 1797, Bengal Secret and Political Consultations, N.A.I., 10 April, 1797, No. 1.

47. C.U. Aitchison, op. cit., p. 57. See also the article of Yogesh Praveen which gives an detailed information of how Asaf-ud-daula died—*Dharamyug*, 20 May 1979, p. 24.
48. Munshi Sital Prasad, op. cit., fol. 81.
49. H.C. Irwin, op. cit., p. 86.
50. Maulana Fayzbaksh, Tarikh-i-Farahbaksh, Abdus Salam Collections, Persian MS 486/7, Aligarh Muslim University, Aligarh, fols. 243b-244a.
51. Ehtesham Abidi, *A Brief Sketch of the Life and Achievements of Maulana Shaikh Muhammad Ali Hazin*, an unpublished manuscript, p. 1; see also Sayyad Hassan Askari, 'The Political Significance of Hazin's Career in Eastern India' —*Bengal Past and Present* 63 (1943), pp. 1-10.
52. Ehtesham Abidi, op. cit., p. 2.
53. Sayyad Hassan Askari, op. cit., pp. 1-10.
54. It is interesting to note that Hazin got the patronage of the Hindu *raja* Balwant Singh of Benares. He was given land and cash gifts. Even Chait Singh who became the next *raja*, gifted Hazin 40,000 *asharfis*—Ghulam Husayn Khan, Balwand-namah, Persian MS 2210, N.A.I., pp. 154-5. Further, in 1756, when Shuja-ud-daula came to crush the revolt of *raja* Balwant Singh, the great Shia scholar and poet urged the *nawab* to come to terms with the *raja* and finally Shuja-ud-daula had to follow his advice—Ghulam Husayn Khan, op. cit., pp. 125-6. Even before the battle of Buxar, Shuja-ud-daula and Shah Alam II visited Hazin in Benares. This time the poet advised them not to fight against the British, and if they chose to do so, then they should mainly depend on their cavalry — Sayyad Hassan Askari, 'The Political Significance of Hazin's Career in Eastern India' — *Bengal Past and Present* 63(1943), pp. 1-10.
55. Though Hazin was a Shia theologian and scholar, he also had a secular approach. It so happened that *raja* Balwant Singh decreed a land of seven and a half acres in the name of Hazin (which included the locality of Aurangabad). The Shaikh out of gratitude composed the following verse in Persian and sent it to the Maharaja, which abundantly reveals his secular approach—

    As banaras na rawam mabad-i-aam ast eenja,
    Har brahman pisar-i-lachman u ram ast eenja.

    The meaning of the above verse is that, 'I would not like to go out of Benares; (Because) here is a worshipping place for all people. Here every Brahmin is the son of Rama and Lakshman'—*Shama*, Hasan Manzil, Shahganj, Agra, p. 27.
56. For details of Kashmiri's biography see Ghulam Ali Naqvi, *Imdad as-Saadat*, Lucknow, 1897, pp. 155-7; Muhammad Ali Kashmiri, *Najum as-sama takmilah*, Vol. II, Lucknow: Matba-i-Jafri, 1302/1884-85, pp. 323-8; Purnendu Basu mentions that during Kashmiri's stay in Calcutta, he developed fluency in English as well as Latin. To his credit he translated scholarly works on European mathematics and physics. At the same time he also compiled *hadiths* and wrote on Islamic philosophy with equal command. He had but one vice, from Shia point of view, his love for music.—Purnendu Basu, *Oudh and the East India Company 1785-1801*, Lucknow, 1943, pp. 23-4.
57. In this context Cole has cited Abdul Halim Sharar, *Guzashtah Lakhnau: Mashriqi Tammadun ka Ahkri Namunah*, Lucknow, 1974, p. 120. But he further

contradicts this reference by stating this on the basis of his interview with Muhammad Riza Ansari (Lucknow, February 1982) and says there is no direct reference to his studying there in the primary sources. But he also accepts that the Nizami syllabus played a crucial role in shaping Dildar Ali's thought and philosophy—J.R.I. Cole, *Roots of North Indian Shi'ism in Iran and Iraq: Religion and State in Awadh 1722-1859*, Delhi: O.U.P., 1989, p. 62, n. 63.

58. Sayyad Ijaz Husayn Kinturi, Shudhur al-'iqyan fi tarajim al-a 'yan, Vol. I, Calcutta National Library, Bukhar Collections (an unpublished Arabic source), fol. 136a.
59. Ratan Singh, op. cit., fol. 271; see also W. Hoey, op. cit., p. 1.
60. For a detailed study of the Shia faith, see S.H.M. Jafri, *The Origins and Early Developments of Shia Islam*, London, 1979, W.M. Watt, *The Formative Period of Islamic Thought*, Edinburgh, 1973, A.A. Sachedina, *Islamic Messianism: The Idea of the Mahdi in Twelver Shi-ism*, Albany, 1981.
61. Meer Hasan Ali, *Observations on the Mussulmans of India*, London, 1832, Vol. I, p. 23; E.S. Harcourt & Fakir Hussain (Trans.), op. cit., p. 86.
62. J.R.I. Cole, op. cit., pp. 128-36; 149-51.
63. Zaynu'l Abidin Shirvani, Riyad-as-siyahah, Moscow, 1974, Vol. III, pp. 1051-2. It is interesting to note that till 1775, Shuja-ud-daula 'still minted coins and had the Khutbah read in the Emperor's name for the sake of protocol, but for all practical purposes he was an independent prince.'—R.B. Barnett, *North India Between Empires: Awadh, the Mughals and the British—1720-1801*, Berkeley & Los Angeles, 1980, pp. 21-22.
64. Emma Roberts, *Scenes and Characteristics of Hindoostan*, Vol. II, London, 1835, pp. 178-9.
65. Abdul Latif Shustri, Tuhfat al-alam, Allahabad Regional Archives, fols. 197b-198a, see also Ali Bakht Azfari, Vaqiat-i-Azfari, ed. by T. Chandrashekharan, No. 65, Madras, 1957, pp. 104-5.
66. See M. Sadiq, *A History of Urdu Literature*, London, 1964, Chapter IX; R. Rusell & K. Islam, *Three Mughal Poets: Mir, Sauda, Mir Hasan*, Cambridge, 1968, E.S. Harcourt & Fakir Hussain, op. cit., p. 84.
67. M.H. Fisher, op. cit., pp. 235-6 n. 92.
68. E.S. Harcourt & Fakir Hussain (trs.), op. cit., pp. 147-8.
69. C.M. Naim & Carla Petievich, 'Urdu in Lucknow/Lucknow in Urdu', *Smarika*, 6 May 1995, Purvottar Railway Mahila Sansthan, Lucknow.
70. Ibid.
71. Acharya Ramchandra Shukla, *Hindi Sahitya Ka Itihas* (Hindi), Kashi: Nagri Pracharini Sabha, 1994, 28th edn., pp. 170-1.
72. Yogesh Praveen, *Lucknow Monuments*, Lucknow, 1989, p. 7.
73. Ibid., p. 29.
74. Ibid.
75. Ibid., p. 14.
76. Yogesh Praveen, op. cit., pp. 15-17.
77. Ibid., pp. 17-19.
78. Yogesh Praveen, op. cit., pp. 19-21.
79. Ibid., pp. 21-3.

80. Ibid., pp. 112-13.
81. E.S. Harcourt & Fakir Hussain (trs.), op. cit., p. 142.
82. Yogesh Praveen. op. cit., pp. 113-14.
83. Ibid., pp. 121-2.
84. Rosie Llewellyn-Jones, *A Very Ingenious Man: Claude Martin in Early Colonial India*, New Delhi: O.U.P., 1992, p. 14.
85. Najmal Ghani, *Tarikh-i- Awadh.*, Vol. III, Lucknow: Newal Kishore Press, 1919, p. 206.
86. Rosie Llewellyn-Jones, op. cit., p. 70.
87. Yogesh Praveen, *Bahare Awadh*, Lucknow, 1987, p. 16.
88. Christopher Hussey, *English Country Houses*, Vol. III, London, 1956, pp. 27. 85.
89. Rosie Llewellyn-Jones gives an interesting account regarding Polier's death, 'Polier was killed at Avignon, where he had settled with his French wife and daughters. Accounts of his murder vary—it was said to have been carried out by 'a band of brigands' who accused him of supporting Robespierre, while others believe it was a party of sans-culottes, jealous of Polier's obvious wealth, brought back from India. Whoever the perpetrators were, their act symbolised the general lawlessness in the wake of the Revolution (French Revolution of 1789).'—op. cit., New Delhi: O.U.P., 1992, p. 183.

Plate 1: Bara Imambara

Plate 2: Procession of Asaf-ud-daula

CHAPTER IV

Island of Awadh (1798-1837)

Asaf-ud-daula died in September 1797. With his passing away a glorious chapter in the history of Awadh came to an end. He was succeeded by his son and heir apparent Wazir Ali.[1] His succession was confirmed during the lifetime of Asaf-ud-Daula with the Governor-General Sir John Shore. Wazir Ali was married at the age of thirteen with the daughter of Ashraf Ali Khan, a noble in the *nawab's* court.[2] This marriage was celebrated with much pomp and glamour. About thirty lakhs were spent on this marriage. The *nawab* himself had walked on foot leading the precession of the bridegroom.[3] Wazir Ali used to look after the important administrative functions of the government during the lifetime of his father, and to receive the Governor-General or the members of the Governor-General's Council as part of protocol.

Wazir Ali was twenty when he ascended the *masnad* of Awadh.[4] He devoted his attention on his army and resented the interference of the East India Company in the affairs of Awadh. He felt his father had died because of the shock caused by illegitimate interference by the Company in the governance of his state. He wanted to reorganize his army and had a lurking hope of driving the English away from Awadh if possible.[5] In the very first year of his reign, the Governor-General himself came to Lucknow and demanded increase the Company's forces. The *nawab* refused. The Governor-General did not find it easy or convenient to depose the *nawab* right away. He went back to Calcutta and left the Resident to deal with the *nawab*. When the Company officials started searching for somebody else to be the *nawab* of Awadh, Saadat Ali Khan, brother of Asaf-ud-daula attracted their attention. Saadat Ali Khan had been driven out of Awadh after the unsuccessful conspiracy to kill Asaf-ud-daula in 1776. The Governor-General thought that a very good bargain could be struck with Saadat Ali Khan since he was living without any hope for the future particularly after the accession of Wazir Ali.[6] Stories were concocted and spread against Wazir Ali. An effort was made to challenge the legitimacy of his birth. Finally a plan of action was evolved by which it was decided to propagate that Wazir Ali was born of a woman of low origin who was already pregnant when she entered the harem. Surprisingly Asaf-ud-daula's mother Bahu Begum also joined the group along with Tafazzul Hussain, the *wazir* and Almas Ali Khan.[7] Wazir Ali was called for a conference at Bibiapur (Hardoi District) and was arrested by the British forces under the Resident Cherry.[8] When Saadat Ali Khan was informed about these development in Benares, he was overwhelmed. When Cherry said what would he give in exchange for the *nawabi*, Saadat Ali Khan, choked with emotions, replied that he would give away half the kingdom. He did not realise what he said at that weak moment, would become an article of faith with the Company officials. Ultimately that was what Saadat Ali was forced to do by two treaties, first in 1798 with Sir John Shore[9] and then in 1801 with Lord Wellesley[10]—the famous 'treaty of friendship'.[11]

Wazir Ali was taken to Benares. In his youthful rage he took to arms and killed Resident Cherry.[12] He was arrested and sentenced to life imprisonment at Fort Williams, Calcutta where he died in captivity in 1817.[13] This was not the first instance of this kind. Later also whenever the Company suspected any of the rulers harbouring ideas of independence they were similarly dealt with. Such were the cases with Munna Jaan and Wajid Ali Shah. Although Bahu Begum was part of the conspiracy to depose Wazir Ali, she could not apprehend the deep and ulterior motives of the English. Masi-ud-din Khan in his book *Oude: Its Princes and Its Governments Vindicated*, wrote:

> Asophood-dowlah was succeeded by his natural son, Vizier Allie and his succession was at first recognised by the British Government, but Sir John Shore, seeing that a better bargain could be made with the brother of the deceased *nawab* than with his son, repaired to Benares, and proposed to the *nawab* Saadat Allie to dethrone Vizier Allie, upon the condition that the subsidy should be increased from 5,55,000 pounds a year to 7,50,000 pounds. To this bargain Saadat Allie cheerfully consented in.[14]

The story of the illegitimacy of Wazir Ali was totally trumped up. Robert W. Bird has said that it was found after an enquiry that

Wazir Ali's birth was illegitimate, but which enquiry?[15] It was also put on the wings of gossip that Asaf-ud-daula was impotent from birth as quoted by some historians (or so-called). Now the writing of history should not be bereft of the knowledge of biology. No body can be 'impotent since birth' unless one is a born eunuch. Impotence is a malady at the time of youth. But in his prime, Asaf-ud-daula had a merry time with many women. The English succeeded in their game more because persons like Bahu Begum, Hassan Raza Khan, Almas Ali Khan and Tikait Rai were parties of the conspiring elite. But a new dimension had been added to the powers of the Company. Not only was their assent critical for the succession of a new *nawab*, they now assumed the power of even deposing a ruling *nawab*. This lesson went a long way in creating a sense of terror on the minds of all the succeeding rulers of Awadh.

On his accession Saadat Ali Khan entered into the first treaty with the East India Company in 1798. By this treaty among other arrangements, the payments to the British Company were raised to 76 lakh rupees and the minimum British force to be maintained in the province was fixed at ten thousand men. At the same time the *nawab-wazir* made an agreement with Bahu Begum granting her certain *jagirs* in Gonda and Faizabad under the guarantee of the British Government. In addition, the Company took over the Fort of Allahabad, along with allocation for its maintenance.[16]

Dismemberment of Awadh

In May 1798, Lord Wellesley set foot on the soil of India. He was a convinced imperialist and his tenure was marked by his incessant endeavour to take over as much as he could of the princely states and territories of this country. At this time Marathas were the only force to reckon with. The conflict between the English and the Marathas was imminent but it was to come later to the total advantage of the Company. Wellesley first turned his attention to Mysore, destroying Tipu in 1799. Then came the time of Awadh. He resorted to an earlier decision of his predecessor Sir John Shore, who had directed the Resident in Awadh to dislodge the *nawab* from the areas of the Doab.[17] After the matters related with Wazir Ali were settled, Wellesley again thought of some new schemes by which more pressure could be exerted on the *nawab*. He conveyed that the *nawab* should increase the number of British detachments and pay for them.[18] The *nawab* declined to accept this proposal, but later by dangling the fear of an Afghan invasion under Zaman Shah, the Company forced him to take on the additional liability of more British forces.[19] At one stage, when the pressure became too much for him to bear Saadat Ali Khan expressed a wish to abdicate.[20] But no agreement could be reached about his successor. The Company said that the question of a successor may not arise because the lineage of the *nawab* may be discontinued. On this suggestion, Saadat Ali Khan immediately retracted from any such course of action.[21] In 1800, the Governor-General despatched armed forces to Awadh from Calcutta. The hapless *nawab* was left with no other option, but to accept the burden of these extra forces and the *nawab* was asked to reduce his own forces by an equal number. It was a wonderful ploy: The power of the *nawab* became weaker and he paid for his becoming weak.

In February 1801, the Governor-General wrote a letter to the *nawab* that he had unnecessarily taken on the burden of two armies under him; he might as well abdicate and live in peace on a pension. As an option, he was politely asked to surrender half his territories to the Company as a one-time payment for the Company forces![22] The *nawab* equally politely replied that since no payments were due from the State of Awadh, none of the proffered options was relevant. The Governor-General was enraged at this audacity and a new factor was added in the Company's communication to the *nawab*.[23] It was conveyed to the *nawab* that the Company could not sit idle and keep on looking at the deterioration of the civil and military administration and the suffering of the people of Awadh. It was a fresh ruse against a native state. The British Imperialism at that point of time in history professed to take upon itself the benign responsibility of the people of the kingdoms it had taken over or was soon going to take over.[24] The *nawab* resisted for about five months, but ultimately had to surrender. In November 1801 the famous *Treaty of Friendship* was signed between the Company and Saadat Ali Khan. By the major conditions of the treaty half the territories of Awadh with total revenues of 1.35 crores were taken over. The *nawab* surrendered Ruhelkhand, Etawah, Kanpur, Fatehgarh, Allahabad, Azamgarh, Basti and Gorakhpur.[25] The Awadh army was totally disbanded. The *nawab* was provided British bodyguards.[26] The *nawab* was required to abide by the 'friendly' advise of the Company Resident. The districts skirting Awadh were formed into Ceded provinces and Henry Wellesley was appointed the President and Lieutenant Governor of these districts.[27] Henry Wellesley, the brother of Lord Wellesley was later to become the Duke of Wellington, the victor of Napoleon at Waterloo. His initial training was in India. The British had given up the policy of keeping Awadh as a buffer state. Except for the north, it was surrounded on all sides by territory under British arms and administration.[28] The seeds of later take over of Awadh were firmly planted.[29] Nothing explains better the attitude and approach of the Company than the preface of the official version of *Treaties and Engagements in Awadh* as published by the British Government:

The Vizier's army was an armed rabble, ill-disciplined, and would have been rather a source of danger than a help had the invasion of Zaman Shah from Afghanistan, with anticipations of which the people of India were periodically alarmed, taken place. In 1799, therefore, the Marquis Wellesley addressed the Vizier, with a view to induce him to disband his troops and replace them by a British subsidiary force. Major Scot was deputed to conduct negotiations for the above purpose, and to secure, by a cession of territory from the Vizier, a resource for the regular payment of the subsidy. The Vizier was very reluctant to agree to the proposals made to him, and threatened to abdicate in favour of his son. But at length, after protracted negotiations and the deputation of the Honourable Mr. Wellesley, the Governor-General's brother, to Lucknow, a Treaty (No. XXXVII) was signed on 10th November, 1801, by which the Vizier ceded to the British Governments lands in the Doab yielding a revenue of Rupees 1,35,23,474, in lieu of the subsidy, and all future expenses incurred in defeating his nujeebs, 2,000 cavalry and 300 golundaz; and agreed to introduce a good system of government in his remaining territories. The Treaty also provided for the free navigation of the Ganges and other rivers, where they formed the mutual boundary of the British territories and Oudh. At a personal interview with the Vizier in Lucknow, the Governor-General, after some discussion, settled various points arising out of the Treaty of 10th November which remained to be adjusted, and explained the general principles which should regulate the connection and intercourse between the two States as resulting from the Treaty. The results of this conference were embodied in Memorandum (No. XXXIX), of which a copy, signed and sealed by the Governor-General, was denied to the Vizier.[30]

His Excellency (the *nawab-wazir*) has also engaged always to advise with, and to act in conformity to the Council (counsel) of the officers of Honourable Companies. Those Councils will always be offered to His Excellency in the form of friendly advice, and in the spirit of reciprocal confidence, and of mutual regard and respect. . . . Under these regulations the Governor-General expects that the

Nabob Vizier will act in conformity to the advice and representations of the Resident, and as no question of difficulty remains between the British Government and His Excellency, the Governor-General entertains a confident hope, that no future vexation can occur in the transaction of affairs.[31]

The high handed intervention of Lord Wellesley continued on all fronts. In 1802, he took over Farrukhabad. The Marathas, the last vestige of native power in India were subjugated by the war that followed the Treaty of Bassein in 1802. The Mughal emperor, who till then was under the protection of the Marathas, automatically became a pensioner of the East India Company in 1803. British power had become supreme. Wellesley himself carried his policy of aggrandisement, with its financial costs, too far. But the things had become too hot for him and he was criticised in Parliament. In 1805 he was recalled. It is not without some surprise that one finds Awadh managing to survive till 1856, even after what it received at his hands.

Internal Administration of Awadh

After the Treaty of 1801 and the surrender of Ruhelkhand and ceded districts to the Company and the overall dismemberment of the Mughal empire, Saadat Ali Khan devoted himself to the internal administration of whatever was left of Awadh.

The above narrative clearly proves the point that although Saadat Ali Khan had a clear dependence on the Company for his political survival, he still emotionally believed that he continued to be the *nawab-wazir*, a subordinate to the Mughal emperor. In 1798, when he was installed on the *masnad* of Awadh, the existence of Mughal emperor was still propped up by the receding power of the Maratha arms. Meanwhile the Marathas set on a course of internecine struggle among themselves. After the death of Nana Phadnavis in 1800 the Holkars and the Scindhia fought the last battle over the control of Poona *peshwai*. The *peshwa* sought the help of the British by the Treaty of Bassein in 1802. By this treaty he accepted the Subsidiary Alliance and lost his independence as the price of British protection. The other Maratha *sardars* took umbrage against the treaty and continued with their isolated attempts to fight the British but one by one they lost ground and had to surrender. Scindhia accepted the Subsidiary Alliance in 1803 by the Treaty of Suji-arjan-gaon and surrendered Broach, Ahmednagar, Doab, as well as Agra and Delhi.

This also led to the aged emperor Shah Alam coming under the British protection. But during this time although the *nawab* of Awadh did not present any *nazar* to the Mughal emperor and no *khilat* of office seems to have been sent by the emperor, the title of *wazir* was implicitly bestowed through correspondence by the Mughal court to Saadat Ali Khan. On this occasion Saadat Ali Khan '. . . expressed a wish to celebrate the mark of royal distinction by some public act of rejoicing . . .'[32] but the idea was not appreciated by the British Resident at Lucknow and it was dropped. The Company perhaps did not want Awadh to look beyond its boundaries. The state of Awadh was reduced to an *island* surrounded by omniscient presence of British Company all around.

Saadat Ali Khan having lost the territories of Ruhelkhand, Farrukhabad, Varanasi, Gazipur and Ballia, concentrated his attention on the remaining territories under his command.[33] The theory that all agricultural land belongs to the state had continued from the olden times. It was for the state to grant the tenure of the landholding and decide the conditions thereof. In Asaf-ud-daula's time a very large area of land had been granted by way of *jagirs*.[34] The *jagirdar* had the right to collect the revenue from the area under his jurisdiction and had to yield a definite proportion of it to the controlling authority of the state. A large number of officers and troops of the British East India Company were to be paid through the state treasury. The word used was *tankhwahs*, meaning salary. In case of default of payment of salary, the British officers appropriated to themselves a certain area of land and collected the land revenue in lieu thereof. This system bypassed the authority of the State of Awadh. Similarly certain area were given to *ijaradars*, or contractors who collected the land revenue as contractors of the state. Saadat Ali Khan slowly established control over all these conduits that bypassed his authority. The recalcitrant *jagirdars* were brought to book by a judicious use of force comprising of the British troops and officers appointed in Awadh to look after the security of the state as well as the *nawab*. In the beginning the officers protested but later on when the payments from *jagirs* became regular, the need for the use of force became much less. He also resumed many of the rent-free grants which had been lavished by Asaf-ud-daula. The system of *ijarah* was abandoned and greater use was made of the bureaucracy of *nazims* and *chakladars*. The money came directly to the treasury. The protests of *jagirdars* were brushed aside. Sometimes the Resident tried to intervene, but the *nawab* held his ground.[35] The treasury reflected the prosperity of the agriculture and trade of Awadh. As compared to the *jagirdars*, he looked after the interests of the general public much better and started enjoying their confidence. After Wellesley was recalled in 1805, the *nawab* was left free to consolidate his command on the administration of the state. *Raja* Dayakrishna continued to be the *diwan* and the entire *diwani* was manned by Hindu officers.[36] The *nawab* made Tafazzul Hussain Khan his *naib-wazir*.[37] Tafazzul Hussain was his tutor in the days when Saadat Ali Khan was the *nazim* of Bareli.[38] When Saadat Ali Khan finally had to make his way to Benares, he went along with him. He had gone to Calcutta and gained social acceptance in the British circles with his knowledge of English.[39] Tafazzul Hussain Khan belonged to a family of Khatris.[40] His family had converted to Shia Islam for the sake of getting into the service of the state. Tafazzul Hussain maintained good relations both with the East India Company as well as with the *nawab*—a typical officer of the state at that time in Awadh. He died in 1800.[41] After his death the *nawab's* second son, Mirza Shams-ud-daula became the *wazir*.[42] He was a man of balance and great dedication. In 1812 after Shams-ud-daula's death, the *nawab* appointed Hakim Mehdi Ali Khan the *wazir*.[43] Mehdi Ali Khan proved a great asset to the *nawab* and the administration of the state improved considerably.

After Saadat Ali Khan became the *nawab*, Bahu Begum went back to Faizabad, but the relations between them remained indifferent. But Saadat Ali Khan often visited her and paid her due respect more to ensure that she might not give away her property to someone else. But the *begum* did not fully trust him and she left her inheritance in the protection of the Company rather than leaving it to Saadat Ali Khan. The decision was ironic since she was responsible for Saadat Ali Khan being made the *nawab* after the deposition of Wazir Ali.

Buildings and Culture

The control of the collection of land revenue brought money into the state treasury and the *nawab* could now pursue the customary activity of Awadh lineage by undertaking construction of public buildings. His first work of public good was building of the market named Saadatganj to commemorate his rule. It was located in the west of Lucknow and became the centre of trade with Doab. The other markets which came up during his time were Rakabganj, Mangliganj, Maqboolganj, Golaganj and Rastogi Mohalla.[44] The foundations of Chattar Manzil, named after his mother Chattar Kunwari, a Rajput Raikwar princess, were laid.[45] The *dargah* of Hazrat Abbas situated in Rustom Nagar was given a bigger facade: it was converted into a big building which housed the metal crest of a banner belonging to Hazrat Abbas, which was brought from Iraq.[46] An outstanding event of his time was the construction of Hanuman Mandir in Aliganj. His mother Chattar Kunwari basically a Hindu princess had great faith in Hanuman. She had named Saadat Ali Khan *mangli* during his childhood. The word *'mangli'* is derived from *mangal* (Tuesday), the day of the week considered specific for the worship of Lord Hanuman. The temple carries the crescent moon on its spire, a unique example of the communal harmony of that period.[47] Saadat Ali Khan also constructed a mausoleum at Golaganj for his mother *janab alia* (Chattar Kunwari). The dome of this building is perhaps the biggest in Lucknow, and the second biggest in Awadh. The dome of the mausoleum of Bahu Begum at Faizabad is rated to be the largest.[48]

The buildings that came up during his time carry a definite imprint of Saracenic influence. But he had also started emulating European architecture. The two most outstanding buildings of his reign were Dilkusha on the outskirts of Lucknow, and the Lal Baradari, the coronation hall of the *nawabs*. The building is fittingly named *Qasar-ul-Sultan*. The residential complex of the *nawab* had shifted from Macchi Mahal to another site on the banks of Gomti, called Moti Mahal.[49] In this complex new buildings named Shah Manzil, Mubarak Manzil and Neeli Baradari were laid out. Kothi Farahbakhsh, originally named as Farhatbakhsh (meaning pleasure-giving) provided a much-needed health resort to the *nawab*. This Kothi is now part of the huge complex of Chattar Manzil.[50] Close to Moti Mahal he bought a house built by a European and named it Kothi Noor Baksh (Light-giving).[51] It has a *baradari* in its compound named Jahoor Baksh. This building is now the residence of the Collector of Lucknow. Another building, Noor Manzil, came up in its vicinity. One of the sons of Saadat Ali Khan lies buried there. A building of great interest is Khursheed Manzil which was built for his wife

Khursheedzadi (the present La Martinere Girls College),[52] built by a European. The Residency was completed during his time. The *baradaris* meant for music programmes, played an important role in the social life of Lucknow. They bear the influence of Rajput architecture.[53] Badshah Manzil in the Moti Mahal complex and the Chandiwali Baradari built near the China Bazar Gate provide demonstrable elements of influence of Hindu architecture on these buildings.[54]

Saadat Ali Khan had spent the best years of his life in Benares and kept his contacts with the Company officials through his tutor Taffazul Hussain Khan. He tried to import certain Western ideas into his edifices. He encouraged people to adopt new ideas in science and technology. He imported an Iron Bridge from London which some how could not be laid during his lifetime. Its installation was completed by Nasir-ud-din Haider across the Gomti at Daliganj and is known as *lohe ka pul* (Iron Bridge).[55]

In the field of Urdu poetry the two poets who created a great name at this time were Nasikh and Mir Anees. Mir Anees is famous for his epoch-making composition of elegiac *marsiyas*. The recitation of *marsiyas* with their ringing rhythms created an atmosphere of pathos at the time of Moharram celebrations.

During the time of Saadat Ali Khan, *kathak* dance was patronised. The three celebrated classical dancers of this age were Hallalji, Prakashji and Dayalluji.[56] The school of *kathak* which was initiated during the time of Asaf-ud-daula, continues even to this day and every generation has had masters contributing to the exposition of the style. A new institution of *tawaifs* had developed. This institution is erroneously put on par with the prostitutes. The *tawaifs* were fairly respectable singing girls with accomplishments in the field of music almost in a classical mould. Their sessions were like the evening clubs where the people of standing and culture came to enjoy their leisure with elan and elegance. Classical *ghazal* singing came out of these *kothas*. In style they could be compared to 'salons' of Paris.

A large number of Europeans entered the *nawab's* service because of his association with them during his stay at Benares and contacts at Calcutta. Before the treaty of 1801, Europeans got employment in the military service of the *nawab*. With this treaty the British Company took over the army responsibilities and the *nawab* was left with a very small force at his command which had a few

Europeans. After the passing away of Claude Martin, no other outstanding French or European seems to have made his mark. An Englishman, Robert William Bird, had taken service with Saadat Ali Khan in 1812 and remained in employment with successive *nawabs*. He was granted pension in 1832.[57] He is the celebrated author of the book *Dacoitee in Excelsis: or, the Spoilation of Oude by the East India Company* and presented a very sincere account of the happenings of that period because of his close association and detailed knowledge of the people of Awadh. The *nawab* kept in his service an English engineer MacLeod who was instrumental in the placement of the order for the Iron Bridge in Lucknow.[58] He was also the consultant in the construction of Khursheed Manzil, a building named after the *nawab's* Begum Khursheed Mahal.[59]

Saadat Ali Khan, however, imposed some restrictions on the non-official Europeans settling in the city. There is one reported incident of Carvalho, a Portuguese, who was evicted from his house. Another such case is of one Mr. Paul, who tried to establish himself in the city, but was not successful.[60]

In Saadat Ali Khan's time Lucknow continued to grow. The treasury was full and there was general prosperity. He was undoubtedly an intelligent person and one of the best administrators of the Lucknow dynasty. He personally looked after the details of the administration and kept a safe balance between the *diwani* and his political administration. He was sagacious and competent. In the restrained words of John W. Kaye,

> If there was at any time, hope for Oude, under purely native administration, it was during the *wazeership* of Saadat Ali, for he was not a bad man and he appears to have rather enlightened view with respect to some important administrative questions.[61]

Hakim Mehdi Ali Khan was appointed *wazir* in 1812 after Shams-ud-daula.[62] He proved to be a very successful administrator and gained a lot of confidence of the general public. The revenues came to the treasuries in full measure and the total collections were reported to be fourteen crore rupees. In 1813, Lord Hastings came to India as Governor-General. Lord Hastings was obliged to Saadat Ali Khan, who had given him a financial help of rupees one crore by which Hastings was able to meet his personal liabilities. Saadat Ali Khan was naturally happy about the appointment and even entertained a distant hope that the areas which were taken away from him by the Treaty of 1801 could now be regained by him on payment of a certain amount of money. His confidence emanated from the 14 crores he had accumulated with him. But Col. Bailey who was Resident at this time felt greatly uncomfortable at the prospect of Saadat Ali Khan establishing direct links with the new Governor-General. He therefore organised a conspiracy to kill the *nawab*. He bought off his brother-in-law, Ramzan Ali Khan, and had the *nawab* poisoned through his unsuspecting attendant Jawahar Ali. The *nawab* died in sleep in his Moti Mahal residence. This shows up another unsavoury aspect of the Company administration of Awadh. A ruling *nawab* could be deposed; a ruling *nawab* could also be killed by conspiracy.[63]

Saadat Ali Khan's was succeeded by his son Rafat-ud-daula who sat on the *masnad* of Awadh under the name Mirza Ghazi-ud-din Haider. The succession was only slightly less dramatic than that of his father. It was organised by Col. Bailey resident who had been instrumental in the poisoning of the late *nawab*.[64]

Saadat Ali and his Three Sons

Saadat Ali Khan had three sons, Rafat-ud-daula, Shams-ud-daula and Nasir-ud-daula.[65] They were born in Benares where Saadat Ali Khan was living in a state of total despair on the yearly pension of three lakh rupees granted by Asaf-ud-daula his half-brother. Saadat Ali Khan also entered into some side business to add to his income. But the overall position of the family was not happy and they still had to live within their limited means. This experience contributed to the parsimonious habits of Saadat Ali Khan. But when he became the *nawab* this habit stood him in good stead.

Rafat-ud-daula succeeded Saadat Ali Khan after his death and assumed the name of Ghazi-ud-din Haider on his ascension to the *masnad* in 1814. He also assumed the title of King in 1819.[66] He was succeeded by his son Nasir-ud-din Haider (1827-37). These two occupants of the *masnad* have brought such a bad name to the throne of Awadh that even the passage of time has not been able to obviate the calumny attached to its reputation.

The second son of Saadat Ali Khan was Shams-ud-daula. He was made *wazir* by his father after the departure of Tafazzul Hussain Khan. He died during the lifetime of his father in 1812. He was a very sincere and devoted person and maintained a dignified public profile. Hakim Mehdi Ali succeeded him as *wazir*.

The third son was Nasir-ud-daula who ascended the throne in 1837 under the name Mohammad Ali (1837-42). According to Islamic law, he may not have had a chance to succeed. But the string of illegitimacies sprung up during the reigns of Ghazi-ud-din Haider and Nasir-ud-din Haider did not let a proper successor come up after Nasir-ud-din Haider and the line stopped there. After Muhammad Ali, luckily the succession was smooth and undisputed. He was succeeded by his son Amjad Ali Shah (1842-7), and he by his son Wajid Ali Shah (1847-56).

The story of the lives and times of Ghazi-ud-din and Nasir-ud-din Haider are worthy of narration. Rafat-ud-daula (Ghazi-ud-din Haider), the eldest son was born in Benares, during his father Saadat Ali Khan's exile there. He was married to the daughter of Mushabbir Khan, a friend of Saadat Ali Khan in Benares.[67] She is later known in history as Badshah Begum. She was a religious person and was well versed in Islamic theology. She became very haughty and assumed an attitude of self-importance. And because she followed a strict religious regimen, she began to look down her husband. Her prudish sense of religiosity began to create difference of attitudes between the husband and wife, and slowly the couple drifted apart. Badshah Begum gave birth to a daughter, who was named Moti Begum, but no son was born to her. Agha Mir, the *khansaman* (Steward) helped Rafat-ud-daula in the pursuit of physical pleasures and looser side of life. He brought in a concubine (*kaneez*), Subah-e-daulat for the company of Rafat-ud-daula, and it was she who bore him a son. Badshah Begum took away this infant into her keeping and had Subah-e-daulat killed. She was buried in an unknown place in total anonymity.[68] This son later ascended the throne as Nasir-ud-din Haider. Almost till the end of his life he believed that Badshah Begum was his mother. Only when the court intrigues became hot, the real facts were conveyed to him. When he came to know about it, he unearthed the remains of his mother and built a respectable mausoleum for her.[69]

Bahu Begum wanted to exercise total control on Nasir-ud-din Haider and keep him away from the influence of his father, even as prince and heir-apparent. She provided him a lavish living style. Prurient women found their way into his harem. Two of them played the most important and infamous role in his life. The first was Sukhchain. When she gave birth to a son, she was given the name Afzal Mahal. This son is known in history as Munna Jaan.[70] The second woman was Malika-e-Zamani. Reportedly she entered the 'Harem' with a son from an earlier liaison. This son is known to us as Kaiwajah. And here began the epic fight between three *begums*—Badshah Begum, Afzal Mahal and Malika-e-Zamani.[71]

It has been mentioned earlier that Rafat-ud-daula had drifted from his wife Badshah Begum. Badshah Begum tried to have complete control on his son Nasir-ud-din Haider, who became King in 1827.

When Nasir-ud-din Haider himself fell under the spell of Malika-e-Zamani, she started exercising the real power behind the throne.[72] Badshah Begum having lost her influence on Nasir-ud-din Haider took Munna Jaan and his mother, Afzal Mahal under her wing and wanted him to succeed. On the other hand Malika-e-Zamani, who was able to bring Nasir-ud-din Haider back in favour with his father Ghazi-ud-din Haider, wanted to advance the claims of Kaiwajah. At this period of time the Lucknow *darbar* was full of sensuality and carnality. Since the rulers were sunk in self-indulgence, this became the pattern for all people in high positions. Everybody was dissipated in licentiousness. Unsavoury liaisons had become the wont in which the high of the land became mightily involved. Everybody was angling for power, money and the control on the throne. Players in the game, were the British Residents, court factions and the *begums*. The stories of the personal life of Nasir-ud-din Haider had become a subject of much light-hearted gossip all over. The reason for the lack of respect for the ruler was partly because of his comic adoption of English dress and customs.[73] The British society in Lucknow and Calcutta made great fun of him. Saucy tales of his lifestyle were published in London in 1855 in a book titled as *The Private Life of an Eastern King*.[74] The damage he did to the institution of rulership of Awadh was immense. It could not be undone by the saner rulers, who came after him, namely, Muhammad Ali Shah, Amjad Ali Shah and Wajid Ali Shah.

Succession of Ghazi-ud-din Haider

Just as Bahu Begum had a poor opinion of her husband Rafat-ud-daula, so had his father Saadat Ali Khan. Reportedly Rafat-ud-daula is said to have been confined to his house if not actually imprisoned by his father. When Saadat Ali Khan's life came to an abrupt end, Rafat-ud-daula approached the Resident with the help of two nobles of the court—Mirza Hazi and Mirza Jafar.[75] Bahu Begum also helped them in this effort. Col. Bailey thought that Rafat-ud-daula would be an easier person to manage compared to his father and would be under obligation to the Company, and so he recommended his case for succession. With his blessings Rafat-ud-daula sat on the *masnad* of Awadh on 14 October 1814, assuming the title 'Ghazi-ud-din Haider'. The Governor-General, Lord Hastings himself came to Lucknow on this occasion and was offered a gift of rupees one crore. He accepted this as a loan for the Company. The gesture pleased the new *nawab* and he offered another rupees fifty lakhs to the Company.[76] The accession of Ghazi-ud-din Haider thus brought rupees one and a half crores to the coffers of the Company. The gifts to the Resident and other officials were in addition. So the custom that every new *nawab* must give more to the Company officials and surrender some more of his powers became an accepted procedure with the Awadh dynasty. Hakim Mehdi Ali continued to be the *wazir*. Since the *nawab* was a weak person the palace simmered with conspiracies in which Agha Mir, the *begums* and the Residents, all played their roles. The Resident's interference increased in Awadh's internal administration in violation of the treaty obligations of 1801. But the *diwani* under *raja* Jaggannath and the economy of the State continued to flourish.[77]

The year 1814 saw the Company drawn into a war with Nepal. The Gurkhas had overthrown the ancient ruling dynasty of Nepal in 1768 and extended their control over the whole hilly region from the frontier of Bhutan on the east to the Sutlej on the west. They sought to extend their dominions over the plains. Since the boundaries between the British and Gurkha territories were ill-defined, there was constant friction. In 1814 they occupied the districts of Butwal and Sheoraj. On their refusal to withdraw, Lord Hastings declared war. The war continued for about two years and came to an end in 1816 with the Treaty of Sagauli. The Gurkhas withdrew from Sikkim, ceded Garhwal and Kumaon and the area west of Kali river to the Company. Although the British dominions were extended by these wars, the Company was now in need of money. The *nawab* was coerced into advancing another loan of one crore. As a sop, the Khairagarh territory (present districts of Sitapur and Lakhimpur Kheri) was given to the state of Awadh.

The Charter granted to the East India Company in 1793 was renewed in 1813. The British Parliament was under pressure to break the monopoly of the East India Company of the trade with the east. The Court of Directors of the Company naturally wanted to retain their rights and put up a very strong fight. Ultimately the matter was resolved by a compromise. The Company was allowed to retain its monopoly of the China trade, but the Indian trade was thrown open to all Englishmen. The new Charter allowed the Company to continue the administration of its territorial acquisitions, 'without prejudice to the undoubted sovereignty of the British Crown'.[78] The sovereignty of the Crown which was limited to the island of Bombay up to this time was now enlarged to cover all the Company's possessions in India. This brought Parliament in touch with the happenings in India and the actions of the Company became a subject of parliamentary scrutiny. This added to the responsibility of the Company and it had to be prepared at all times to be answerable to the public opinion in England. Whether the Indian rulers took any advantage of this situation is a matter of doubt. A new dimension was added to the activities of the Company and they organised themselves for dissemination of information in such a way that the conduct of Indian rulers was always presented as perverse.

Hakim Mehdi Ali Khan, who continued as *wazir* under the new *nawab*, was an able and upright administrator. Mirza Jafar who was tipped to become the *wazir* on the accession of Ghazi-ud-din Haider died of shock at his failure to get the office. Another claimant for the *wizarat*, Agha Mir, now organised a conspiracy for the removal of Hakim Mehdi Ali Khan with the help of the Resident. Hakim Mehdi Ali Khan was charged with the murder of Rai Amar Singh, the *chakladar* of Baharaich, and was removed. Agha Mir, the old *khansaman*, became the *wazir*.[79] He was a man of low origin and on assuming *wizarat* did not grow in stature. He gathered together a set of people of his own flock. The activities of the administration became mean and selfish in approach and attitude. Agha Mir and his gang exploited the power which came to them and amassed tremendous amount of wealth.

Badshah Begum was a religious person and was brought up in an atmosphere where Shia thought and legend had become part of her bearing. She took her religious rites to an extreme and began to celebrate the *chatti*, the sixth day of the birth of Imam Mehdi, almost on the pattern of Krishna Janmastami. The *jhanki's* (replicas of Kerbala) of the various Imams were decorated. In her palace complex she constructed mausoleums of the Twelve Imams. Like the *devadasis*, one untouched maiden was dedicated to serve each Imam. This novelty was not acceptable to the Shia theologians but they dared not oppose the Badshah Begum. Sometimes Ghazi-ud-din Haider also participated in these celebrations.[80]

The attention of the *nawab* was more and more distracted by the atmosphere of permissiveness infiltrating the palace. But it was typical of the heritage of the *nawabs* of Lucknow that despite their diversions they were constantly engaged in works of public utility. In front of Moti Mahal a boat bridge was constructed across the Gomti to connect the palace complex with the orchards of the *nawab* on the other side. He constructed a mausoleum for Saadat Ali Khan in a typically Persian style, but the architecture of this building is unique. The dome stands out with abundant individuality without the support of any auxiliary structure like the minarets. Another mausoleum dedicated to Saadat Ali Khan's wife Khursheed Mahal was constructed adjacent to this building.[81] These two mausolea are elegant in conception and the quality of their construction. He also started construction of another building on the lines of the mausoleum of Hazrat Imam Ali, and named it Najaf-e-Ashraf. As chance would have it, he was himself buried in this mausoleum, and it is now called Shah Najaf.

Ghazi-ud-din Haider as King

In 1819 he was inspired by the British to cut off the last lingering relationship with the Mughal court and assume independent title as King.[82] His preoccupation with Shia theology and sectarianism led him to believe that his line of succession descended directly from Imam Moosa-al-Kazim, the seventh of the Twelve Imams. Shias believe that the Twelve Imams were the genuine spiritual successors of the Prophet, so by their lineage, they are the inheritors of the world. The genealogy of Saadat Khan, the founder of the Awadh dynasty, was traced from Kara Yusuf, son of Kara Muhammad, who ruled western Iran in the fifteenth century.[83] The Awadh line of succession was therefore considered to be of longer standing and hence superior even to the Mughal, and the Awadh ruler could now claim that he did not need to subordinate himself to the Sunni Mughals. This thinking was encouraged by the Company officials and enthused Ghazi-ud-din Haider to make a clean break with the Mughals and assume kingship. The game of the Governor-General Hastings was to break the concept that the Mughals were the rulers of India and propagate the idea of British paramountcy. The British were supreme and everybody else was subordinate to them. Ghazi-ud-din Haider, amidst his various diversions could not understand the larger objectives of British policy and fell an easy prey to a false sense of his importance. He was proclaimed 'King' and sat on the throne. The day chosen for his coronation was the day on which Prophet Mohammad had declared Hazrat Imam Ali his successor. Ghazi-ud-din's sense of vainglory was fully satisfied and on 19 October 1819 he was proclaimed *padshah* of Awadh. He gave to himself the honorifics of *Padshah-e-Ghazi*, *Shah-e-Zaman*, etc. The crown was put on him on that occasion by the Mujtahid, head of the Shia Ulemas.[84] His assumption of the kingship was jeered at by the Mughal court as well as the *nizam*.[85] He had been cut off from the stream of Mughal tradition. Yet as King, when he was offered *nazar* by the rulers of Rampur and Chakeri, he was not allowed to accept that honour.[86] His letters to the British monarch were intercepted by the Company and were not allowed to be presented before the British sovereign. His isolation was complete and his authority was reduced to a political island. His protestations to be a sovereign King were put on the shelf. Now he had to redefine his relationship with the people of Awadh, who had been brought up in the traditions of the Mughal empire. On the fourth anniversary of his coronation it was not the chief Ulema who put the crown on his head, it was the British Resident. His son Nasir-ud-din Haider was also crowned by the Resident when he sat on the throne. The *padshahs* of Awadh were thus made subordinate to the Company.

Mirza Agha Mir continued to be the *wazir* and carried on his nefarious activities. The people suffered under his administration. But he pandered to the fancies of the King and surrounded him with more and more women of easy virtue. Once, even the Badshah Begum revolted, but her protests were put down with heavy hand.

The court intrigues were in full swing. Although Nasir-ud-din Haider was being reared as the heir apparent, rumours were floated about the illegitimate birth of Nasir-ud-din Haider himself. On the other hand, a *kaneez* who had entered the harem of Nasir-ud-din gave birth to a son, Munna Jaan. His birth also raised many doubts. The conflict arose about the succession of both—Mirza Nasir-ud-din Haider, after Ghazi-ud-din Haider, and then in the generation after him about Munna Jan. At this stage Ghazi-ud-din Haider was so disgusted that he disinherited both of them. The administration fell more and more into the quagmire of uncertainty, but Agha Mir succeeded all this time in his efforts to be the chief recipient of the King's favour. The governance suffered. The *ijaredari* system, meaning collection of revenue through contractors was adopted again. The Amani system by which Saadat Ali Khan had so assiduously built up his finances, was again put aside. The administration was so weak that the people of Awadh were put to much hardship, but the social customs and the milieu of mutual understanding in the society were such that compared to the Ceded Districts the people in Awadh were happier.

In 1823-4, the Company was engaged in the First Burmese War and again demanded more money on loan. The *nawab* was once again coerced to advance another loan of two crores. On the other hand, constant fight between the courtiers and *begums* of Awadh and the effort by the factions to advance the cause of the pretenders, whose birth from royal blood was doubtful, became the subject of any number of controversies. In such an atmosphere Ghazi-ud-din Haider died of consumption in 1827.

The rule of Ghazi-ud-din Haider was marked by a fall in the standards of administration and formulation of state policies. There was hardly any time for thinking on the matters of state. The Hindu hegemony of *diwani* under Dayakrishna and his son *raja* Balkrishna continued to provide the basic money for the running of the state. Among the works of public utility started in his time was the Ghazi-ud-din Haider Canal which would have connected the Gomti with Ganges. It is a matter of surprise that a system of administration which was surrounded by so much of laxity, had visualised a project of such grandiose proportions as the Ghazi-ud-din Haider Canal. But such things could happen in Awadh. It is a different matter that the project was left midway more because of the intervention of the Company. The *nawab* had thought of importing an Iron Bridge from London but its implementation was put off till the time of Muhammad Ali Shah. Where the court failed in providing the leadership to society, the routine understanding between the communities and the general prosperity of agriculture and commerce filled in the gap. Even in its isolation Awadh nurtured a society of deep understanding and culture. During Ghazi-ud-din Haider's reign the total loans advanced to the Company went up to 4.5 crore rupees, and much money went too by way of gifts to officials. This was undoubtedly a heavy drain on the economy of Awadh.

SHAH NASIR-UD-DIN HAIDER (1827-37)

On the death of Ghazi-ud-din Haider, his son Nasir-ud-din Haider came to the throne. He was twenty-five when he became King[87] At that time he was under the influence of the current consort Malika-e-Zamani. She had come to the royal household with a son from her previous liaison, Kaiwajah by name. On the assumption of power by Nasir-ud-din, she became the real power behind the throne. She was opposed by the mother of Nasir-ud-din, Badshah Begum, who championed the cause of Munna Jaan. The reign of Nasir-ud-din Haider was plagued by the unending tussle between these two *begums*. They had no vision beyond their own interests.

The history of Awadh was now at a stage where the stream of Mughal influence had nearly dried up. The weaklings on the throne became petty figures under the shadow of British paramountcy. Yet the power of the native spirit was slowly articulating itself and gaining strength and momentum.

Besides Malika-e-Zamani as the power behind the throne, Agha Mir remained the *wazir* and *raja* Darshan Singh succeeded to the position of *diwan*. Moncton was the British Resident.[88] Nasir-ud-din Haider very soon fell under the outward charm of the English manners and culture. He began to wear trousers and jackets even in his *darbars*.[89] Agha Mir had the tacit support of the Company, and he amassed a lot of wealth, by unscrupulous means. Because of his conduct, he had become very unpopular with the public, and an outcry was raised against him. Nasir-ud-din Haider wanted to remove him but was obliged to seek the permission of the Governor-General. At long last Agha Mir was dismissed from *wizarat*. The King wanted to confiscate the wealth he had illegitimately accumulated, but the Resident intervened. Almost after two years of attrition and protection in the Residency at Lucknow he was allowed to get away with his wealth and settle in one of the ceded districts. The King found himself helpless in this situation.[90] Fazal Ali was appointed the new *wazir*.[91]

In 1829, the Sikh wars broke out and again the Company asked for a loan of Rs. 62.40 lakhs. In a surprising development, it was negotiated that the interest accruing on this loan was to be paid as pension to the King's relatives by the Company. It appeared that king had lost faith even towards his own successors. Fazal Ali could not last for a long time. He was succeeded by Iqbal-ud-daula and then *raja* Ram Dayal. In 1830, Hakim Mehdi Ali Khan was recalled and appointed *wazir*.[92] By this time he had also become an Anglophile. This was in keeping with the temperament of the time since Nasir had himself become Anglicised in his customs and behaviour. But this did not prevent him from continuing with the Imam's *chhati* celebrations in which he went to the length of total stupidity by acting as a pregnant mother.[93] The King of Awadh became the butt of jokes all over. To add to the clamour against him, he fell under the influence of the consorts Dhania Mehri and Diwai.

On being constantly reminded of his responsibilities of good government and subsequent threat of removal, he was prompted to act and control the lawless elements. This was the time of the Reform Movement in Bengal. Lord William Bentinck and Raja Ram Mohun Roy, were the leading lights with whom Nasir-ud-din Haider associated his name unknowingly, by issuing an order which prohibited *sati*.[94]

A very important role was played by the growth of Hindi literature during this time. In the middle ages, when the Mughal empire was at its peak and there was no chance of a political redemption the Hindi literature had turned towards escapism and that period is known as the *bhakti kaal*—an era of devotional poetry. The two poets who rendered yeoman service to the growth of Hindi poetry were Surdas in Braj (Mathura region) and Tulsidas in Awadh. Tulsidas is the famous writer of *Ram-Charit-Manas*. He has also written some other scholarly poetry, but *Ram-Charit-Manas* captured the imagination of the people and brought to them a sense of pride in their traditions. The book is also a masterpiece of Hindi literature from which many idioms have originated. The contribution of Tulsidas to Hindi literature and Hindu ethos is greater than what Shakespeare did to England and English. Towards the beginning of the eighteenth century the Muslim hegemony was showing cracks. The path was shown by Shivaji, who proclaimed an independent Hindu rulership. The poet who sang to his glory was Bhushan and his poetry is path breaking. He is the creator of a school of poetry known as *veer ras*—a poetry of valour. The other poets who were attached with some court or the other also wrote in praise of those kings and their heroic battles. Hindi poetry also adopted the expressions of *shringar*, romance and embellishment of physical beauty. This period known as *riti kaal* is full of poetry of either valour or of physical enjoyment. Hindi poetry also adopted words and expressions of Persian and even Arabic. Hindi and Urdu have a common syntax and grammar. Each contributed to the growth of the other. Acharya Ram Chandra Shukla, the first and foremost historian of Hindi literature has observed that the growth of scholarly works of this period was mostly in Awadh. In this geographical area there were greater experiments in the evolution of native literature. Lucknow was duly influenced by this trend. Poetry had broken the confines of scholarly pursuits and had come closer to the common man. Along with Urdu prose, Hindi prose and ideas started circulating in a much greater measure.

By sheer momentum of the tradition, Nasir-ud-din Haider continued to take interest in the construction of public buildings. The Chattar Manzil was completed in his time. The Tarewali Kothi meant as an observatory was also completed.[95] During the later period of his life, Nasir-ud-din Haider was totally consumed by sensuality and even effeminacy. To add to the infamy, his life in private and even public was controlled by a very voluptuous woman named Dhania Mehri. She was of low origin and suddenly became important. Naturally, she became greedy of power and money. Such people usually play crucial roles in conspiracies, and she did. A plan to eliminate the King was hatched and Dhania Mehri played the pivotal role.[96] The Resident, Col. Low won over Dhania Mehri and the King was given a lethal dose of poison. He died on 8 July 1837.[97] He was buried in the incomplete mausoleum at the Kerbala of Iradat Nagar by the side of Begum Qudasia Mahal. This is located in the rear compound of the present-day Shia College. His reign was the most ignoble in the history of Awadh. Some of his actions as King were laughable and his surrender to the atmosphere of lewdness was total. He did not realize that he was not merely losing his grip as a ruler, he was also squandering his life away, to an ungrateful set of people surrounding him.

The period of this chapter covers the reign of Saadat Ali Khan, Ghazi-ud-din Haider and Nasir-ud-din Haider. During the time of Saadat Ali Khan, Awadh was reduced to a territorial island, surrounded on all sides by the British. During Gazi-ud-din's time, his assumption of the title of King, made *Awadh a political Island.* But because of the loans given to the Company, two districts Sitapur and Lakhimpur Kheri (being addressed by their present names) were added to Awadh expanding its frontiers up to Ruhelkhand. The reign of Nasir-ud-din Haider was an island where depravity and loss of social standards had become supreme. All this led Awadh into the twilight zone, when the new King took over and was forced to enter into another treaty—the treaty of 1837.

NOTES

1. Michael H. Fisher, *A Clash of Cultures: Awadh, the British and the Mughals*, New Delhi, 1987, p. 90. Wazir Ali remained *nawab* from June 1797 to January 1798. He was the brother of Asaf-ud-daula and Saadat Ali Khan and was one of the fifty-seven children of Shuja-ud-daula. There was also a hint of Wazir Ali's connection with the Afghan Zaman Shah who had invaded the Panjab twice in 1790s. This tenuous connection made him dangerous both for the British. Wazir Ali's last act on leaving Lucknow before his pursuit of Cherry was to raid the *aina khana*—the treasure house of late Asaf-ud-daula. Much treasure was taken, and only a few items were ever recovered—*The Oxford History of India*, Oxford, 1958, p. 554; *The Asiatic Annual Register (1807)*, pp. 204-5. Further it is believed that Wazir Ali was a son of a Farrash, who sold his pregnant wife to Asaf-ud-daula for sake of money—W. Hoey, *History of Asaf-ud-daulah*, Lucknow, 1971, pp. 87-8.
2. Jagdish Sahai, *Awadh Mein Nawabi Shasan* (Hindi), Faizabad, n.y., p. 107.
3. Ibid. See also *The Asiatic Annual Register (1804)*, Vol. IV, pp. 9-10; W. Hoey, op. cit., pp. 30-1, 57.
4. Jagdish Sahai, op. cit., p. 108.
5. Resident to Governor-General, 24 September 1797, Bengal Secret Consultations, N.A.I., 2 October, 1797.
6. C. Macfarlane, *Our Indian Empire*, London, 1848, Vol. II, p. 30.
7. It is interesting to note that there were seven persons responsible for the dethroning of Wazir Ali: Tafazzul Hussain Khan, Tahsin Ali, Tikait Rai, Almas

Ali and Ashraf Ali, Hasan Raza Khan and Bahu Begum—see Jagdish Sahai, op. cit., p. 109 n. 3. Further Tahsin Ali Khan was regarded with special favour by the British since, as a result of his confidential relations with Asaf-ud-daula, he had been able to provide necessary evidence to disqualify Wazir Ali from succession—*Oudh Papers*, p. 596.

8. After the arrest of Wazir Ali he was sent to Benares on 21 January 1798—Jagdish Sahai, op. cit., p. 109. See also Governor-General to Council, 14 January 1798, Foreign Secret Proceedings, N.A.I., 30 January 1798 for a detailed description.
9. C.U. Aitchison, *A Collection of Treaties, Engagements, and Sunnads Relating to Indian and Neighbouring Countries*, Calcutta, 1909, Vol. II, pp. 125-9.
10. R.W. Bird, *Dacoitee in Excelsis: or, the Spoilation of Oude by the East India Company*, Lucknow, 1971, p. 50; C.U. Aitchison, op. cit., Vol. II, p. 131.
11. R.W. Bird, op. cit., p. 49 cited in Mirza Ali Azhar, *King Wajid Ali Shah of Awadh*, Karachi, 1982, pp. 127-8.
12. R.C. Majumdar, *An Advanced History of India*, London, 1948, p. 720. According to E.S. Harcourt and Fakir Hussain, Wazir Ali was sent to Chunar Garh as a prisoner where he died—E.S. Harcourt and Fakir Hussain (trs.), *Lucknow: The Last Phase of an Oriental Culture*, p. 49. While Dr. Jagdish Sahai is of the opinion that Wazir Ali was imprisoned in a bungalow in Calcutta. Nobody was allowed to meet him and in this bungalow he had to spend seventeen years, three months and four days all alone—Jagdish Sahai, op. cit., p. 113.
13. For a detailed version of Wazir Ali's revolt see J.F. Davis, *Wazir Ali Khan and the Massacre of Benaras*, London, 1844.
14. Cited in Safi Ahmad, *British Aggression in Awadh*, Meerut, 1969, p. 36.
15. R.W. Bird, op. cit., p. 23. But what is the evidence on which this story was invented is not very clear.
16. Rajendra Pandey (trs.), *Awadh Ki Loot* (Hindi), Lucknow, 1966, pp. 25-26; Jagdish Sahai, op. cit., pp. 116-17. The treaty further stated that '. . . all correspondence between the Nabob Saadet Ali Khan and any foreign power of state, shall be carried on with the knowledge and concurrence of the Company.'—C.U. Aitchison, op. cit., Vol. I, pp. 118-22.
17. Governor-General to Resident, 23 January 1798, E.M.S. Add. 13526, fol. 33b, British Library, London, cited in Michael H. Fisher, op. cit., p. 93.
18. In this context the Governor-General wrote to the Court of Directors of the Company that it would '. . . reduce your military expense by transferring the charge of a very large body of your troops to the funds of the Nabob Vizier. . . .' Governor-General to Secret Committee, 25 January 1800, HMS, British Library, London, 579:518.
19. James Mill is of the opinion that the main reason behind such a policy was that Wellesley wanted that for the future pursuit of British policies related with north India a total security of Awadh as well as its isolation from other powers was necessary. Further he had a strong desire for the total annihilation of Awadh's native army—James Mill, *History of India*, Vol. IV, London, 1858, p. 229.

20. Sunder Lal, *Bharat Mein Angreji Raj* (Hindi), pp. 355-8, cited in Jagdish Sahai, op. cit., p. 119.
21. James Mill, op. cit., Vol. II, p. 156; P.E. Roberts, *History of British India*, p. 116.
22. R.W. Bird, op. cit., p. 33.
23. Ibid., pp. 31-2.
24. It is interesting to note the reasons given by Wellesley for taking over the country: 'I am satisfied that no effectual security can be provided against the ruin of the province of Oude, until the exclusive management of the civil and military government of that country shall be transferred intact to the Company under suitable provisions for the maintenance of His Excellency and his family. No other remedy can effect any considerable improvement in the resources of the state, or can ultimately secure its external safety and internal peace.'—James Mill, op. cit., Vol. IV, p. 229. On hearing such a decision Saadat Khan exclaimed, 'If such be, indeed, the case it will not be long ere the remaining portions of the country will be wrested from me.'—R.W. Bird, op. cit., p. 49.
25. C.U. Aitchison, op. cit., Vol. II, pp. 131.
26. R.W. Bird, op. cit., pp. 49-50.
27. When Lord Wellesley's letter of 14 November 1801, about appointing his brother Henry Wellesley, as President of the Board, reached the Court of Directors, they lost 'no time in condemning the appointment of Mr. (Henry) Wellesley, who was the Private Secretary to the Governor-General, and directed that Mr. Wellesley be removed forthwith.'—James Mill, op. cit., Vol. VI, pp. 266-7, 245, 246.
28. The Company took away a huge chunk of land from Saadat Ali Khan which had an annual estimated demand of Rs. 13,523,474. The *nawab* was left only with the province of Awadh, surrounding him on three sides by Company territory and on the fourth by Himalayan frontier with Nepal—C.U. Aitchison, op. cit., Vol. I, pp. 123.
29. John Kaye has given the more conscientious statement that, 'the condition of Oude soon attracted his (Wellesley's) attention, not because its government was bad and its people were wretched, because that country might either be a bulwark of safety to our own dominions, or a sea of danger which might overflow and destroy us.'—*History of Indian Mutiny*, Vol. I, London, 1888, p. 83.
30. C.U. Aitchison, op. cit., Vol. I, pp. 57-8.
31. Ibid., pp. 104-11.
32. Resident to Governor-General, 28 April 1800, Foreign Secret Consultations, N.A.I., 15 May 1800.
33. The explanation given by Saadat Ali Khan for paying attention to the remaining territories under his command was: 'Of my territory that now remains in any possession; if I continue to distribute this little to jagierdars, I shall by and by have no authority whatever. . . . I have no intention. . . but the preservation of my authority.' Vizier to Resident, recd. 21 March 1811, Bengal Political Consultations, N.A.I., 3 May 1811.
34. Asaf-ud-daula had bestowed approximately 1/6th of the total gross revenue of his lands in *jagirs* to his dependents, relatives and favourites. For a detailed

analysis of the distribution of *jagirs* under Asaf-ud-daula see Richard B. Barnett, *North India Between Empires: Awadh, the Mughals and the British*, Berkeley, 1980, pp. 173-81. Further he also awarded various sources of revenue which could otherwise had become a part of Awadh Treasury. For example, he appropriated revenues including the *abkari* (liquor tax) and license tax on 'dancing girls' in Faizabad to Bahu Begum, the former worth 900 and the latter 800 rupees (annually?)—see List of Revenues appropriated to the Bhow Begum, 25 August 1805, Bengal Political Consultations, N.A.I., 4 June 1807.

35. Saadat Ali always denied the right of the Resident to interfere in the internal affairs of the state of Awadh, which is clear from the following statement: 'The fact is this: the affairs of my household are distinct from the duties and obligations of my government, and my right to control the affairs of such relations as my mother and sister, etc. are totally unconnected with, and independent of, my duties and obligations as a prince. . . . [I have] absolute control and authority over every branch of my household.'—Political letter from Bengal, 15 October 1811, *Papers Respecting A Reform in the Administration of the Government of His Excellency the Nawaub Vizier. .* , London: Court of Proprietors of E.I. Stock, 1824, p. 764, cited in Michael H. Fisher, op. cit., p. 103.
36. Ratan Singh, Sultan-al-Tawarikh, Persian MS, Tagore Library, Lucknow University, Lucknow, fol. 354; Bahadur Singh, Yadgar-i-Bahaduri, Persian MS Regional Archives, Allahabad, fols. 604-605b; Munshi Ram Sahai, *Ihsan-c Tawarikh*, Lucknow: Tamanni Press, 1876, pp. 126-9. Dr. Nigam asserts that Dayakrishna was replaced in 1815 unofficially, but we find no supporting evidence to this statement of Dr. Nigam—see Gazi-ud-din Haider: The First King of Oudh—1814-1827, Ph.D. Dissertation, Tagore Library, Lucknow University, Lucknow, 1947, p. 61.
37. Resident to Governor-General, 24 May 1794, Home Miscellaneous Series, London: Commonwealth Relations Office, 447, fol. 234; see also Resident to Governor-General, 21 July 1795, London: Commonwealth Relations Office, 448, fols. 395-446.
38. M.A. Kashmiri, *Najum-as-sama takmilah*, Lucknow, 1302/1884-1885, pp. 323-8.
39. Purnendu Basu, *Oudh and the East India Company—1785-1801*, Lucknow, 1943, pp. 22-4.
40. Kalikinkar Datta, 'Raja Jhow Lal of the Oudh Court', *Journal of the Bihar and the Orissa Research Society*, 23, Part 4 (1937): 507.
41. W. Hoey, op. cit., pp. 15-18; Resident to Saadat Ali Khan, 26 July 1777, Foreign Department Secret Consultations, A.I., 8 September 1777, No. M; Hamid Afaq Qureshi, Nawab Wazir Ali Khan: Life and Career—1780-1817, Ph.D. Dissertation, Tagore Library, Lucknow University, Lucknow, 1981, p. 191. See also *Asiatic Annual Register, or A view of the History of Hindustan, and of the Politics, Commerce and Literature of Asia, for the Year 1803*, London, 1804, pp. 1-8; Governor-General to Vice-President in Council, 5 April 1797, Bengal Secret and Political Consultations, N.A.I., 10 April 1797, No. 1.
42. Michael H. Fisher, op. cit., p. 109.

43. Jagdish Sahai, op. cit., p. 128.
44. *Gazetteer of the Province of Oude*, Allahabad, 1877, Vol. II, p. 368.
45. Pawan Kumar Singh and R.R. Kidwai hold that the name Chattar Manzil was given due to its *chattar* or gilded dome, which seems a misconception—Pawan Kumar Singh, *Shahar-e-Lucknow* (Hindi), Lucknow, 1990, p. 68; R.R. Kidwai, *Lucknow: The Lost Paradise*, Lucknow, 1993, p. 48. But Yogesh Praveen who is an authority on the history of Awadh, is clearly of the opinion that Chattar Manzil was built by Saadat Ali Khan, in the memory of his late mother Chattar Kunwar—Yogesh Praveen, *Lucknow Monuments*, Lucknow, p. 71.
46. Sikander Raza (ed.), *Wajid Ali Shah and Monuments of Awadh*, Lucknow, 1974, no pagination.
47. Rekha Misra, *Women in Mughal India*, Allahabad, 1967, pp. 92-9.
48. Ibid.
49. After the annexation of Awadh, Moti Mahal came into the possession of the British and was used at first as a commissariat. Later it was sold to Maharaja of Balrampur, who made alterations to the buildings and the 'Pearl Dome', which was a unique architectural achievement, disappeared, See G. H. Rouse (ed.), *Lucknow Album*, Calcutta, 1874. p. 19.
50. This building was bought for four thousand pounds by Joseph Queiros, which was sold shortly afterwards to Saadat Ali Khan. This building almost became the nucleus of Chattar Manzil complex—Rosie-Llewellyn Jones, *A Very Ingenious Man: Claude Martin in the Early Colonial India*, O.U.P., 1992, p. 217.
51. Maria Nugent, *A Journal From the Year 1811 till 1815*, Vol. I, London, 1839, p. 303.
52. Paripurnanand Verma, *Wajid Ali Shah Aur Awadh Rajya Ka Patan* (Hindi), Uttar Pradesh, 1949, p. 19. But Rosie-Llewellyn Jones holds that Khursheed Manzil is situated at Alambagh, that is, east of Lucknow, which is totally incorrect—Rosie-Llewellyn Jones, *A Fatal Friendship: The Nawabs, the British and the City of Lucknow*, Delhi: O.U.P., 1985, p. 153.
53. Yogesh Praveen, *Lucknow Monuments*, p. 163.
54. E.S. Harcourt & Fakir Hussain (trs.), op. cit., p. 64. Yogesh Praveen, op. cit., p. 163.
55. Dr. Hamid Afaq Kureshi, *Some Aspects of Science and Technology During* 1722-1756, n.d., pp. 2-4,5 & 10-11.
56. E.S. Harcourt & Fakir Hussain (trs.), op. cit., p. 142.
57. Rosie-Llewellyn Jones, op. cit., p. 25.
58. Bengal Political Consultations, 11 October 1811, N.A.I., Nos. 21 & 22.
59. Foreign Political Consultations, N.A.I., 3 November 1815, No. 5.
60. Rosie-Llewellyn Jones, op. cit., p. 39.
61. John Kaye, *History of the Sepoy War in India*, London, 1870, Vol. I, p. 118.
62. Jagdish Sahai, op. cit., p. 128; Amrit Lal Nagar, *Shatranj Ke Mohre* (Hindi), n.y., pp. 306-7.
63. Amjad Ali, *Mukhtasar-Tarikh-e-Awadh*, pp. 139-40; Yogesh Praveen, 'Nawabene Awadh' (Hindi), *Dharamyug*, 20 May 1979, p. 38.

64. Amjad Ali, op. cit., pp. 141-3.
65. H.C. Irwin is of the opinion that Shams-ud-daula was the eldest son of Saadat Ali Khan. He writes, 'Shams-ud-daula, eldest son of Saadat Ali, had died before him and his children were therefore excluded from inheritance under the rule of Mohammedan Law known as *Mahjub-ul-irs* in favour of the second son, Ghazi-ud-din Haider'—H.C. Irwin, *The Garden of India Or Chapters on Oudh History and Affairs*, Vol. I, Lucknow, 1973, p. 97.
66. James Mill, op. cit., Vol. VIII, p. 504; Michael H. Fisher, 'The Imperial Coronation of 1819: Awadh, the British and the Mughals'. *Modern Asian Studies* 19(1985), pp. 239-77.
67. Jagdish Sahai, op. cit., p. 131.
68. Ibid., pp. 132, 144.
69. Sibte Muhammad Naqvi, *Amjad Ali*, p. 56.
70. Abdul Halim Sharar, *Guzishta Lakhnau Mashriqi Tammadum Ka Akhri Namuna*, New Delhi, 1971, pp. 42-3. But according to some scholars like Amrit Lal Nagar, the birth of Munna Jaan from Sukh Chain is a concocted story—*Shatranj Ke Mohre*, pp. 44-5, cited in Jagdish Sahai, op. cit., p. 143 n. 3.
71. Ibid.
72. Jagdish Sahai, op. cit., p. 144.
73. Resident to Secretary to Government, 17 April 1823, Bengal Political Consultations, N.A.I., 9 May 1823, No. 51; Annual Report of British Subjects, 7 February 1833, Foreign Political Consultations, N.A.I., 19 February 1833, No. 50. A. Mukherjee, 'King Nasirud Din Haidar of Awadh (1827- 37)', *Journal of Indian History* 45, pt. 2 (August 1967): 582-607; D.B. Diskalkar, 'Foundation of an Observatory at Lucknow', *Journal of the U.P. Historical Society* 10 pt. 1 (July 1937), 7-32.
74. William Knighton, *Private Life of An Eastern King*, New York, 1856.
75. Jagdish Sahai, op. cit., p. 133.
76. R.W. Bird, op. cit., p. 64.
77. *Akhbar of 1810, 1839*, Andhra Pradesh Central Library, Hyderabad.
78. *The English Charter of 1813.*
79. H.C. Irwin, *The Garden of India*, pp. 97-107.
80. E.S. Harcourt & Fakir Hussain, op. cit., pp. 36-7; Jagdish Sahai, op. cit., p. 136; Yogesh Praveen, *Bahar-e-Awadh* (Hindi), Lucknow, 1987, p. 18.
81. Ibid.
82. Resident to Secretary to Governor-General, 23 November 1814. Foreign Department Political Consultations, N.A.I., 13 December 1814, No. 3.
83. Hashim Ali Rizvi, Mirat al-Bilad, Persian MS 2551, Regional Archives, Allahabad, fols. 144a & B, Amir Ali Khan, *Wazir Nama*, Kanpur, 1876, p. 28, Kunwar Durga Parshad, *Bostan-i-Awadh*, Sandila, 1888, p. 413.
84. Resident to Secretary to Government, 12 October 1819, Bengal Political Consultations, N.A.I., 20 November 1819, No. 98.
85. Resident Hyderabad (Russell) to Governor-General, 22 January 1820, Bengal Secret Consultations, N.A.I., 22 January 1820, No. 13.
86. *Arzdasht* from *Raja* Bijy Bahadur of Churkurry to the Address of the King of Oudh, Bengal Political Consultations, N.A.I., 3 February 1821, No. 5.

87. Resident to Governor-General, 20 October 1827, Bengal Political Consultations, N.A.I., 16 November 1827, No. 15.
88. Michael H. Fisher, op. cit., p. 251 (Appendix 1c).
89. B. Saiyid Abu Muhammad, 'Some Autographs of King Nasiruddin Hyder', *Journal of the U.P. Historical Society 12*, pt. 1 (July 1939): 40-8.
90. C.U. Aitchison, op. cit., Vol. I, p. 101; Resident to Secretary to Government, 2 February 1828, Bengal Political Consultations, N.A.I., 22 February 1828; King of Oudh to Governor-General, 17 August 1830, Foreign Political Consultations, N.A.I., 24 September 1830, No. 46; Munshi Sital Parshad, op. cit., fol. 301; Resident to Secretary to Government, 29 December 1827, Bengal Political Consultations, N.A.I., 2 January 1828, No. 36; Secretary to Government to Resident, 2 October 1828, Bengal Political Consultations, N.A.I., 11 October 1828, No. 22; Minute of Metcalf, 17 September 1830, Foreign Political Consultations, N.A.I., 24 September 1830, No. 59; Minute of Governor-General, 14 September 1830, Foreign Political Consultations, N.A.I., 24 September 1830, No. 58.
91. Munshi Sital Parshad, op. cit., fols, 301, 307. Ratan Singh, op. cit., fol. 400, Abd al-Ahad, *Tarikh Badshah Begam (Waqa i-idil Pazir)*, tr. by Muhammad Taqi Ahmad (Allahabad, 1938), pp. 17, 20-21, 57; Resident to Secretary to Government, 29 December 1827, Bengal Political Consultations, N.A.I., 11 January 1828, No. 36; Abd al-Ahad, op. cit., p. 57. Resident to Secretary to Government, n.d., Bengal Political Consultations, N.A.I., 10 April 1829, No. 31; Resident to Deputy Secretary to Government, 30 June 1829, Bengal Political Consultations, N.A.I., 18 September 1829, No. 34.
92. H.C. Irwin, op. cit., p. 104.
93. Abdul Halim Sharar, op. cit., p. 92.
94. There were many serious debates raised by Hindu leaders as the policy was considered an unwarranted governmental interference in Hindu religious custom. Resident to Secretary to Governor-General, 6 October 1829, Bengal Political Consultations, N.A.I., 23 October 1829, No. 40.
95. D.B. Diskalker, op. cit., pp. 10-11.
96. Yogesh Praveen, 'Shahane Awadh', *Dharamyug*, 27 May 1979, p. 37.
97. Jagdish Sahai, op. cit., p. 155.

Plate 3. Chhatar Manzil

Plate 4: Mausoleums of Saadat Ali Khan and Khursheed Zadi

CHAPTER V

The Twilight (1837-47)

After the death of Nasir-ud-din Haider, his foster mother Badshah Begum once again tried her hand to control the levers of power. She was married to Rafat-ud-daula who had ascended the throne as Ghazi-ud-din Haider. During her lifetime she made constant efforts to keep control over Nasir-ud-din Haider as the Prince and heir apparent and kept him away from the influence of both Ghazi-ud-din Haider, his father, the King and Agha Mir, the *wazir*. To an extent she succeeded. But Nasir-ud-din Haider himself fell prey to the charms of two women one after the other. The first, Afzal Mahal, gave birth to Munna Jaan, the apparent successor. The second, Malika-e-Zamani, came to the harem with a son whose name was Kaiwajah. Malika-e-Zamani became the controlling power behind the throne in the time of Nasir-ud-din Haider. Badshah Begum thus lost the second round. Having lost the power over her husband and her foster son, she made third attempt to make Munna Jaan succeed the throne. Nasir-ud-din Haider was so thoroughly irritated with the conflicting claims and sponsors of Munna Jaan and Kaiwajah, that in a moment of sheer despair, he conveyed his decision to disinherit both of them in writing to the Resident. Sensing this opportunity to be almost like the one which brought Saadat Ali on the *masnad* of Awadh, after Wazir Ali, Nasir-ud-daula the third son of Saadat Ali Khan was enthroned by the Resident.

When the news of the death of Nasir-ud-din Haider was confirmed, Badshah Begum actually led a detachment of forces from Almasbagh to Lal Baradari, the Coronation Hall. At the same time the Resident was preparing to seat Nasir-ud-daula on the throne. But the Begum beat him to it and reached the Coronation Hall before the Company forces. Soon the Company forces coming from Madiaon Cantonment also arrived there. British Resident Col. Low was leading the Company troops. He asked Badshah

Begum to withdraw from the scene, but she refused and proclaimed that succession belongs to Munna Jaan. On her refusal to withdraw, Resident directed his cannon fire on the building and the people assembled there. About forty persons were killed. The Company forces entered Lal Baradari and looted it to the last piece of its jewellery. At about 3 a.m., the sixty-three-year-old Muhammad Ali was woken up, installed on the throne and given the title 'Muhammad Ali Nausher-wane-Adil'.[1] Badshah Begum and Munna Jaan were arrested and taken to the Residency. After five years of confinement they were sent to the Chunar Fort. Munna Jaan died on 10 January 1846 and Badshah Begum on 30 July 1847. They are both buried in Chunar Fort.[2]

While Badshah Begum was engaged in this drama the Resident directed his assistants Lt. Shakespeare, along with Latafat Hussain Khan, the *Mir Munshi*, of the Residency and Maulvi Ghulam Yahia Khan, the *darbar-vakil*, to go to the house of Naseer-ud-daula and present to him an agreement drafted in Persian. The translation of that so-called 'deed of engagement' is as follows:

> Lt. Col. John Low, the Resident, has apprised me, so Lt. Shakespeare, his second assistant, of the death of Nasir-ud-Hyder, King of Oude. The Resident has also communicated to me the substance of the order of the Government of India respecting the necessity of new engagements on the (part of the) Company's Government with the Oude state; and I hereby declare that in the case of my being placed on the throne, I will agree to *sign any new treaty* that the Governor-General may dictate. (Singed) J. Low.
>
> N.B. At the foot of the paper, the present King wrote the words, *Cubool wo Munzoor ust* (It is accepted and agreed upon), and affixed the impression of his seal.[3]

The Engagement recited above, with the circumstances under which it was obtained, will doubtless be thought a sufficient answer to the Preamble of the Treaty of 1837, as far as the latter testifies to the misgovernment of the Oude Princes. It is reported that the King designate Naseer-ud-daula signed the deed of engagement willingly and without hesitation. He was then installed on the throne under a new name, Muhammad Ali, on 8 July 1837.[4] The Company desired Roshan-ud-daula to continue as *wazir* because of his open help in deposing Munna Jaan. But soon the new King found Roshan-ud-daula to be closer to the Company than to the state of Awadh. In

August 1837, within a month of his enthronement, the king of Muhammad Ali, charged Roshan-ud-daula with disloyalty, had him arrested and sent to Kanpur.[5] Hakim Mehdi Ali who was residing in Farrukhabad was recalled and made *wazir* once again.[6] Muhammad Ali Shah was incharge of the *diwani* in the time of his father Saadat Ali Khan and had rich experience in revenue matters. He was a mature person at the age of 63 and knew about court intrigues. He took personal charge of the affairs of the state. The court was taken out of the mire of lewdness; unseemly expenses were curtailed and economy was enforced in the expenditure of the court as well as the state. He was greatly helped by the experience of Hakim Mehdi Ali. But within three months, the Company enforced another treaty based on the deed of engagement at the time of enthronement. This treaty reversed certain provisions of the earlier treaty of 1801. The preface of this treaty is worthy of attention and is self-explanatory:[7]

Treaty between the Honorable East India Company and His Majesty Abool Futeh Moeen-ood-Deen Nausherewan-i-Audil Sultani Zaman Mahummad Ali Shah, the King of Oude.

Whereas by the substituting alliance the Honorable East India Company and the Oude States, the British Government is bound to defend the Oude territories against the foreign and domestic enemies, the Sovereign of Oude engaging to retain in his service only a small specified number of troops: and whereas, while the British Government has faithfully and scrupulously performed the obligations so imposed on it, the engagement on the part of Oude State has been habitually infringed, there being now in the employment of His Majesty the King of Oude a large and expensive military force; and whereas experience has shown that the execution of all the provisions of the Treaty of 1801 is attended with serious difficulty, and it is desirable and proper that a modified arrangement, consistent with the principles of that Treaty, and conducing to the prosperity and advantage of both States, should be introduced; and whereas the restrictions as to the amount of military force to be employed by His Majesty the King of Oude may with propriety be relaxed, on condition that an adequate portion of the increased force shall be placed under British discipline and control, so as at once to promote the general interests of the Indian empire, and in particular the dignity and safety of the King, providing at a reduced cost for the efficiency of his national military establishment: and whereas the Article 6th of the Treaty of 1801 requires that the Sovereign of Oude always advising with, and acting in conformity to, the counsel of the Officers of the Honorable Company, shall establish in his reserved dominions such a system of administration (to be carried into effect by his own officers) as shall be conducive to the prosperity of his subjects, and be calculated to secure the lives and property of the inhabitants, but provides no remedy for the neglect of the solemn and paramount obligation: and whereas the infraction of this essential engagement of the Treaty, and inattention to the first duty of a Sovereign on the part of several successive Rulers of Oude, have been continued and notorious, and have ever exposed the British Government to the reproach of imperfectly fulfilling its obligations towards the Oude people, and it is therefore just and proper that the defect alluded in Article 6th of the Treaty aforesaid should be rectified; the following provisions have accordingly been arranged and concluded on the one part by Lieutenant-Colonel John Low, Resident at the court of Lucknow, in the name and on behalf of the Right Honorable Lord Auckland, Governor-General of India in Council, and on the other, by Abool Futeh Moeen-ood-Deen Nausherewan-i-Audil Sultani Zaman Mahummad Ali Shah, the King of Oude, for himself and his heirs; and this agreement is to hold good from generation to generation to the end of the time.

The 1801 Treaty had given the *nawab* the right to keep his own army for his personal security and for the defence of the state. This provision was now withdrawn and the right of the *nawab* to keep any army under his command was completely negated. The treaty also put an additional expenditure of Rs. 16 lakhs for an army detachment which was to be controlled and manned by the British officers.[8] The most important Article—*Article 7* of this treaty read as follows:[9]

In modification of the Article 6th of the Treaty above referred to, it is hereby provided that the King of Oude will take into his immediate and earnest consideration, in concert with the British Resident, the best means of remedying the existing defects in the Police, and in the Judicial and Revenue Administration of his dominions, and that if His Majesty should neglect to attend to the advice and counsel of the British Government or its local representative, and if (which God forbid) gross and systematic oppression, anarchy and misrule should hereafter at any time prevail within the Oude dominions, such as seriously to endanger the public tranquility, the British Government reserves to itself the right of appointing its own officers to the management of whatsoever portions of the Oude territory, either to a small or to a great extent, in which such misrule as that above alluded to may have occurred, for so long a period as it may deem necessary, the surplus receipts in such case, after defraying all charges, to be paid into the King's treasury and a true and faithful account rendered to His Majesty of the receipts and the expenditure of the territories so assumed.

This article for the first time propounded the concept of take over of the administration of Awadh. The king protested but ultimately gave in. In the preface of the *Treaties and Engagements* the matter has been made clear:

The assent of the King was most reluctantly given to this treaty. The Home Government therefore disallowed it and directed the restoration of the relations with Awadh to the same footing on which they previously stood. The King was thereupon informed of the determination of the Government to relieve him from all that was onerous in the conditions respecting the subsidiary force established under the treaty, and to defray from the British treasury the expense of the portion of it already organised, but the formal abrogation of the treaty was not intimated to him.[10]

In other words the treaty was not accepted by the Court of Directors in England. A question has been raised whether the entire treaty was disallowed by the Home Government or only that part which imposed on the Awadh state the expense of the auxiliary force. On 8 July 1839, the king of Awadh was informed that he was relieved of the cost of maintaining the auxiliary force which the British Government had taken upon itself. However, one school of historians has maintained that the whole of the treaty was disallowed, but the then Governor-General and his successor kept the fact under hiding in a very sly manner.[11] But the treaty or the philosophy thereof surfaced time and again. Sir John Kaye admits '*years after this date even in Lucknow Residency the treaty was held valid.*' In October 1853, Col. Sleeman wrote to Sir James Hogg:[12] 'The treaty of 1837 gives our Government ample authority to take the whole administration on our selves.' And again, in 1854, to Col. Low: 'Our Government would be fully authorised at any time to enforce the penalty prescribed in our treaty of 1837.'

The King of Awadh was constantly under the impression that the treaty signed by him and the Resident and endorsed by the Governor-General was final. It continued to be published in Hutchinson's *Collection of Treaties and Engagements*, an important official publication. The Governor-General and his officials kept the abrogation of the treaty a deliberate and well-guarded secret to serve a certain objective; to use when it suited their purpose. In 1856, at least, the Treaty with its Article 7 was decided to have never been in force, and total annexation was put into effect.

The signing of the treaty once again dampened the spirit of the King and his government. But like his father Saadat Ali Khan, after the detachment of Ruhelkand from Awadh, he got down to work for the good administration of Awadh. He changed the atmosphere of the court and reinstated a measure of dignity. Unfortunately Hakim Mehdi Ali, his able *wazir*, died soon after.[13] He was succeeded by Yahiya Khan, who was a Sunni and was the only exception to the line of *wazirs* who were invariably Shias or Hindus. He was appointed and given the title 'Zaheeer-ud-daula'.[14] His close attachment to the Resident was an additional factor in favour of his appointment. But he too died within six months.[15] He was succeeded by Mehdi Ali's nephew, Munawar-ud-daula and like his uncle was a great support to the King of Awadh.[16]

The King reorganised the administration of Awadh. The *amani* system was reinforced and the treasury of Awadh began to show signs of prosperity in agriculture and commerce.

In 1838, the First Afghan War broke out and the King of Awadh as usual was approached for a loan once again and a sum of one lakh pound sterling was given to the Company. In 1839 the Company very generously conveyed the redemption of the annual subsidy of rupees sixteen lakhs which had been enforced on the King of Awadh under the Treaty of 1837. Muhammad Ali Shah, thereafter, engaged himself in the construction of public buildings. He was the second greatest builder of Lucknow after Asaf-ud-daula. He laid the foundations and completed the Hussainabad Imambara.[17] This Imambara is popularly known as Chotta (small) Imambara. This complex of buildings, like the Asafi Imambara, has two entry gates, the miniature replicas of Roomi Darwaza. Adjacent to this complex came up two other buildings—Jama Masjid and a proposed seven storeyed tower—known as Satkhanda. Both remained incomplete in his lifetime. The Jama Masjid is one of the most ornate buildings of Lucknow, native in its idiom. Muhammad Ali Shah died before this could be completed. The work was left to his second wife Malika Jahan.[18]

Malika Jahan was a lady of great dedication. She had no issues. After the completion of Jama Masjid, she went on pilgrimage to Kerbala in Iraq. She was received as a royal personage but died on this journey and lies buried there. Satkhanda, a tower erected to watch the Id moon remains incomplete to this day—a monument to a very foolish idea that had been floated by the people around the courts that if a successor would undertake to complete the works of his predecessor, bad luck would come to him.[19] It could hardly be a divine inspiration, but it took away the sense of basic sanity from the court that continuity is a mark of good government. A few buildings in Lucknow specifically the Satkhanda and the Mausoleum of Naseer-ud-din Haider are living testimony to this stupidity. Even so, the skyline of Lucknow had been changed and assumed a certain grace. Lucknow came to be known as the *Babylon of India*.

The most important factor of the Awadh administration at that time was the creation of the Hussainabad Trust. Over a period of time a total sum of thirty-six lakh rupees was entrusted to it, the interest accruing to be used for the maintenance of the Trust and for grant of pension to the long list of relations of the King. The interest was fixed at 3½ per cent.[20] The sum remained deposited with the Company, the succeeding British Government and then the Government of India. The beneficiaries of this deposit were called *vaseekadars* and despite the penury in which they live at present, they feel a sense of honour. The interest on this deposit continued to be 3½ per cent,[21] till eighties in the twentieth century.

The author of this book as Commissioner and Chairman of the Hussainabad Trust had approached the Government of India to increase the rate of interest to bring it in line with current rates. I was told that about 250 crore of rupees had been deposited by the various erstwhile states and this could be a strain on government resources. The matter was further pursued that a deposit going above 150 years cannot be taken lightly. Ultimately the Government relented and now the deposits bring in much better returns to the delight of Trustees who call themselves *mutwallis*, the protectors of the Trust. To me it has remained a matter of conjecture as to why a King with all the embellishments of sovereignty had to deposit money with an external agency to care for his heirs and successors. Either he lacked confidence in the future of his throne or else was particularly farsighted. In any case, the future of the state of Awadh had passed into the hands of the British.

During the time of Muhammad Ali Shah many Europeans hitherto employed on very high salaries were either dismissed or their emoluments were considerably reduced. Among them were Maj. Davidson, a military officer, Dr. Clarkson, Walker and Adolf William, the European attendants at the *darbar*.[22] Muhammad Ali Shah in

Anglophile pursuits had invited one Professor Leddon to set up a college in Lucknow; he was also dismissed. The Hindu officials came in for a more favourable treatment and the percentage of Hindus in state service went up to 39 per cent as against 26 per cent in the time of Ghazi-ud-din Haider.[23] There were numerous instances recorded in Muhammad Ali Shah's court diary of the King's order for setting free a number of prisoners on the auspicious occasion of Diwali.[24] The King himself participated in the Dussehra celebrations and the heir apparent and other members of the royal household also took part. It was a time of awakening in India when practices like *sati* and female infanticide were greatly curbed. On their part Hindus showed great respect for the Muslim customs. In particular the *tazia* processions drew large crowds of Hindus, the *tazias* receiving respectful obeisance. It almost appeared that they were praying in front of their own temples. Hindu officers and rich persons spent a lot on these occasions, possibly to court favour with the King.[25]

Muhammad Ali not merely reigned but also ruled. He personally looked after the details of the administration. Since he had appointed Amjad Ali Shah, the heir apparent as his *wazir*, the political heads of the administration remained only as *naibs* (Vice-Regents) to the *wazir*. The King was able to break the power of the cabal and consequently some reforms could be brought about. The revenues improved considerably, corruption and disorder were controlled. Muhammad Ali was undoubtedly one of the best rulers of Awadh. Like his father Saadat Ali Khan he exercised great control on his kingdom and administration. Whether Muhammad Ali Shah understood it at that time or not, his rule contributed to the extension of the twilight zone of the Awadh dynasty by nearly twenty years after the ominous treaty of 1837. His rule was without much turmoil or any important external event other than the Afghan war.

Amjad Ali Shah (1842-7)

Amjad Ali Shah[26] succeeded his father without any dispute or trouble. Muhammad Ali had given him the charge of *diwani*[27] and his mother Malika Afaq had reared him in a cultured atmosphere. Since Nasir-ud-daula was the third son of Saadat Ali Khan, there was hardly any chance for him to become a successor to the throne according to Muslim law. But the imbroglio over Munna Jaan cleared the way for his father and him. The childhood and youth of Amjad Ali Shah were therefore punctuated by a sense of restraint and discipline. His world was confined to religion and a mind-set where intellectual liberalism came slowly to be excluded. When his father became King by a sudden turn of events he was about 37 years of age. Once he was given the *wizarat*, his fortunes rose and he had his share of marriages and concubines. A sense of physical enjoyment did enter his life, although at a late stage.[28] But he never made a public fool of himself. The ways of the court and the life of his nobles were kept under a certain restraint.[29] His father Muhammad Ali Shah had two wives, Malika Afaq his own mother, and Malika Jahan, who had no issues. So he never had to face the bickering claims and counter-claims which had become rife during the reigns of Ghazi-ud-din Haider and Nasir-ud-din Haider.

Amjad Ali conducted himself in public in the manner of a religious divine. He laid great emphasis on the purity of physical conduct and his ambition was to enjoy the reverence due to a great religious personage. This earned him the honorific of *hazrat saheb* in public parlance. The new bazaar which was set up during his lifetime is named Hazratganj and has remained the most fashionable shopping centre of Lucknow for more than 160 years.[30] The Maqbara of Amjad Ali has also been built adjacent to this shopping area and is known as Maqbara Sibtenabad.

Immediately after Independence in 1947 there was a surprising indifference towards the maintenance of these historic buildings. One portion of the mausoleum was 'allotted' under the Rent-Control Act to the office of the Registrar Census Operations at Lucknow, the other part to a 'refugee' for setting up a furniture workshop. Turning lathes, the scraping of wood and the hammering of nails are strange tributes to a man who valued peace and tranquillity in his life! Hazratganj remained a spot for the social evenings of Lucknow. It was the fashion centre. As against this, Aminabad which was set up by Ameen-ud-daula, the *wazir* of Amjad Ali, became the business centre. Hazratganj was famous for its relaxed evenings and respectful loitering called *Gunjing*. The *Gunjing* was best described by a keen social observer as 'the art of seeing others and being seen'. The style and glory of Hazratganj have continued undiminished.

Amjad Ali appointed Ashraf-ud-daula, hitherto his own *naib* (deputy), as his *wazir*.[31] Initially Ashraf-ud-daula was a great loyalist of the Company but the conduct of his King made such an impact on him that he became more loyal to the king. Since the real power vested with the Company, he was removed from that office within four months. He was replaced by Imdad Hussain Khan who was given the honorific of Ameen-ud-daula.[32] He remained in his office for about a year. He was succeeded by Munawar-ud-daula, a nephew of Hakim Mehdi Ali Khan, who had held the office of *wazir* in the time of Muhammad Ali. Because of the Company's interference in the administration he went away for *haj*. After his departure Ameen-ud-daula was reappointed to this office in July 1844.[33] The same year Davidson was appointed as the new Resident, who proved to be exceptionally good and did not interfere with the internal administration of Awadh.[34]

The attitude of the King was in favour of a general good sense in administration, but the capacity for hard decisions was missing. A ruler who wanted to look and behave like a religious divine was not the right person at this time in history for Awadh. The Company was mentally prepared for the take over of Awadh and this undercurrent was there all the time. Efforts were on to create disturbances. Those who disregarded the authority of the King found shelter in the Residency. The Resident had started holding a *darbar*, parallel to the King. The King lived in his own world and the selfishness of his ministers became the deciding factor behind state policy. The zamindars became more and more refractory and became indifferent about payment of dues to the state. The Company was trying to create a situation where according to Articles 7 and 8 of the 1837 Treaty, they could claim to take over the administration of Awadh either in part or as a whole. One great event of Amjad Ali Shah's reign was the Panjab War, in which he did render help to the British. In Panjab, after the death of Ranjit Singh (1839) there was no settled government and the real power was in the hands of army and it was becoming unruly. In an unwise move, the successors of Ranjit Singh diverted the attention of the army by encouraging them to go beyond the frontiers of the Sikh kingdom and create disturbance there. In 1845 Sir Henry Hardinge met the challenge of the Sikhs in the sanguinary battles of Ferozeshah and other engagements. As usual, the Company suffered a drain on its resources and asked Awadh for help. It was provided to them in the form of an army contingent and a loan of Rs. 3.20 lakhs.[35]

The tradition of the construction of the public works continued unabated. The road between Lucknow and Kanpur was constructed and the Iron Bridge imported during the time of Ghazi-ud-din Haider was laid across the Gomti.[36] The Gomti had three bridges now: one near the Macchi Mahal, second the Iron Bridge and the third Nao Ka Pul—the pontoon bridge near Moti Mahal.

The King carried his Shia bias to excess, devoting much time and attention to religious celebrations. He put great faith and reliance on the Mujtahid hierarchy created by Sayyad Dildar Ali. In the previous chapter we have discussed the role of Sayyad Dildar Ali in formulating Shia theology in the State of Awadh. There is no doubt that his learning and scholarship contributed immensely to the organisation of the Shia community in Lucknow and the hinterland of Awadh.[37] When Ghazi-ud-din Haider had become the king, the Shia theologians did much to create among the Shias, a sense of pride in the kingship at Lucknow. Even if the proclamation of Ghazi-ud-din Haider as a king carried him into political isolation, the strength of Shia hegemony was greatly furthered by his new title.

Sayyad Dildar Ali had two sons, Sayyad Muhammad and Sayyad Hussain. Both were brilliant and carried the illustrious mantle of their father. Sayyad Muhammad was born in 1784. He was bred and brought up under his father. At the age of eighteen he completed his religious education and was awarded the *sanad* of *ijtehad*, the highest degree of Shia theological learning. After his father's death in 1820, he carried out the task of leading the Shia community, having been nominated as Mujtahid by his father during his lifetime. According to Shia customs, *madarsas* were not considered the in-thing. The teacher had direct relationship with the students and taught the subjects as he chose, to a limited group of disciples. The Shia teachers were persons of great learning and devotion. During this time works of great merit were authored. Sayyad Muhammad trained a very large number of teachers and had a big following. He came to be known as *Sultan-ul-Ulema*—king among the theologians. He wrote as many as twenty-seven works of outstanding erudition. As a departure from the concept of Shia learning on a limited teacher-taught basis, he set up a school in Lucknow known as the *Sultan-ul-Madaris*.[38] That school continues, and enjoys much repute, but not the glory of yonder years.

The younger brother Sayyad Hussain was born in 1796. He upstaged his brother by completing his *sanad* of *ijtehad* at the age of seventeen. He assisted his elder brother throughout his life and the two together continued to hold the leadership of Shia community.

Starting from the days of Sayyad Dildar Ali, Shia theology acquired a certain zest. But none of the rulers were influenced by sectarian exclusiveness. It was only Amjad Ali Shah on whom the bias had an over-weaning influence and he showed it. He started the system of giving gifts—*zakat* through the Mujtahid as the supervisor. More than rupees three lakhs were distributed each year as *zakat* during his reign.[39] The court system of Awadh thus acquired a greater inculcation of religious thinking. The appellate courts in Lucknow were looked after by the two Sayyad brothers. The elder brother known as *Sultan-ul-Ulema* had his son Sayyad Muhammad Baqar appointed *munsif*.[40] A Shia Mufti was posted by every *nazim* in every district known as *chaklas*.[41]

Shia hegemony did not mean that other streams of Islamic thought had been completely eclipsed. The Sunni scholars of Firangi Mahal attained outstanding eminence as theologians and authors. Maulvi Zahir-ul-lah (1760-1840) was one of the greatest *alim* of his day and served the state as *mufti-e-adalat* for forty years. He was an expert on Koranic interpretation. Maulvi Abdul Razzaq (1821-89)[42] was well-known for his scholarship and wrote a large number of books on Sunni theology. He was the one who was openly in favour of declaring Islamic *jehad* in the Hanumangarhi incident. Maulvi Wali-ul-lah (1768-1853)[43] wrote a seven volume commentary on Koran in Persian, a landmark in the history of religious writing in Lucknow. Muhammad Abdul Wali, Maulvi Anwar-ul-Haq, Maulvi Noor-ul-Haq and Maulvi Abdul Hai were other names of repute. Mulla Moin wrote a treatise on the illegality of *mutah* (temporary) marriage. This temporary marriage contract is prevalent among the Shias but is considered illegal by Sunnis.[44]

The ascendancy of Shias in Awadh led to constant friction on the occasion of Moharram. *Tabarra* was encouraged by Shia theologians. The Sunnis started a new concept called *madde-sahiba*, in which they praised all the four Caliphs. To this Shias replied with *kadde-sahiba*, in which they again came back to the condemnation of the first three Caliphs and praised the Imams. As usual this led to intense clashes and bloodshed. During the first ten days of Moharram the gates of Firangi Mahal use to remain closed. One of the great scholars of Firangi Mahal Maulana Bahr-ul-Uloom left Lucknow for ever.

Shia-Sunni conflicts did not come in the way of the cordial relations, Hindus had with both sects. The mutual tolerance and good will was a pleasant feature of this society. The Muslims had in many cases absorbed many of the superstitions prevalent among the Hindus. Hindus basically believe in one God, but the devotion of a single individual may consecrate in him part of the powers of the Ultimate Divine. That individual is worthy of emulation and reverence is offered to that person. Worship comes naturally in such cases. These great individuals are enumerated as 'gods' like Hanuman, Maha Kaali, *èt al.* The worship of such 'gods' may give to a human being inspiration for creative work or fortitude on occasions of adversity. The idea is that above an individual there is a natural or a supernatural power. In such an atmosphere the logic is defied and faith in the power beyond becomes a natural corollary, where reason stops and superstitions take over. To any human being such belief is likely to appeal as a short-term measure. Some Muslims also adopted such beliefs. Butter, writing in 1839, remarks,

> The religious excitability of the Muslims of Awadh seems to range lower than that of their co-religionists in Ruhelkhand, in Hyderabad or even in Bengal. People of Awadh could hardly be accused of bigotry or intolerance.

Irwin observed, 'Speaking generally, it may be said that all our Musaalmans are more or less Hinduised.'

Sufi thought also continued to exert influence during this period and brought about greater understanding among the Hindus and Muslims. The widespread saint worship and Hinduised customs and beliefs percolating among the Indian Muslims created a reaction among some fundamentalist Islamic thinkers. They organised themselves as *Ahl-i-Hadis*, popularly called *wahabis*. The leader of this sect was Sayyad Ahmad, a resident of Rae-Bareli district in Awadh. He was born in 1782 in Rae-Bareli, and became a disciple of Shah Abdul Aziz of Delhi and preached against the abuses which he thought had crept into the beliefs and social practices of Indian Muslims. He found a great following and moving to Afghanistan with many of his followers died fighting the Sikhs near Peshawar in 1833. But he had few supporters in Awadh. In Awadh fundamentalism did not find much ground.

Amjad Ali carried his total involvement with Shia philosophy almost to an extent of absurdity. The name *Panjtan*—the names of five pillars of Shia philosophy—the Prophet, the Ali, Ali's two sons—Hassan and Hussain and their mother Fatima could not even be written on state papers by anyone other than a Shia.[45] Shia calligraphers were appointed to write religious state papers. Whatever may have been the effects of his religiosity on matters of state, Amjad Ali brought sanity and discipline to the court and the behaviour of his nobles. He died of cancer in 1847 and was buried in the Sibatanabad Imambara constructed near Hazratganj.[46] He carried on the good work of his father to redeem falling standards of behaviour, current during the time of his predecessor. His religious preoccupation did not leave him time or dedication towards the intricacies and details of administration. His father Muhammad Ali Shah was able to stem the rot and postpone the evil day as pronounced by the Treaty of 1837. Amjad Ali Shah also made his humble contribution in continuing the good work.

The Island of Awadh was now fighting for survival. It was the court of Awadh *versus* the coterie of the Resident. Everybody who was anybody was trying to curry favour with the Resident to influence the King and administration of Awadh in his favour. On the other hand, the court conspiracies constantly enfeebled the state. The King had hardly any vision to look beyond the confines of Lucknow. The great hinterland of the State of Awadh had begun to feel the lack of power and force in the administration. Even if land revenue administration continued unabated in the solid performance of its duties, lack of policy encouraged officials towards selfish pursuits against the interests of the state. The judiciary and *diwani* kept some semblance of order but the lack of purpose began to hasten the state towards the end of the *Twilight*.

NOTES

1. Resident to Political Secretary to Government of India, 24 July 1837, Foreign Secret Consultations, 7 August 1837, N.A.I., No. 10; Yogesh Praveen, 'Shahane Awadh', *Dharamyug*, 27 May 1979, p. 29.
2. Jagdish Sahai, *Awadh Mein Nawabi Shasan* (Hindi), Faizabad, n.y., p. 159; John Pemble, *The Raj, the Indian Mutiny, and the Kingdom of Oudh—1801-1859*, New Delhi: O.U.P., 1977, p. 82.
3. R.W. Bird, *Dacoitee in Excelsis: or, the Spoliation of Oude by the East India Company*, Lucknow, 1971, p. 85.
4. Resident to Political Secretary to Government of India, 24 July 1837, Foreign Secret Consultations, N.A.I., 7 August 1837, No. 10—gives a detailed description of this incident.

5. Jagdish Sáhai, op. cit., p. 162. But Michael H. Fisher says: 'Despite these bonds between the new *wazir* (Roshan-ud-daula) and the Awadh Padshah, the examples of the sudden disgrace of his three predecessors apparently led the Minister to seek strong guarantees for his security from the British. The resident reported that an emissary from the new *wazir* approached him offering to exchange policies favourable to the Company—notably release of Company troops stationed in Awadh, and paid for in perpetuity by the cession of half the territories of Awadh ruler in 1801, for use elsewhere—for a guarantee of the Wizarat for life. When this was rejected, a series of alternative bargains were offered, each demanding less benefit for the *wazir* than the previous one. Finally the *wazir* simply begged for the goodwill of the British should he be dismissed from office (Resident to Political Secretary to Government of India, 16 January 1834, Foreign Political Consultations, 23 January 1834, N.A.I., No. 42). When the *wazir* was indeed dismissed from his post by the new Padshah, Muhammad Ali Shah, he was permitted to retire to the protection of British territory (P.D. Reeves (ed.), *Sleeman in Oudh: An Abridgement of W.H. Sleeman's 'A Journey through the Kingdom of Oude in 1849-1850'*, Cambridge, 1971, pp. 237-8)' is cited as the authority for these statements by Michael H. Fisher, op. cit., pp. 192-3.
6. Munshi Sital Prashad, Mirat al-Auza, Persian MS 2149, Raza Library, Rampur, fol. 333 Resident to Political Secretary to Governor-General, 7 January 1838, Foreign Political Consultations, N.A.I., 24 January 1838, No. 43.
7. C.U. Aitchison, *A Collection of Treaties, Engagements, and Sunnads Relating to Indian and Neighbouring Countries*, Calcutta, 1909, Vol. I, p. 138.
8. Safi Ahmad, 'The Treaty of 1837', *Medieval India—A Miscellany*, 2 (1972), pp. 282-90.
9. C.U. Aitchison, op. cit., Vol. I, p. 140.
10. Ibid., p. 61.
11. J.W. Kaye (ed.), *A History of the Sepoy War in India*, Vol. I, London, 1870, p. 127.
12. Ibid., p. 129.
13. Jagdish Sahai, op. cit., p. 164; Michael H. Fisher, op. cit., p. 193.
14. Munshi Sital Prashad, op. cit., fol. 333; Resident to Political Secretary to Governor-General, 7 January 1838, Foreign Political Consultations, N A.I., 24 January 1838, No. 43.
15. Ratan Singh, Sultan al-Tawarikh, Persian MS, Lucknow University Library, Lucknow, fols. 445-6.
16. Munshi Sital Prashad, op. cit., fol. 390; Ratan Singh, op. cit., fol. 445; P.D. Reeves (ed.), op. cit., pp. 237-8.
17. Kamal-ud-din Haider, *Sawanihat-i-Salatin-i-Awadh*, Lucknow, 1896, p. 355; Officiating Resident to Officiating Secretary to Government of India, 11 January 1839, Foreign Department Political Consultations, N.A.I., 22 May 1839, Nos. 63-5; Mirza Ali Azhar, *King Wajid Ali Shah of Awadh*, Vol. I, Karachi, 1982, p. 187.
18. Safi Ahmad, *Two Kings of Awadh: Muhammad Ali Shah and Amjad Ali Shah—1837-1847*, Aligarh, 1971, p. 158.

19. Abdul Halim Sharar, *Guzishta Lakhnau Mashriqi Tammadun Kā Akhri Namona*, New Delhi, 1971, p. 44.
20. Kamal-ud-din Haider, op. cit., p. 355; Officiating Resident to Officiating Secretary to Government of India, 11 January 1839, Foreign Department Political Consultations, 22 May 1839, N.A.I., Nos. 63-5; King of Oudh to Acting Resident, 26 February 1839, enclosed with Acting Resident to Officiating Secretary to Government of India, 13 March 1839, Foreign Department Political Consultations, 12 June 1839, N.A.I., Nos. 38-40. It is quite interesting to note that Muhammad Ali Shah did not name Shia Ulema as trustees of the Imambara and its mosque; this honour was conferred on Sayyad Imam Ali Khan and Azimullah Khan, and their descendents after them—Safi Ahmad, *Two Kings of Awadh: Muhammad Ali Shah and Amjad Ali Shah—1837-1847*, Aligarh, 1971, p. 30.
21. Safi Ahmad, op. cit., p. 30.
22. Secret Consultation No. 9/11, 21 August 1837 (Translation of an official note from the King of Oude to the Resident, Col. Low, dated 9th August 1837), Political Consultation No. dated 27 February 1837 (No. 1 of this date), (Letter of Col. Low, addressed to W.H. Macnaughten, Secretary to the Government of India, 7 February 1837).
23. *Kitab Akhbar Deorhi Badshah Oudh*, dated 27th *Shaban* 1255 A.H. corresponding to 5 November 1839.
24. *Kitab Akhbar Deorhi Badshah Oudh*, dated 9th Shaban 1255 A.H. corresponding to 15 October 1839.
25. Mrs. Meer Hasan, *Observation on the Mussulmauns of India*, Vol. I, p. 48.
26. The real name of Amjad Ali was Srraiyajah—Muhummad Ali Naqvi, *Amjad Ali Shah*, pp. 80-2, cited in Jagdish Sahai, op. cit., p. 169. Sayyad Muhammad Quli Kinturi has referred him as *misdaq as-sultan al-adil* or '*The Just King*'—*Akham-i-adalat-i-alaviyyah*, Lucknow, 1259/1843, p. 3.
27. Sayyad Muhammad Quli Kinturi, op. cit., p. 3.
28. Sayyad 'Abbas Ardistani', *Al-hism-al-mutin fi ahwal al-wuzara wa's salatin*, 2 Vols., MSS 235a, 235b, N.A.I., New Delhi, pp. 143-4. Amjad Ali ordered that the houses of male prostitution should be closed down. This order was followed with a series of arrests and banishments of the male prostitutes. Only those were spared who gave up their *saris* and agreed to have their locks shorn—Muhammad Mihdi Lakhnavi Kashmiri, *Najum-as-sama: takhmilah*, Vol. I, pp. 236, 263-4; see also Tota Ram Shyam, *Tawarikh-i-Nadir al-asr*, Lucknow, 1863, p. 112.
29. There is a difference of opinion among contemporary historians regarding whether the court and life of Amjad Ali was really under certain restraint or not. W.H. Sleeman and Kamal-ud-din Haidar, in their respective works, believed that Amjad Ali practised certain restraints in his life. The main reason behind this may be that they wanted it to be understood that it was Wajid Ali Shah and not Amjad Ali who was responsible for the downfall of Awadh empire. But Mirza Rajjab Ali Suroor (*Fasanay-e-Ibrat*, Lahore, 1942) gives an opposite tradition.

30. Paripurnananda Verma, *Wijid Ali Shah Aur Awadh Rajya ka Patan* (Hindi), Lucknow, 1949, p. 60.
31. Munshi Sital Prashad, op. cit., fol. 429.
32. Ibid., fols. 439-45, 501.
33. Kamal-ud-din Haider, op. cit., Vol. I, p. 382.
34. Jagdish Sahai, op. cit., p.174; W. Bird, op. cit., p. 66.
35. Resident to Political Secretary to Government of India, 18 May 1842, Indian Political Consultations, N.A.I., 15 June 1842, No. 37.
36. Paripurnananda Verma, op. cit., pp. 62-3.
37. Sayyad 'Abbas Ardistani', op. cit., Vol. II, p. 139.
38. Kamal-ud-din Haider, op. cit., Vol. I, pp. 371-2.
39. Ibid., p. 371; Mirza Muhammad Taqi, *Tarikh-i-Aftab-i-Awadh*, pp. 138-9, W.H. Sleeman, *A Journey Through The Kingdom of Oude*, Vol. I, pp. 309-10 : 'Out of the reserved treasure, the Zukaat, or two and a half per cent is ever year paid to the mojtahid for distribution among the poor of the Sheea sect at Lucknow. No person of the Sunni sect is permitted to partake of this charity. Being a Sayyad, (the Mujtahid) neither he nor any member of his family can legally take any part of this charity for themselves, except for the bonafide purpose of paying debts, but they get over the difficulty by borrowing large sums before the money is given out, and appropriate the greater part of the money to the liquidation of these debts, though they all hold large sums in our Government securities. To his friends at court he sends a large share, with a request that they will do favour to undertake the distribution among the poor of their neighbourhood. Only a small portion is actually distributed among the poor of the Sheea sect.'
40. Kamal-ud-din Haider, op. cit., p. 371.
41. Ibid.
42. M. Muhammad Inayat Ullah, *Tazkira-i-Ulema-i-Firangi Mahal*, pp. 92-100.
43. Ibid., pp. 197-200.
44. Muhammad Azmat Ali, *Muraqqai-Khusravi*, p. 221; M. Muhammad Inayat Ullah, op. cit., p. 174.
45. Tota Ram Shayam, op. cit., p. 112; Najmul Ghani Khan, op. cit., Vol. V, p. 23.
46. Abdul Halim Sharar, op. cit., p. 187. The formal confirmation of death was given by the Residency Surgeon Dr. Logan, who was also the Superintendent of His Majesty of Oude's Hospital and Dispensary at Lucknow—Kamal-ud-din Haider, op. cit., Vol. II, p. 1; cited in Mirza Ali Azhar, op. cit., Vol. I, p. 193.

Plate 5: Entry Gate of Chhota Imambara

Plate 6: Chhota Imambara

Plate 7: Jama Masjid

CHAPTER VI

The Last Struggle (1847-56)

Wajid Ali Shah, the most famous name in the history of Awadh, succeeded his father at the young age of twenty-five on 13 February 1847.[1] He had been declared heir apparent in the lifetime of his father. Col. Richmond, the Resident, wanted to intercede in favour of his elder half-brother Mustafa Ali Khan, but Amjad Ali Shah strongly refuted the idea and there was no change in the decision of the king.[2] Wajid Ali Shah took over at a simple function at the Lal Baradari.[3] The administration remained unchanged with Ameen-ud-daula and *raja* Balkrishna, continuing as *wazir* and *diwan*. His first act as the king was a decision to construct a mausoleum for his father in Hazratganj.[4]

Wajid Ali Shah was born on 30 July 1822,[5] when Ghazi-ud-din Haider was the king and his son Nasir-ud-din Haider was clearly in the line of succession. Wajid Ali Shah's grandfather Nasir-ud-daula was the third son of Saadat Ali Khan, and was not likely to become the king. He lived as a noble of the court. The luck of Wajid Ali Shah changed when the Company refused the enthronement of Munna Jaan, after the death of Nasir-ud-din Haider. Wajid Ali Shah's grandfather was woken up late at night on the fateful day of 8 July 1837, and was set up on the throne of Awadh under the canon fire of Company forces with the new name, Muhammad Ali Shah. Wajid Ali Shah was present at the time of coronation of his grandfather. At that moment he became the possible king of Awadh. He was at the formative age of fifteen and that event marks a clear line of demarcation in the evolution of that young man.[6]

Wajid Ali Shah's education started at the age of six.[7] His father Amjad Ali Shah was a devout Muslim, who was brought up under the strict religious regimen of his mother Malika Afaq. During the infancy of Wajid Ali Shah, his father was living on the pension granted by the court. The child was brought up in the strict family discipline, in which his father Amjad Ali Shah played an important role and the basic tenets of Shia religion were inculcated in the mind of the young man. Sayyad Imdad Hussain Khan was appointed his *ataleeq*,[8] to initiate him in moral conduct and education. Wajid Ali Shah was a brilliant young man and his schooling was in Persian. The standard of his writings in Persian is regarded very high by scholars. He also had a natural gift for music. He was a handsome man and one may say that his was a well-rounded personality.

Muhammad Maseeh-ud-deen, who accompanied the Oudh Commission as the Special Envoy of Wajid Ali Shah to England to represent the case against the Awadh Annexation, to Queen Victoria and the people of England, says:

> His present Majesty (Wajid Ali Shah) who has received a liberal eastern education, is well versed in ancient and modern history and literature, and, besides being the author of several Persian and oordoo poems of considerable merit, has written many useful and popular works which are found in most of the public libraries of Europe.[9]

Although no details are available about his tutors who gave him lessons in the different branches of learning, he was regarded as a scholar of substance by his contemporaries. His writings both in Urdu and Persian show his instinctive understanding of the subject and felicity of expression.

> Of an amiable disposition, rendered still more attractive by affable and engaging manners, Wajid Ali is much beloved and respected by his subjects from the highest to the lowest, from the rajah to the ryot, and this the more so, as he has ever discharged the duties of his high office with justice tempered by mercy.[10]

Maulana Abdul Halim Sharar, the well-known Urdu novelist, who had spent his childhood and youth 'under the protection of the King' at Matia Burj (Calcutta), speaks very highly of his literary attainments. Sharar says that:

> Wajid Ali Shah's literary taste was of a very high order. In fact he had a natural gift for *(i)* Literature and poetry, and *(ii)* for Music. . . . His literary attainments were very high. Although not an Arabic scholar but in Persian he was probably a little less proficient than Abdul Fazal (of Akbar's court, the well-known author of *Aieen-e-Akbari*). He could write, in a very short time, Persian prose of the highest diction which would remind one of the best classical writers in that language. Similarly, it was difficult to find another more naturally gifted poet than Wajid Ali Shah. He composed hundreds of Marsias, Salams, etc., and wrote so many

books in prose and poetry that it is difficult to remember them now; and every composition had a different and natural style. . . . He could dictate Marsia and Salams, to two different scribes simultaneously. . . .[11]

In the inaugural lecture at the Ecole Imperial at the opening of a course in December 1856, M. Garcin de Tassy, Member of the Institute and Professor of Hindostani, referred to Wajid Ali Shah as:[12]

I do not want merely an appreciation of this resolution which is politically oriented; neither do I want to estimate the qualities and faults of Wajid Ali, as a Sovereign; but I am interested in him as a distinguished literary figure and an eminent Hindustani poet. (Translation of the original French).

S. Ameer Ali Khan a leading *vakeel* of the Sudder Diwani Adalat, Calcutta, and minister (with the title of *wazeer-us-sultan*) of the king, at Matia Burj, says that eminent scholars and *ataleeqs* were appointed to educate and train Wajid Ali Shah in his childhood and, being very intelligent, he mastered the subjects in a very short time.[13]

The atmosphere of Lucknow was adopting a permissive style of living. There was escapism in the air all around. Since the real power of decision-making had slowly drifted away from the native rulers, the Residents were playing an increasingly decisive role in matters of administration. In the field of literature, the earlier school of Urdu poetry of elegance and sobriety initiated by masters like Mir, Sauda and Soz was giving way to writings of sensuous content. 'Atish', 'Nasikh', 'Shaq', 'Rind' had taken over the literary firmament of Lucknow. Wajid Ali also came under the influence of this school and adopted 'Atish' as his *ustaad* and began to write poetry[14] under the pen-name 'Akhtar'.[15] His written works show an excellence in the quality of his writing and also his liberal mental makeup and vision. His very famous observation at the time of the Hanumangarhi conflict in Ayodhya was

Hum ishque ke bande hain mazhab se nahin vaqif
Gar kaba hua to kya butkhana hua to kya[16]

We are the votaries of Love and unacquainted with religion;
to us it does not matter, whether it is Kaba or a temple.

This shows that the man had risen above the narrow domestic walls of the sectarian beliefs. He represented in the truest sense the much talked about *Ganga-Jamuni* or composite culture of Awadh.

Wajid Ali Shah took over in July 1847 and immediately started reorganising his army. He took the duties of the king seriously. The troops were regularly paraded. The Company officials immediately became apprehensive. The king was advised that he should desist from army exercises. When he did not go by their advice physicians and *hakims* were drafted in the service of the Company. The filial piety of Malika Kishwar, the king's mother, was also appealed to. She was advised that her son's physical well-being would be adversely effected by strenuous exercise. The king was literally stopped from commanding the army. The Company did not want a king who could ride a horse or command an army. The concern of physical well-being of the king was merely a ruse. He lived till the ripe old age of 75 and died in 1887.[17]

Wajid Ali Shah gave a lot of attention to the administration. He went and attended his office regularly. The administration was also made responsive, and a regular system was evolved to establish direct contact with the public. He introduced placement of complaint boxes on public streets. When the king moved in procession, two silver boxes were carried in front of the procession. The keys of these boxes were kept by the king himself. These boxes were called Mashghala-e-Nausherwani or Masghala-e-Sultani.[18] Because of the amiable nature of the king and his poetic disposition, he was well-loved by the people of Lucknow and was addressed as *jaane alam*. Then two things happened.

Ameen-ud-daula, the competent *wazir* since the days of Amjad Ali Shah was physically attacked by some miscreants near his residence in Golaganj.[19] By this incident it was made to appear that a *wazir* who could not maintain his own security, was not fit for the high office. Although the miscreants were taken into custody, the Resident intervened and had them released. The *wazir* was removed. A plain reading of the situation would show that the people who attacked the *wazir* in full day light must have had the support of the Resident. And so it was. The interference of the Resident had reached that mean level of behaviour. One does not have to go far to understand the objective of this behaviour of the Resident. His purpose was to bring a bad name to the governance of the king.[20]

Ameen-ud-daula was succeeded by Amir-ud-daula, and then another incident occurred. It was conveyed to the king that Gulab Rai, a jeweller, was constructing a new temple, and on the day of the installation of the idol, a Brahmin boy would be offered as a sacrifice. The king became very angry and ordered that the human sacrifice be prevented. The orders were conveyed through the *wazir*, but the subordinate officials went beyond their brief and demolished the dome of the temple. This naturally raised tempers and the Hindu shopkeepers went in a procession to the Resident. When this came to the notice of the king, he directed the temple to be reconstructed. The *wazir* was charged with defalcation of duty and removed.[21] Ali Naqi Khan succeeded to the post on 5 August 1847.[22] Among other reasons for his selection was his old association with the king. Before his enthronement Ali Naqi Khan had built a palace Anand Sabha as a pleasure haunt for the young Prince. Ali Naqi Khan was a man of duplicity and kept his options open on both sides, king and Resident. He maintained good relations with the Resident and married his daughter to Wajid Ali Shah. So now the king's father-in-law was his *wazir*. His influence in the court grew. Ali Naqi Khan remained *wazir* till the time of deposition of Wajid Ali Shah. He also accompanied the king to Matia Burj.[23]

Lord Hardinge, the Governor-General visited Kanpur in 1847. In the discussions there with the king he admonished the latter about the poor state of affairs in Awadh and gave him two years grace to improve conditions. After this visit, Hardinge prepared his long report (July-August 1847), in which charges levelled against the administration were repetitive and assiduously blamed the conduct of the king 'given to debauchery'.

About three months later the *wazir* contacted the Resident about 'a plan for the introduction of the British system of administration into his dominions, to be tried in the first instance, in such portions of the king's dominions as adjoined the British territories'.[24] Col. Richmond, the Resident, sent his assistant Captain Bird to Agra to communicate personally with Thompson, the Lieutenant-Governor of the north-western provinces. The king wanted the guidance of the Lieutenant-Governor for evolving a scheme of administration which was in line with British methods and procedures. Thompson gave his views on most points suggested in the Report to Sir Henry Elliot, Secretary to the Government in the Foreign Department in Calcutta, who rejected the scheme outright on the ground that 'if His Majesty the King of Oude would give up the whole of his dominions the East India Company Government would think of it, but that it was not worthwhile to take so much trouble about a portion'. This was the first in a long series of rebuffs to the King of

Awadh. By 1848, Dalhousie had taken over as Governor-General and he had come mentally prepared for the take-over of not only Awadh but also of most of the states in India.[25]

After this incident, Wajid Ali Shah issued a book, '*Dastoor-e-Wajidi*' or *Royal Book of Rules and Orders*. There are sixty-six directions contained in this book.[26] This is a compendium which in most countries of the world could be taken as a model text. It is a comprehensive documentation of government actions and policies for public welfare. There are directions about maintaining registers on the disposal of civil, revenue and criminal cases. Directions to the military officers for removing oppression committed by soldiers and *nizamat* employees. Directions regarding control of corruption and bribery. And direction regarding rules about Holi celebrations, prohibition of *sati* and female infanticide are also there. In the economic field this compendium contemplates the system of fixing minimum purchase price for foodgrains coming from the rural areas to the *mandis* to help the farmers to get a proper price for their labour in the field. This was the most progressive step to improve the finances of the agriculturists. Directions about court etiquette, Moharram celebrations, schemes of public welfare and such other important matters. Yet the continuous interference of not only the Resident but also his minions set at naught any changes that could bring about prosperity and justice. Even the appointment of lower officials was controlled by the Resident, reducing the efficacy of the king. But the king was successful in bringing about a profound change in the field of social conduct of the public. He introduced a special cap, '*alam pasand*' for his courtiers.[27] He also introduced many attractive designs in clothes and *khilats* and put into fashion many new styles. Lucknow had become one of the most culturally oriented town in the country.

At this point when he was giving rein to his natural abilities, the pressure of the Company curtailed his activities. Till the end of his life, Wajid Ali Shah remained a person of suppressed genius. The number of women he kept possibly gave satisfaction to his manhood. This is not unusual for the people of outstanding ability, even today, not excluding some Presidents and outstanding sportsmen of the Western democracies. In an interview with Hakim Safdar Nawab of Lucknow, a new angle on the concept of female company was put across. Wajid Ali Shah provided a modern stage to Lucknow.

He needed female actresses. Since the stage was not considered to be a fitting place where respectable citizenry should make its appearance, Wajid Ali Shah contracted a large number of *muta* marriages, and those ladies acted on the stage of Lucknow. One more point which came up during discussions was that Wajid Ali Shah apprehended a constant threat to his life. Two earlier rulers had been poisoned with the collusion of the Residents. Some of the females married to him were trained soldiers. Since they were married, they remained loyal and the life of the king was secured. An experiment of trained female soldiers as bodyguards has been tried with success in the twentieth century in a north African state.

Wajid Ali Shah's benefactions in the field of music and theatre were outstanding; few people can match the originality of his contribution. He brought literature and the 'stage of Lucknow' to a point where he came face to face with his people. His annual fair at Qaiserbagh was an occasion for rejoicing which broke the barriers of high and low, rich and poor, Hindus and Muslims. Wajid Ali Shah was the embodiment of what we now call a composite culture.

The entire reign of Wajid Ali Shah is the story of an uneven fight between the King of Awadh and the colonial power. It was a time of unbridled imperialism. All the European countries were expanding their tentacles on the rich, but comparatively unprotected countries of Asia and Africa. The science, the industry and the rapacity of the European countries made the peoples of Asia and Africa their hapless victims. Of the three streams of history which were merging in Awadh in the eighteenth and nineteenth centuries, the Mughal strain had by now become empty of significance. Now it was only native Awadh which was fighting the British. There was only a perverted romance in it. How could a man erudite, creative and upright face a situation in which he was confronted with a set of crafty people with vastly enhanced resources.

Here lies, also, a story of the people of India who were slowly learning to rise. The Reform Movement had started all over the country. There was dissemination of knowledge, science and communication. The telegraph had made its appearance.[28] The lessons of dealing with a devious foreigner were beginning to be learnt. Since the advent of Islam as a power in the eleventh century in India, the Muslims had adopted this country as their own. The dynasties that ruled the country from Delhi did not share administration with the native Hindus. The Hindus, despite their majority, were tolerated as a society of a subject people. In Awadh, right from the beginning, except for the *masnad* of the *nawab* or the King, Hindus shared political administration and rose to be *wazirs*. It was only after the propagation of sectarian Shia philosophy that the *wazirs* were mostly Muslims—nay, Shias. Since the choice became limited, incompetent people were given the responsibility of the *wizarat* leading to a quick turnover. It was only in the time of Wajid Ali Shah, that after the first changes, Ali Naqi Khan remained in that position throughout. But the *diwani* and the revenue administration remained the undisturbed citadel of Hindu administrators, led by *raja* Balkrishna.

Native strength was therefore a great support to the Awadh dynasty. There was progress in agriculture, there was progress in commerce and there was general prosperity. When peace was disturbed and the Company insulted the sovereign, time and again, there was resentment. The people of Awadh had a feeling of being robbed. Whatever financial prosperity the state gained because of good administration, was taken by the Company either by way of loan or outright extraction. The rulers of Awadh had shown continuing interest in works of public utility which gave to a large number of people their means of livelihood. The public lived well and dressed well. The army, on the other hand, was totally under the control of the Company. Only the personal protection of the king was somehow managed by the king himself; otherwise the army detachments were entirely controlled and managed by the British officers. If there was a disturbance of order or reluctance shown by the zamindars in payment of revenues, it was the Company forces that were sent for action (after 1801). When the dynasty of Awadh began under Saadat Khan there were conflicts and skirmishes, but it were the Indian forces on both sides. But in the time of later rulers it was a *firangi* who was leading the forces. Since they were better trained and better armed, the English won. The native pride was hurt. Slowly the idea gained ground that Indians lost against our own people fighting under a different flag and a superior command. The insult and hurt spread far and wide in the hinterland of Awadh. Awadh was the granary, and also the ground of recruitment for the healthy, brave young man who provided bulk of the Company forces. The insult to the king was felt more by the inhabitants of the province who were away from the court and its conspiracies. The people at the court had their own axes to grind, since some of them were seeking direct or indirect benefits from the Resident. The rural folk were more simple in their perception of loyalties. If the sovereign was insulted, they felt insulted in equal measure. The idea that India was a nation in its own right was already in the air. When the fires were finally stoked in 1857 and a conflagration took place, it were not merely the sepoys who broke into mutiny, it was the entire population which rose in revolt. Details apart, it was again the Mughal throne representing India as a symbol, confronted the *firangi*. Since people from almost all parts and all sections of the country participated, it was incontrovertibly the First War of Independence. It cannot be called a Sepoy Mutiny simply because India lost the war.

The American War of 1776 is invariably spoken of as the War of Independence. It was a war fought between the native forces of America against the British colonial rulers. Cornwallis who later came to India as Governor-General was the Commander of the vanquished British forces. In America itself there were a very large number of 'loyalists' who fought for the British masters. But the seaboard Colonies organised themselves better. The native leaders from their various areas of influence, came together and fought against the common enemy—the Great Britain. The autonomous constitutions of the various 'uniting states' of America arises from this basic idea of loyalty of local forces, which kept their own autonomy. Originally, the Federal Government had only limited functions. The United States as a nation has grown later with history. The claim that theirs was a War of Independence while ours was a Sepoy Mutiny should not be accepted as such by impartial writers of history. India was fighting to regain its house and to regain the lost paradise.

The British writers have repeatedly cast aspersions on the effete culture and society of Awadh, which is quite contrary to the facts. If Lucknow and Awadh was an effete culture, its inhabitants would not have fought for one and a half years with such dogged determination. It was not the people of India who were responsible for the failure of the struggle, it were the leaders. In India the configuration of the society has been so miserably divided among the higher and the lower castes, that people belonging to different castes regard themselves as separate entities. The caste is so badly ingrained in the Indian mind that it is deemed a divine dispensation. Slavery is not unknown in the history of other countries. When one country conquered the other in the olden days, they brought with them the wealth, the women and the young men as part of the loot. The young men worked as slaves, subservient to the masters, they were sold to. They remained in the life-long service of their masters. But there was no untouchability. In India, the lower castes belonging to the same religion, Hinduism, were considered as people who should not be touched, and even their shadows were to be avoided. In Awadh, even a society like this underwent a change. There was a large-heartedness everywhere. Large heartedness was described as *darya-dili* ('ocean of generosity'). Rigid social barriers were loosened or broken. This society of Awadh found in Wajid Ali Shah a person who had looked after their well-being and given them a sense of pride and glory. They fought in 1857 to regain their lost pride and that is how the struggle of 1857 should be seen.

Some historians have tried to underplay the depth of hostility of the populace in general, and Awadh in particular, towards the *firangis*. They have also tried to belittle the expanse of the area involved where the people took up arms and overthrew British rule. Awadh was taken over by the order of the Governor-General and Outram was appointed as the Chief-Commissioner in February 1856. The resistance against his rule started building up slowly in the beginning and vociferously later. The elder brother of Wajid Ali Shah, Mirza Mustafa Ali, was being persuaded to lead the forces and throw off the yoke of Company administration. On hearing this, Mustafa Ali was arrested along with Mohammad Hassan Khan by the Company. Ruknu-ud-daula, Mirza Haider Shikoh and Humayun Shikoh, members of the Mughal *darbar* who were staying in Lucknow, were also arrested. All of them were kept under confinement guarded by the Company detachments. But the incinerating fires were not confined to Lucknow. The entire countryside was agog with the news of the incarceration of their leaders and subversion of their social traditions and administration. Even before the famous incident of Mangal Pandey in Meerut (14 May 1857), the Awadh Irregular Contingent had risen in revolt (2 May 1857) in Lucknow. It was quickly put down. But by the end of May, the movement was in full swing in Lucknow and had gone into the whole of Awadh. By 10 June 1857, Sitapur, Aurangabad, Gonda,

Baharaich, Sultanpur had swept aside British administration. The English suffered a massive defeat and many casualties in Kanpur. The newspapers in London screamed 'Cawnpore Massacre' in their headlines. By 29 June 1857, the British were confined to the Residency in Lucknow. Awadh was free and proclaimed Brijis Qadar its ruler. Begum Hazrat Mahal, the Regent was declared *nawab alia* and given control of the administration. At this point a 'Sainik Panchayat' came into being. In India the voice of 'Panchayat' is hallowed as divine. In this 'Sainik Panchayat', the participants were General Barkat Ahmad, Umrao Singh, *raja* Jaipal Singh, *raja* Raghunath Singh, Shahb-ud-din and Ghamandi Singh. Maulvi Ahmad Shah Danka, later joined the elite group. The 'Sainik Panchayat' entered into an agreement with the Ruler that the Government administration would be conducted with 'the aid and advice of the *panchayat*'. For the first time a democratic ingredient was put in the governance of Awadh.

Nationalist forces attacked the Residency in July 1857. The resistance put up by the British in the Residency with the help of the Sikhs is a legend in the history of the British empire. This was the only building where after the proclamation of Queen Victoria, the Union Jack flew day and night and was never lowered after the sunset, as is generally done on all government buildings. The Residency was saved but the Commanders Henry Lawrence and Major Banks were killed in action. Havelock and Campbell led the forces from Kanpur and met the nationalist forces in Alambagh, on the outskirts of Lucknow. The fight continued, inch by inch, in Sikandar Bagh, Moti Mahal and Shahnajaf. On 23 November 1857, Havelock entered the Residency after a heroic battle. The Residency was relieved of the pressure. Outram was in command, but Havelock was killed in the battle. After this battle Campbell went back to Kanpur. After the fall of Delhi, Jhansi and Kalpi, Campbell came back to Lucknow in February 1858 and the fight was resumed. Each road and each street of Lucknow was a battlefield. Blood was shed in defence of honour and pride of the country. But the forces of empire were mightier and a bleeding Lucknow had to surrender. On 16 March 1858, Begum Hazrat Mahal was forced to leave Lucknow, but her battle lines continued via Bharawan in Hardoi, Bitawali, Shahjahanpur and then Bareilly. The nationalist forces reassembled in Chauka Ghat in Gonda district *Raja* Narpat Singh,

Ram Baksh, Chandan Singh, Gulab Singh, Devi Baksh Singh and Beni Madhav carried on the torch of freedom. In October 1858, *raja* Madhav Singh was killed. The *begum* moved on to Bondi in Baharaich district, on the border of Nepal. In November 1858, the famous proclamation of Queen Victoria was issued. The Crown had taken over the administration of the East India Company which ceased to exist as a political entity. The Proclamation was answered with a ringing call of defiance on the part of the Awadh rebels. After losing the last battle, Begum Hazrat Mahal left the sacred soil of India and found refuge in Nepal. For the time being the War of Independence had been lost. This is only a brief narrative of what happened during a period of a year and a half. Many misleading books have been written about this period. What I wish to emphasise in this brief description is the utter misconception that Awadh was a decadent culture and the people of Awadh were unhappy with their rulers. Had it been so, why did they take up arms and suffer privations of such a long and a protracted war? They could have easily said 'British Masters, trample on us and take us over'. Why did the people of Awadh fight in the name of their rulers and under their command? If this point has been made let us come back to the history of Awadh beginning with 1849.

Sleeman was appointed Resident in 1849.[29] He toured Awadh for about a year, went to various places and created dissension against the king wherever he went. According to Maj. Bird:

> . . . his appointment sealed the doom of Oude and its dynasty. Col. Sleeman was the emissary of a forgone conclusion. He effected to inspect and make a report, but the character of his report was determined for him before he entered Oude. He professed to examine, but he was under orders to sentence; he pretended to try, but he was instructed simply to condemn.[30]

Sleeman charged rupees three lakhs from the court of Awadh as expenses of his travels.[31] Never before in history has a foreigner ventured inspection of an area not under his own sovereign. Expectedly this report was highly prejudicial and weighted in favour of the take over of the administration of Awadh. He was, however, against annexation because 'our good name in India would inevitably suffer; and that good name is more valuable to us than a dozen of Oude's'.[32] But Dalhousie did not seem to have been impressed. It appears that Residents everywhere were sending such reports to the

Governor-General. On a report from Fraser, the Resident at Hyderabad, he observed:

> Gen. Fraser makes mountains of these mole hills, sends me more official papers on the march of a Subedar's party of the contingent than were produced by the battle of Waterloo, and dins into the government, day after day with provoking pertinacity his one remedy—the assumption of the government by us, that is, by himself.[33]

It seems the reports of Sleeman gave Dalhousie similar feelings. The reports on Wajid Ali Shah's physical and mental health sent by Sleeman also did not corroborate the reports of the Residency doctor. Sleeman repeatedly described Wajid Ali Shah as an imbecile or lunatic, but he was fit and healthy.

Dalhousie from the outset was busy enforcing the notorious Doctrine of Lapse and had taken over the smaller States of Satara (1848), Jaipur (1849) and Sambalpur (1849). After Sleeman's appointment as Resident in Awadh, more and more States were taken over, including Baghat (1850), Udaipur (1852), Jhansi (1853), Berar (1853) and Nagpur (1854). After Sleeman left in 1854 two other states were shackled in 1855—Carnatic and Tanjore. Awadh came later—the crowning act of Dalhousie's reign.

The Doctrine of Lapse was capricious. It also left most kings and Princes in a state of uncertainty. In Hindu philosophy the body is mortal but the soul is immortal. A Hindu never dies, his soul merely transmigrates from one body to the other. When a Hindu breathes his last his physical remains are given a final offering '*tilanjali*' by his son or successor. Without this, it is believed his soul will not rest in peace. For a Hindu, this action by his son is his 'spiritual' necessity. Much later this plea was taken by a very famous lawyer of India (Pandit) Mohammad Ali Jinnah before the Privy Council. This theme of Hindu philosophy was agreed upon and adoptions thereafter became a legally accepted norm even under the British rule in India. But in Dalhousie's time, his decisions had a vicious finality: no adoption was permitted to rulers. It is not surprising that his policies prepared the ground for the War of Independence in 1857.

In 1854 Sleeman departed and Gen. Outram took over as Resident.[34] He continued the dirty work of Sleeman and kept on sending reports based on the data collected during the time of Sleeman and retained in the Residency at Lucknow. Awadh continued to get a bad name in the British press. But its people enjoyed life and peace much better compared to the Company ruled provinces. In England the media publicised and even insisted that why should England not take over the entire country because the people of India lived under great tyranny of the native rulers.

A great test of his efficacy as a ruler came for Wajid Ali Shah in the form of an incident at Ayodhya.[35] In Ayodhya there are two famous and important temples. One is the *janamasthan* or birthplace of Lord Ram (on which stood a mosque till December 1992). The other temple is Hanumangarhi. Hanuman was a great devotee of Lord Ram and was his great general. He is the ruling deity of Ayodhya. His temple Hanumangarhi is a veritable fortress built on a hillock, surrounded by protective walls on all sides. These walls were constructed by the munificence and patronage by *raja* Tikait Rai, the important noble in the time of Asaf-ud-daula and anointed his *wazir* between 1790 and 1792.

The first named important structure in Ayodhya is known as *Ram Janambhoomi-Babri Masjid* complex. According to the *White Paper* issued by the Government of India,

> The structure is commonly known as *Ram Janambhoomi-Babri Masjid* complex was erected as a mosque by one Mir Baqi in Ayodhya in 1528. It is claimed by some sections that it was built at the site believed to be the birth spot of Shri Ram where a temple had stood earlier. This resulted in a long-standing dispute.[36]

Some historians writing about 1855 incident have confused the two different structures. Prominent among them being Michael H. Fisher.[37] This structure which in modern times is referred to as *Ram Janambhoomi-Babri Masjid* complex has a history of its own. According to the pamphlets brought out by some Hindu institutions, it is said that one great sage Baba Shyamananda had his abode in Ayodhya. He was a great *siddha* (a man of attainments) and his fame spread far and wide in whole of north India. A Muslim *faqir* Hazrat Kajal Abbas Musa Ashiqan Qalandar Shah came to Baba Shyamananda and sought his blessings. Baba Shyamananda accepted him as his disciple and offered him his sagacious teachings. The catholicity of Baba Shyamananda was such that Qalandar Shah was provided teachings according to Islamic traditions. He also became a *siddha* after some time and learnt yogic exercises while staying in the *ashram*. Jalal Shah was another Muslim *faqir* and he also came to Ayodhya and learnt that *Janambhoomi* is a *siddha-*

peetha. The devotion and prayers at this place provide recompense to the devotee in ample measure. The story goes further like this—when Babur lost his first battle against the Rajput confederation led by Rana Sanga, he visited Ayodhya and came under the spell of these two Muslim *faqirs*. They blessed him, but took a promise that if he won the next battle for the kingdom of India, he would destroy this Ram Janambhoomi temple and build a mosque. After his victory against Rana Sanga in the battle of Khanua, near Agra in 1527 Babur came back to Ayodhya and to redeem his promise made to Jalal Shah Qalandar and Kajal Abbas, he ordered his commander Mir Baqi to destroy the old temple and build a mosque.[38]

In the other story as brought out in the pamphlets issued by the Quran Society of India,[39] it has been stated that an army commander of Sikander Lodi named 'Babarik' or 'Babarak' built a magnificent mosque in Ayodhya to commemorate his victory over Bengal. In colloquial usage Babarik became Babri. One more story according to this pamphlet is that Babur visited India as a *faqir* and had a chance meeting with two Muslim saints—Shah Jalal-ud-din and Hazrat Musa Ashiqan. These saints prayed for the success of Babur and commanded that if his wish was fulfilled, he should construct a mosque in Ayodhya. When Babur conquered the empire in India, he ordered Mir Baqi, his army commander to construct a mosque on a barren hillock in Ayodhya. The facts of the case are under examination of the High Court at Allahabad in a long drawn contest. But the common factor in both these pamphlets issued by Hindu as well as Muslim organisations is Babur's meeting with two Muslim divines Qalandar Shah and Jalal Shah and the construction of a mosque after the fulfilment of his wish of the conquest of Hindustan. Whether a temple existed on that site is a matter of judicial enquiry at the highest level. But the fact is that the place were Ram Janambhoomi-Babri Masjid complex stood once could not have been a barren land. It has greenery all around and the area surrounding it is known as *kuber tila*. Kuber is God of Wealth in the Hindu pantheon.

The structure of Babri Masjid had granite pillars generally used in temple constructions. There were two separate panels of inscriptions—one inside the mosque and the other on the external gate. The inscriptions are in Persian and refer to Babur by name as well as his pen-name 'Qalandar'.[40] The mosque also had the Sharqui mosque architecture with minarets assimilated to gates.

There is a long sequence of stories about Hindus trying to recover this complex, but the incident of 1855 was not concerned with this structure.

The incident of 1855 starts with a Sunni *faqir*, who was brought up in the *ashram* of Hanumangarhi. His name was Ghulam Hussain.[41] This was not the first incident of its kind, the large heartedness of Hindu centres at that time was such that many Muslims were brought up and were provided livelihood in these *ashrams*. Since Hindus did not accept conversions, the Muslims lived and stayed as Muslims. For some reason after an altercation one day, this Ghulam Hussain came out of Hanumangarhi and went round to the Sunnis all over and claimed that the *bairagis* had destroyed a mosque inside the Hanumangarhi. A large congregation of Muslims attacked the Hanumangarhi. The Hindu *bairagis* pushed them out and a sanguine conflict ensued. It left 11 Hindus and 75 Muslim dead. The Muslims were buried by the *naib-kotwaal* of Faizabad Nasir Hussain. This place is known in common parlance as *Ganj-e-Shahidan*—burial of the martyrs.[42] A small *mela* used to be held at this place every year for a long period. After the affray, Muslims sought shelter in the other structure called Ram Janambhoomi-Babri Masjid complex. Ghulam Hussain Shah was also there, but managed to escape. He is not heard of any time in future. The Babri Masjid provided shelter to this runaway group of Sunni Muslims, but the building was not touched by the Hindus. It was in 1857 that an agreement had nearly been reached between Hindus and Muslims, but the sudden end of the war did not let the understanding take concrete shape. After 1857, the British government aborted the agreement and the matter remains contentious to this day.[43]

The Muslims presented a petition to the king and beseeched him to intervene as a Muslim. On this plaint, Wajid Ali Shah made his famous observation—'We are people of love and are not guided by sectarian religious considerations.' He instituted a commission of enquiry consisting of *raja* Man Singh, Agha Ali Khan, the *nazim* at Faizabad and Capt. Orr of the Company.[44] The Commission reported that there was no mosque within the precincts of Hanumangarhi.

They went to Ayodhya and succeeded in bringing the Hindus and Muslims together. An agreement between the parties was arrived at and a deed of compromise was executed between the Hindus and Muslims which was submitted to the Government.[45]

The Muslims particularly the Sunnis were not satisfied with this decision. A Maulvi at Amethi named Ameer Ali signalled disagreement. Amethi had become the centre of Sunni revivalist Muslims and soon the voices of *jihad* were heard. Wajid Ali Shah sought the intervention of the Mujtahid Sayyad Muhammad Nasirabadi and specifically put these two questions to him:

(Q 1) What is your guidance concerning those who go to Faizabad to fight the Hindus?

(Q 2) For they desire to take revenge on them for their uncivilized behavior with the mosque and the Quran. According to the law is it permissible for them to go there and fight, and will this be rewarded? Or is it forbidden?

The Mujtahid gave this opinion:

Without the participation and aid of the customary-law ruler or the Islamic-law ruler, such actions are in no wise permissible. God knows best.[46]

Fortified with this reply, the idea of *jihad* was rejected by the king. But Maulvi Ameer Ali went ahead and obtained help and organised a large force.[47] The news of *jihad* also attracted the Pathans and they also joined the party.[48] The forces under Maulvi Ameer Ali assembled near Rudauli in Barabanki district and prepared to proceed towards Ayodhya. At this point Wajid Ali Shah intervened effectively and sent his army to stop the motley troops under the command of Maulvi Ameer Ali. At Rudauli, they fought a decisive battle. Maulvi Ameer Ali was killed, and his troops were scattered. The matter came to an end.[49] The Resident and the Governor-General praised Wajid Ali Shah for his firmness and act of statesmanship. At this point of time Awadh was saved.

The incident of 1855 and its successful handling by Wajid Ali Shah provided only a brief reprieve to the kingdom. Dalhousie, the Court of Directors and the Home Government in England were actively considering steps to take over the kingdom of Awadh. Sleeman's Report had been so biased and one-sided that even Dalhousie desisted from taking action on it. When Outram followed Sleeman as Resident of Lucknow, he sent another series of loaded reports. Based on these, Dalhousie wrote his *Minutes* on 15 June 1855.

The East India Company Office in Calcutta started exploring the possible procedures for the take over of Awadh. The files containing the treaty of 1837 were put up before the new Governor-General. Although the treaty had been signed by the then Governor-General-in-Council, the Company Court in London had not accepted the treaty. The decision not to accept the treaty had not been conveyed to the King of Awadh at Lucknow. Dalhousie thought that if the treaty of 1837 had not been declared null and void in public, something could be done by making use of it. It had for the first time, advanced the principle of take over of the administration of Awadh and the appointment of Company officials therein, but with the consent of the king. So Dalhousie reverted to the idea of declaring this treaty null and void and turned to the treaty of 1801 in which the then *nawab* of Awadh had ceded half his territory in perpetuity to maintain the British forces for his protection. The 1801 Treaty also said that should the people of Awadh suffer from misgovernment under the State of Awadh, the British Company would be there to help them. According to Article 6,

> His Excellency engages that he will establish in his reserved dominions such a system of administration, to be carried into effect by his own officers, as shall be conducive to the prosperity of his subjects, and be calculated to secure the lives and property of the inhabitants; and His Excellency will always advise with, and act in conformity to, the council of the officers of the said Honorable Company.[50]

So charges of misgovernment and fear of life and security of the subjects were levied on the king and his administration and the Minute was sent to the Court of Directors in London.

> On the arrival of these Minutes in England, the cabinet was consulted and in accordance with their advice the Court of Directors issued their final orders for the assumption of the government of Oude. Their despatch of 21st November, 1855, is a specimen of the art of writing important instructions so as to avoid responsibility, but it expresses their disapproval of Lord Dalhousie's plan of obtaining the prior consent of the king to a new Treaty, and in case of his refusal, of cancelling the Treaty of 1801, and withdrawing from Oude; and it directs that unless it was 'the conviction of the Governor-General that the king's alarm at such a threat would render his acceptance of the Treaty a matter of virtual certainty', that alternative should not be offered to him; and it authorizes 'the only other course by which our duties to the people of Oude can be fulfilled — that of assuming authoritatively the powers necessary for the permanent establishment of good government throughout the country, leaving all questions of detail to the wisdom of the Governor-General, in conjunction with the other members of your

government'. The Court of Directors, in fact, supported the opinions of the members of Council against that of the Governor-General.[51]

The Court of Directors contended themselves with observing 'that the best course was to take no step whatever and to leave matters as they stood until some particular question arises, which must be dealt with according to circumstances'.[52]

The question arises: why the British authorities went through this length of hair-splitting arguments when annexation had already been decided. The answer is: since treaties were supposed to be strictly observed; and the British Parliament keenly scrutinised the activities of the Company's government, the sham of following the law had to be observed. Victorian England at that time suffered from a sense of 'priggish self-complacency'. So the Cabinet and the Court of Directors decided the objectives and matters of principle and left the execution to officials in the field.

British public opinion had to be fed with the information that the kings of Awadh were really decadent, unfit, and incompetent; that the people of Awadh therefore suffered great hardship under their rule. In England,

> this was the high noon of liberalism, and its imperialist message—that western trusteeship and western method of administration were conducive to the greatest happiness of the greatest number of any black population — had so intoxicated the Victorian mind that even the East India Company's inveterate critics assumed that the people of Awadh must prefer British rule. Seizure of the kingdom was therefore widely preached as a moral duty, the performance of which would earn the British nation the eternal gratitude of the native population.[53]

The British press carried lurid stories about the lewd *nawabs* of Awadh. The book *Private Life of an Eastern King*[54] appeared in 1855. This was reportedly narrated by a European attendant, attached to the household of Nasir-ud-din Haider, to William Knighton, Assistant Commissioner with the British Resident. The descriptions are prurient and inconsistent, but the book hit its mark. If there was any chance that any Englishman at that time in London had any sympathy for the governance of Awadh, the book was designed to stifle it completely. The Englishmen in London associated the scandals of the court of Nasir-ud-din Haider with the court and activities during the time of Wajid Ali Shah. The book and the press filled in the gap in the decision-making process of the policy-makers in London and annexation was ordered.

A mere reading of the preface to the first edition of *Private Life of an Eastern King* (London, 1855), fully reveals the game-plan. The preface was written by the 'Member of the Household' to keep the anonymity. Even the title page carries this inscription—'Compiled for a Member of the Household of His Late Majesty, Nussir-U-Deen, King of Oudh'. It will be worthwhile to quote the preface to the first edition verbatim:[55]

> The following narrative is a record of facts — not in any case fictitious. It has been compiled from the notes I took of passing events during the three and a half years that I lived in the court of Lucknow.
>
> Nussir-U-deen has long been gathered to his fathers; but the principal European members of his household are still alive, and in England. I have not given their names or my own; for the public would know as little of the one as of the other, had I done so. Should the truth of statements be denied, however, or the names considered necessary to substantiate the narrative, I shall have no hesitation in giving them all.
>
> It would have been easy for me to have thrown something of the heroic into the account of my residence at the court of Lucknow; but I have adhered simply to the truth, and have endeavoured solely to describe the inner life of the places as I found it. Much there was that was strange, much there was that was horrible about that life: I witnessed many scenes which I could not describe without offending against conventional propriety; but in all . . . reader will find recorded, exaggeration has been strictly guarded against.
>
> That Oudh is one of the most miserably-governed countries under heaven, is no secret; and that it would be a blessing to its numerous inhabitants were the . . . government to do for it what has been so well done by the Punjab, everyone will admit. I have not wanted a political disquisition, however, but simply a . . . narrative; and therefore the state of the country . . . incidentally alluded to occasionally in the following pages.
>
> My task is done.
>
> London, *October, 1855*

It's a different matter that William Knighton himself never visited India or Awadh until 1859 as Assistant-Commissioner. This was verified by a letter of his son-in-law which is quoted in full:[56]

> The late William Knighton, LL.D., went to Ceylon about the year 1845 to look after a coffee estate which had been left to him by an uncle. Finding that planting did not pay he sold the estate and proceeded to Calcutta, where he remained

about three years. During his sojourn there he wrote his first two books, *Forest Life in Ceylon* and *Tropical Sketches*. Returning to London he became associated with the literary clique which included Carlyle and Emerson. Whilst in Calcutta he made the acquaintance of a member of the household of the late King of Oudh, who, I believe, was 'the tutor', but whose name I am unable to give without a reference to Mr. Knighton's papers, which is impossible at present as they are in England. Later, in London, he again met this gentlemen and about 1855, when residing at Sydenham, he wrote the *Private Life of an Eastern King* from materials supplied to him by the above-named 'member of the household'. Subsequently, about 1858, Mr. Knighton received a nomination in the I.C.S., and proceeded to Fyzabad in 1859 as Assistant Commissioner at that station. This was the first occasion on which Mr. Knighton was ever in Oudh. He only remained in the Oudh Commission, however, for about ten years, as being in a position to consult his own tastes, which were essentially literary, he returned to England in 1868 and devoted the remainder of his life to those pursuits.

The above story will plainly give out that a book which depended on the narratives by a person, who was at best a member of the household created a theatre of the absurd. But the atmosphere in England was such at that time that absurdity decided the policy of the state.

The facts in Awadh were just the otherwise. The king was erudite and hard working. He had written about forty books. His famous opera *Indar Sabha* is his great contribution to the stage of Lucknow.[57] The stage actors till that time were not given respectability in society. Wajid Ali Shah by participating in stage performances changed the acceptability of the stage and its performers in high society. Lucknow was the only town which offered succour to artists from everywhere in India. The Mughal *darbar* had become almost defunct and the rest of India had practically surrendered to the anglicized culture. Lucknow had become the cultural centre of India, in all fields of music, painting and literature. Even Hindi literature had been provided patronage by the court. Journalism had become an accepted area of activity. Journalists, called *akhbar-nawis*, used to send written information from all over the province. The reports were edited and circulated to the nobles of the court.[58] Science had progressed. The state observatory which was closed during the time of Amjad Ali Shah, was reopened. The king was very humane and took care of the problems of his people seriously. It is the Resident who almost every time came in the way of proper dispensation of justice. The roads and the *sarais* (Inns) were well-maintained. The people of Awadh were happy, prosperous and lived under a just government. They had great faith in the king. All these things came to the fore with the Revolt of 1857. The deposition of Wajid Ali Shah was certainly a very important factor in the 1857 Revolt. But in 1855 the decision-makers in Britain thought otherwise and so they did what they did.

In January 1856, the Governor-General's order was conveyed to the Resident, General Outram. It was presented to the king. Surprisingly the seal of the king was already stamped on the new treaty paper.[59] Ali Naqi Khan had been won over by the Company and his collusion in the presentation of the papers is now an established fact. Wajid Ali Shah refused to sign.[60] The wording of the treaty putting the entire blame of maladministration on the King of Awadh was also something to which he greatly objected. His refusal to sign the treaty had something to do with his mental makeup as a Shia personage. For a Shia there is heroism in tragedy. The suffering of Imam Hussain at Kerbala is their ultimate sense of fulfilment. Heroism lies not in sulking, but in rising above suffering. The wording of the treaty was an insult and affront to the king. So the king as a Shia must refuse to bow to it, as Imam Hussain had done. Wajid Ali Shah had understood that the power of British arms was such that to fight them was not possible. The states of India had fought against each other in suicidal wars and the take over by the British forces was a forgone conclusion. Yet he nurtured a childlike faith in the British sense of justice.

On his refusing to sign, Wajid Ali Shah was deposed on 7 February 1856, and Awadh was declared annexed. On 13 March, Wajid Ali Shah proceeded to Kanpur and stayed with his English friend Brandon. During this month, Company officers plundered the nobles of Lucknow loyal to the *nawabs*. Even the *begums* were humiliated. At Kanpur, Wajid Ali Shah was joined by Major R.W. Bird, who resigned his position with the Company. After staying for a month in Kanpur, he went to Benares. He was well received by the Maharaja of Benares. After a week he went to Calcutta by river and stayed there at Matia Burj. In June, Malika Kishwar and Maseeh-ud-din along with Brandon and Bird left for London to present their case to the Empress and Parliament. In England, the king's party met the members of the Court of Directors of the East India Company. For the first time a properly framed series of charges against the king for his dereliction of duties in the governance of Awadh were given to the king's Party. This document is known as *The Oude Blue Book.* It was sent to Wajid Ali in Calcutta, who answered all these charges.

The king's reply consist of seven Chapters, covering 58 pages, under the following heads:

Chapter I: 'Relative to the Submission and Fidelity Evinced by the rulers of Oude towards the East India Company from the Time of Treaty.'

Chapter II: 'Relative to the Acts Performed by the East India Company in Contravention of the Stipulations of Different Treaties.'

Chapter III: 'Relative Matters Contained in the Statements of Col. Sleeman and General Outram, being the Slanders published against the Kingdom of Oude.'

Chapter IV: 'Shewing the Discrepancies in the Observations and Statements of Lord Dalhousie, the Members of the Supreme Council, and General Outram.'

Chapter V: 'Showing Proofs that Oude was Governed with some Ability, and that there was no Misrule in the Kingdom.'

Chapter VI: 'Showing the Invalidity of Setting Aside of the Treaties between the Two Nations.'

Chapter VIII: 'Showing the Crimes, Murders, &c. Committed in the East India Company Territories.'[61]

After the submission of the replies by the king, Malika Kishwar was given audience by Queen Victoria (July 1857), in a special court. By that time the war of independence had started in India. The story of massacre of Englishmen in Kanpur had hit the headlines in the newspapers of London. Wajid Ali Shah was put under arrest and confined to the dingy cells in Fort William in Calcutta The king's party in London suffered from dissensions. Malika Kishwar left London in January 1858, reached Paris and died there. She was buried in Paris. The French government constructed a mausoleum at the place of her burial. Her son Gen. Hashmat, half-brother of Wajid Ali Shah, also died in March 1858. His body was taken to Paris and was buried by the side of his mother. The heir-apparent, son of Wajid Ali Shah, came back to Calcutta. But he also died within a period of six months.

Wajid Ali Shah was a broken man and he accepted the offer of pension by the East India Company in late 1858. The Company reduced the pension to twelve lakhs as against the promised amount of fifteen lakhs. After the end of the war and the proclamation of take over of India directly by the Crown, Wajid Ali Shah was released from Fort William and settled down in Matia Burj. He died in 1887, after leading a life of total devotion to music and art and pursuit of pleasure. Matia Burj became a mini-Lucknow.

After the proclamation by the Crown, Wajid Ali Shah took life with a stoic indifference. He knew that the political power had inexorably passed into the hands of the British rulers. What he did not realize was that his reign would become a symbol of India's *Ganga-Jamuni* culture—the composite culture. After six hundred years of Muslim rule in India, this was the only answer to any foreign intervention. The 1857 War was fought on the plank of Hindustan being a nation entitled to have its own rulers. During the war, the people sank their differences, but the leaders remained entwined in their personal egos and ambitions. The sense of total devotion to a common leadership came to this country sixty years later, after the First World War. But in 1857, the people fought a last struggle to regain their own house and lost pride.

We in India have yet to write a history of our own—free from prejudices and possible self-condemnation. We are a people where the prejudices of caste and creed have been nurtured for centuries. But the speed of communication and the store of information which is now available can certainly help us regain our sense of unity in the midst of several diversities. We must learn from our history. Those who do not learn from their history are condemned to repeat it. The division of the country in 1947 was the latest example. Partition was a crime done to our national life. At some future date it may still be undone, when the recognition of our common cultural heritage and common destiny may yet emerge.

NOTES

1. R.W. Bird, *Dacoitee in Excelsis: or, the Spoilation of Oude by the East India Company*, Lucknow, 1971, p. 98; Najmul Ghani, *Tarikh-i-Awadh*, Vol. V, Lucknow, 1863-5, p. 120.
2. Amjad Ali, *Tajdar-e-Awadh*, p. 14, cited in Jagdish Sahai, *Awadh Mein Nawabi Shasan* (Hindi), Faizabad, n.y., p. 178. Amjad Ali made it abundantly clear that Mustafa Ali was one and a half years old when he was married to his mother—R.W. Bird, op. cit., p. 4.
3. Kamal-ud-din Haider, op. cit., Vol. II, p. 4.

4. Jagdish Sahai, op. cit., p. 178.
5. Masud H. 'Adeeb', *Lucknau ka Shahi Stage*, Lucknow, 1957, p. 13.
6. Kamal-ud-din Haider has mentioned about an interesting incident as well as a peculiar custom related with the funerals of the *nawabs*. The funeral procession of the *nawabs* were not taken out from the main gate. Instead it was taken out from the back door of the palace. The heir-apparent to throne never used to see the face of the cadaver. Further, it was strictly followed that after the death of the *nawab*, the next claimant to the throne was not going to stay in the same palace in which the death took place. The heir-apparents therefore used to get their palaces built in advance. Wajid Ali Shah before sitting on the throne got palaces like Shah Manzil (for winters), Falak Sair Manzil and Huzoor Bagh (for autumn) etc., built in advance—Kamal-ud-din Haider, op. cit., p. 178.
7. Najmul Ghani, op. cit., Vol.V, p. 46.
8. Ibid.
9. M. Maseeh-ud-din Khan Bahadur, *British Aggression in Oudh*, Lucknow, 1964, p. 14.
10. M. Maseeh-ud-din Khan Bahadur, op. cit., p. 41. Maseeh-ud-din Khan Bahadur belonged to Kakori, and 'other members of his family had held high positions in the government of Oudh King'. 'Khan Bahadur Maseeh-ud-din Khan Bahadur had served for five years as the Mir Munshi of the Persian Department of the Governor-General's Secretariat. He must in that capacity have handled a considerable number of Persian as well as English State-papers. We may assume that he was supplied with all necessary material from the Oudh archives.'—M. Habib, Foreword to British Aggression in Oudh, op. cit., p. 4.
11. Maulana Abdul Halim Sharar, *Preface to Huzn-e-Akhtar*, Lucknow, 1922, p. 12. Maulana Sharar's maternal grandfather, Munshi Qamar-ud-din, was *sar-daftar* or Superintendent of the king's office and had accompanied him from Lucknow to Matia Burj. He had also, under the king's order accompanied the Awadh Commission (consisting of the Queen-Mother, the king's brother and the Heir-apparent) to England. On his return from England Mushi Qamar-ud-din remained at Matia Burj and sent for Sharar, aged eight years only, and his father from Lucknow. Sharar spent his childhood and youth in Matia Burj 'under the protection of the King' and in the company of the Princes. He had unique opportunities of observing the king, the *mahlat-e-aliat* (ladies) and the *durbar*. Maulana Abdul Halim Sharar, *Preface to the King's Masnavi: Huzn-e-Akhtar*, Lucknow, 1922, pp. 8, 9.
12. R.W. Bird, op. cit., p. 156.
13. S. Ameer Ali Khan, *Wazeernamah*, Kanpur, 1875, p. 97.
14. Jagdish Sahai, op. cit., p. 178. In an interview with Yogesh Praveen at my residence, Mr. Praveen strongly holds that Dabir was his *ustaad*. In support of his opinion he quotes a couplet of Wajid Ali Shah to this effect: *Main Kamsini Se Ashiq-e Nazme Dabir Houn* ('From childhood I have been a lover of Dabir's verse')—Author.
15. Munshi Medhi Lal, *Maharabaye Gader* (no pagination), cited in Paripurnananda Verma, op. cit., p. 77.
16. Cited in Awadhwasi Lala Sitaram, *Ayodhya ka Itihas*, Prayag, 1932, p. 16.

17. Paripurnananda Verma, *Wijid Ali Shah Aur Awadh Rajya ka Patan*, Lucknow, 1949, pp. 70-1.
18. S. Ameer Khan, *Wazeernamah*, pp. 114-17; Kamal-ud-din Haider, *Qaiser-ul-Tawareekh*, Vol. II, p. 7; Najmul Ghani, op. cit., Vol.V, pp. 123-5. Masud Hassan says, 'The sealed Boxes bore the inscription *Mashghala-e-Sultani, Adl-e-Nausherwani*',—Masud H. 'Adeeb', op. cit., 1950, p. 14. But this is not mentioned in any book and Mr. Masud has not cited any source.
19. Kamal-ud-din Haider, op. cit., Vol. I, p. 382. It was Ameen-ud-daula who completed the construction of the metalled road between Lucknow and Kanpur. This increased the revenues of Awadh.
20. Rajab Ali Beg Suroor, *Fasanaye Ibrat* (no pagination), cited in Paripurnananda Verma, op. cit., pp. 74-5.
21. Najmul Ghani, op. cit., Vol.V, pp. 133-9.
22. Kamal-ud-din Haider, op. cit., Vol. II, p. 26.
23. Munshi Sital Prashad, Mirat ul Auza, Raza Library, Rampur, fol. 501.
24. R.W. Bird, op. cit., pp. 101-2.
25. Ibid.
26. S. Ameer Khan, *Wazeernamah*, Kanpur, 1875, pp. 112-13.
27. Ibid., pp. 123-8.
28. It is quite interesting to note that between March and September 1855 there had been a series of negotiations between Wajid Ali Shah and the Company regarding the establishment of a telegraph line between Lucknow and Kanpur. Though the *nawab* was quite anxious about this project, the Company refused to sell their technology. Instead the Company pressed the *nawab* for exclusive rights to control the enterprise, as its utility at this stage was strictly strategic in nature. But the *nawab* refused to give permission. Thus the arrival of telegraph had to wait until the following year, when the British took over the entire province. For details of these negotiations see Dispatches, Foreign/Political Consultations, 22 March 1855, 7 August 1855 and 25 September 1855, India Office Library, London, cited in Veena Talwar Oldenburg, *The Making of Colonial Lucknow—1855-1856*, New Jersey: Princeton University Press, n.y., p. 43.
29. G.D. Bhatnagar, *Awadh Under Wajid Ali Shah*, Lucknow, 1968, pp. 100-16. R.W. Bird, op. cit., p. 109.
30. R.W. Bird, op. cit., p. 109.
31. Ibid., pp. 129-31.
32. Cited in Mirza Ali Azhar, op. cit., p. 325.
33. Sir W. Lee-Warner, *Life of the Marquess of Dalhousie*, Vol. I, London, 1904, p. 126.
34. L.J. Trotter, *Bayard of India*, p. 129, cited in Mirza Ali Azhar, op. cit., Vol. I, p. 362.
35. For details see Kamal-ud-din Haider, op. cit., pp. 105-25; Kunwar Durga Prashad, *Dastan-e-Awadh*, Lucknow, 1309/1891, pp. 159-60.
36. *White Paper On Ayodhya*, Government of India, February, 1993, p. 1.
37. Michael H. Fisher, *A Clash of Cultures: Awadh, the British and the Mughals*, New Delhi, 1987, pp. 201-2, 216, 228-36.

38. Anon., *Shree Ram Janam Bhoomi Ka Pramanith Itihas* (Hindi Pamphlet), Shri Ram Janambhoomi Mandir, Ayodhya Dham, n.y., pp. 3-5.
39. Faraq Amini, *Babri Masjid Tathayon ke Prakash Mein* (Hindi Pamphlet), Union Printing Press, Delhi, n.y., no pagination (available from New Holy Publishing House, 4153, Urdu Bazaar, Jama Masjid, Delhi).
40. English translation of the Persian inscription on the gateway of the Mosque—*Author*.
41. Kamal-ud-din Haider, op. cit., pp. 110-25; Kunwar Durga Prashad, op. cit., pp. 159-60.
42. Najmul Ghani, op. cit., Vol. V, pp. 235-6.
43. G.D. Bhatnagar, op. cit., pp. 117-40.
44. Captain Orr to Superintendent, Frontier Police, 20 August 1855, Foreign Department Consultations, N.A.I., New Delhi, 28 December 1855. No. 354.
45. S. Kamal-ud-din Haider, op. cit., Vol. II, p. 119.
46. Kamal-ud-din Haidar, op. cit., p. 109.
47. It is also said that the *begum* of Bhopal was also reported to have sent an elephant and sufficient force for Ameer Ali—Officiating Resident to Secretary to Government of India, 8 September 1855, Foreign Political Consultations, N.A.I., 28 December 1855, Nos. 360, 441. On the other side the Hindus received financial and other aids not only from the landholders of Awadh, but also from Maharajas of Gwalior and Jodhpur—Officiating Resident to Secretary to Government of India, 8 September 1855, Foreign Political Consultations, N.A.I., 28 December 1855, No. 415.
48. Mirza Ali Azhar, op. cit., p. 3371.
49. Mirza Jan, *Hadiqa-i-Shuhda*, title page missing, available in Nadwa Library, Lucknow, pp. 177-85.
50. *Treaties & Engagements with Oudh*, Vol. II, p. 102.
51. Sir Charles Jackson, *A Vindication of the Marquis of Dalhousie's Indian Administration*, London, 1865, pp. 144-5.
52. Ibid., pp. 129-30.
53. John Pemble, *The Raj, the Indian Mutiny and the Kingdom of Oudh 1801-1859*, New Delhi, 1977, p. 107.
54. William Knighton, *Private Life of An Eastern King*, New York: J.S. Redfield, 1855.
55. William Knighton, *The Private Life of an Eastern King Together With Elihu Jan's Story or the Private Life of an Eastern Queen*, ed. by S.B. Smith, O.U.P., 1921.
56. *The Pioneer*, May 1918.
57. The court poet Amanat was commissioned to write the drama by Wajid Ali Shah. It is also said that the musical drama *The Court of Indra* or *Indar Sabha* was modelled on a sort of *rahas* or pantomime. In such a style, the Hindu folklore was married to Perso-Urdu forms of versification and Muslim outlook. Thus the *Indar Sabha* was in many ways the epitome of Awadh's composite culture—Masud Hasan Rizvi Adib, *Urdu Drama Aur Stage*, Lucknow 1957, pp. 45-50. It is interesting to note that Freidrich Rosen has called the *Indar Sabha*, 'a Vishnuite *yatra* in Islamic form'—Freidrich Rosen, *Die Indarsabha des Amanat*, Leipzig, 1892, p. 6.

58. The number of these *akhbar nawis* or journalist was about 660. The duty of these *akhbar nawis* was to collect news from different corners and then send it to the *nawab*. There used to be an editor to edit the news. The salaries of these *akhbar nawis* was between Rs. 4 to Rs. 15 per month. According to Sleeman these *akhbar nawis* were very corrupt. They used to fleece money from the zamindars and courtiers by threatening to send false reports to the king. They themselves use to pay 1,50,000 rupees per year to the senior courtiers in order to save their services from getting terminated. According to Sleeman even Malika Kishwar used to take Rs. 12,000 as bribe from the courtiers—cited in Paripurnananda Verma, op. cit., pp. 202-3.
59. *The Oude Blue Book*, Inclosure 4 in No. 4, p. 252.
60. Kamal-ud-din Haidar, op. cit., Vol. II, pp. 134-6.
61. Cited in Mirza Ali Azhar, op. cit., p. 391.

Plate 8: Ornate Entry Gate of Qaicar Bagh

Plate 9: Qaiser Bagh Complex

Plate 10: Wajid Ali Shah in a Dance Drama

Plate 11: Dilkusha

Denouement

We have surveyed the period from 1722 to 1856. It was a momentous time in the history of India. The Mughal empire was falling apart and an alien power was slowly taking over the country. In its evolution, independence and isolation, Awadh became the epitome of the cultural matrix of India. A genuine composite culture grew slowly, illumined by lanterns of understanding, creating a mixed society with firm bonds of emotional integration.

Saadat Khan, a Persian noble of the Mughal court, crossed the Gomti, took Lucknow and made his way to Ayodhya. He set up his capital close to Ayodhya, and a new town grew which later came to be known as Faizabad. He came with Mughal forces and was able to create a new Awadh by subjugating refractory landlords and bringing order in his state. Safdar Jung kept the Mughal formations with him. Shujà-ud-daula, who very unwisely involved himself in the battle of Panipat and dissipated his energies, met his greatest reverse in the battle of Buxar. After this battle he was advised by the Bangash Pathan chief not to depend on the Mughals and to make Faizabad his capital. That was the end of his Mughal association. He was now on his own, and relied more and more on local chiefs. Having parted with the Mughals, the Persians were left alone in an alien land. The nobles of the court were mostly first-generation immigrants and not from established families. The political executives of the *nawabs*, therefore, never stood on a firm ground. The court was always ridden by intrigue, leading to a quick turnover of political advisers.

The *nawabs* of Lucknow began as *subedars*. The literal meaning of *nawab* is 'deputy' or Viceroy in the Mughal empire, and was used as a prefix to dignitaries. In 1748, Safdar Jang was raised to the status of *wazir* of the Mughal empire and was addressed as *nawab-wazir*. His successors carried the title with them. In 1819, the *nawab* of Awadh assumed the title of King. The chief political executive similarly changed his designation: under the *subedars* he was called *naib*, with the *nawab-wazir* he was addressed as *naib-wazir*; when the *nawab* became the King he was given the title of *wazir*. Newal Rai was the *naib* during the time of Saadat Khan. Tikait Rai and Jhao Lal were also anointed as *naib-wazir* for a limited period of time during the reign of Asaf-ud-daula. With the increasing patronage extended to Shia theology all the subsequent chief political executives were invariably Shias. The sole exception was Yahya Khan, a Sunni, during the reign of Amjad Ali. He died within six months, much to the relief of the King. The land revenue system remained invariably with the Hindus, first with the Khatri family of Surat Singh and then with the Kayasthas, Jhao Lal, Tikait Rai, Atma Ram and Balkrishna. The economic prosperity of Awadh was in some measure due to this unbroken chain of command.

All conquerors negate the symbols of dignity of the conquered people. When Muslim came to India, they broke the temples and converted a large number of Hindus to Islam. The British adopted a more subtle policy. They reduced the stature of our crowning glories. The name *subedar* (the erstwhile Governor of a Province) was given to the highest non-commissioned officer of the army, under the British Second Lieutenant. The *angarkha*—the long flowing dress of the *nawabs* was made into the uniform of the orderlies of the officers of the British empire.

It was a matter of chance that the Irani *nawabs* of Lucknow started their life in Faizabad which was close to Ayodhya. Lucknow at that time was dominated by the Sheikhzadas. They were controlling the areas Bijnour (Lucknow), Malihabad, Kakori, Kasmandi and Chotti Amethi. In Chotti Amethi near Gussainganj close to Lucknow is the mausoleum of Mulla Jeewan, the teacher of Aurangzeb in his younger days. The Amethi of Sultanpur was known as Bari Amethi or *raja saheb ki Amethi*. In Ayodhya the *nawabs* and the court were away from the Afghan domination and they evolved independent lifestyle. Faizabad was known as *bangla*. The river Ghagara provided the water transport from Ayodhya to Calcutta and the place received direct influence from Calcutta. In the public it was known as *Chotta Calcutta*. The Hindu customs of Ayodhya slowly found their way in the court of the *nawabs*, first at Faizabad and then at Lucknow. The Dussehra procession inspired the public celebration of Muharram; the public display of lights on Diwali day was adopted to light up private and public buildings on the *qatl ki raat*; the bonhomie of sprinkling colour at Holi became the occasion of a similar gaiety at *nauroz*, the New Year's day in the Persian calendar. Similarly *saawan mela* and *basant mela* were also organised by the rulers. The adoption of Hindu customs reflected the *darya-dili*, the large-heartedness of the Shia rulers.

Socially, life in Awadh displayed a relaxed togetherness. Some writers have spoken about conversions, but in Awadh there were hardly any, except those which were done voluntarily for seeking court favours. A Khatri adopted Shia-Islam, but was nevertheless thrown out of the revenue department. When another Khatri adopted Islam and went through circumcision, his concubine left him. Conversions had mainly taken place earlier during the Delhi Sultanate and Mughal rule. Among the upper castes it was mostly Rajputs who had converted to Islam and among the lower castes, they were Julahas (weavers) and Ghosis (milk vendors). The other lower castes almost in entirety maintained their Hindu identity.

In the field of literature, native similes and metaphors were taken over in Urdu, as against purely Persian cultural symbols. When Anees wrote his *marsiya*, he wrote of Hindu concepts.

Yarab rassol-e-pak kee kheti hari rahe
Sandal se mangh bacchon se, godi bharee rahe

O God! The crops of the pious Prophet may ever remain green, the hair-parting of the ladies may be graced with sandal, and the lap of the mothers may always be full with children.

Now these concepts of the agricultural crops remaining green; the hair parting of the ladies full of sindoor and women always enjoying the progeny, are characteristically Hindu concepts and do not come from Euphrates.

Socially the Shia weddings had totally adopted the customs of Awadh. The etiquette of paying compliment was also changed. A Muslim greets another Muslim with *salam-alaikum* and the other responds with *wa-alaikum assalam*. In Lucknow it became *adab-arz*, I convey my respect to you, very close to *namaskar*—I Bow to thee. In political life there was a great deal of understanding of each other's ideas. A Hindu invariably believed in rebirth and existence of *parmatma*. The Muslim carried on with their own

Koranic beliefs. At the celebration of festivals all came together. A Shia could never think of constructing a mosque where human blood has been shed. There was respect for other religions.

This culture was deposed in 1856. But a greater national culture was to evolve after the war of Independence of 1857, whose seeds were at least partly sown by the callous execution of Awadh.

APPENDIX I

مخطوطہ نمبر ۲۰۸۴۲ تعداد اوراق = ۶۱

موجودات ۱۰۱۳ سائز ۲۲ × ۲۲۰۶

رسالہ فی احکام الارضین / للعلاّمہ السید دلدار علی النصیر آبادی الکھنوی الشیعی

السیّد دلدار علی المجتہد النصیر آبادی کی مختصر حیات

علامہ مجتہد دلدار علی بن محمد معین بن عبد الہادی حسینی نقوی شیعی النصیر آبادی پہلے ایسے آدمی ہیں (شیعون میں) جنھوں نے اجتہاد کا دعوٰی کیا اور جمعہ کی نماز باجماعت قائم کی۔ نجم الدین السبزواری کی نسل سے ہیں۔ سلسلۂ نسب جعفر بن علی تقی تک پہنچتا ہے۔ سنہ ۱۱۶۶ھ میں رائے بریلی سے بیس[۲] میل دور نصیر آباد میں پیدا ہوئے۔ علم کے حصول کے لیے الٰہ آباد کا سفر کیا۔ سنہ ۱۱۹۴ھ میں عراق گئے طف، نجف، کاظمین، مشہد کی زیارت کی۔ باقر محمد البہبائی، علی بن محمد الطباطبائی و علی مہدی بن مرتضیٰ طباطبائی وغیرہ سے مختلف کتابوں کا درس لیا۔ سفر پورا کرنے کے بعد ہندوستان واپس ہوئے۔ لکھنو میں وزیر حسن رضا خاں الشیعی نے اپنے لڑکوں کا اتالیق مقرر کیا۔ اس زمانے میں شیعہ امامیہ اونچی جگہوں پر تھے لیکن ان کا کوئی اجتماع نہیں ہوتا تھا۔ انھوں نے اجتہاد کر کے نماز جمعہ قائم کی۔ پھر اپنے مذہب کو حق ثابت کرنے اور دوسرے مذہب خاص طور پر مذہب احناف صوفیاء وغیرہ کو باطل ثابت کرنے کے لیے جدوجہد کی۔ یہاں تک کہ شیعہ مذہب اودھ میں بہت پھیل گیا۔ اپنے مذہب کی مدافعت میں بہت سی کتابیں لکھیں۔ سنہ ۱۲۳۵ھ میں غازی الدین حیدر کے عہد میں لکھنو میں وفات پائی۔ وہیں حسینیہ میں دفن ہوئے (نزہتہ الخواطر۔ جلد ۷۔ صفحہ ۱۶۶۔ دائرۃ المعارف عثمانیہ حیدرآباد ۱۹۵۹ء)

رسالہ کے بارے میں: شیعہ فقہ کی عربی کتاب ہے جس میں غیر مسلم سے خراج یا مالیات وصول کرنے کے احکام بتائے گئے ہیں۔ ابتداء کتاب یوں ہے:

وبعد فهذه نخبة وافيه ونبذه كافية من مهمات المسائل التى

لها تعلق باموال الکفار و احوال الارضین ۔

(یہ رسالہ کفار کے اموال اور زمین کے احوال سے متعلق اہم مسائل پر مشتمل ہے)

مسئلہ فی الارضین :۔ منقسم باعتبار الشرعیۃ الی اربعۃ اقسام

القسم الاول :۔ ارض اسلم علیہا اہلہا طوعًا

القسم الثانی :۔ ارض الصلح

القسم الثالث :۔ الارض الانفال

القسم الرابع :۔ الارض المفتوحہ

آگے ان چاروں قسموں کی تعریف اور احکام بیان کئے ہیں

وہ اقتباس جس کا حوالہ اطہر عباس رضوی کی کتاب ص ۲۲۵ پر ہے۔ رسالہ میں اس کی عبارت یوں ہے :۔ واعلم ان الکفار لا یخلون من ثلثۃ اصناف . اما حربیون اما ذمیون و اما مستامنون والذمیون عند الامامیہ منحصرون فی کونہم من اہل الکتاب اذا التزموا شرائط الذمۃ واما عند العامۃ فالمشرکون عندہم غیر الحجازئین مع التزام شرائط الذمۃ معدودون من اہل الذمۃ . المستامنون الذی قد امنہم المسلمون مرغیر مرۃ . فالقسم الاول منہم باق علی الاصل لعدم قیام دلیل خروجہم عنہ اما کونہم فی بلاد تجری فیہا احکام الاسلام فمجرد کونہم کک لا یجوب الخروج من الاصل . اما عندنا فلانہم لا یصلحون ان یکونوا من اہل الذمۃ لعدم کونہم من اہل الکتاب ولا ان یکونوا من اہل الامان لان من شروط الامان لا یزید علی سنۃ الامع الحاجۃ ای حاجۃ من حاجات الدینیہ اقتضت الامان المشرکین فی بلاد الهند مع کونہم مظہرین لشعائر الکفر وعبادتہم للاصنام بالاعلان وشرب الخمر و ارتکاب الفجور مع نسوان اہل الاسلام مع اہل الہاشمیات الفاطمیات ونحو ذلک .

(ترجمہ) جان لو کہ کفار کی تین حیثیت ہے ۔ حربی، ذمی، مستامن اور امامیہ کے نزدیک، ذمی صرف اہل کتاب ہیں جب وہ ذمی ہونے کی شرط کو پورا کریں، اور جمہور کے نزدیک حجازیوں کے

کے علاوہ مشرکین بھی ہیں جو ذمی ہونے کی شرائط پوری کرتے ہوں، انہیں ذمی شمار کیا جائے گا۔ مستامن وہ ہے جسے مسلمانوں نے امان دی ہو۔ پس ان میں سے پہلی قسم کے لوگ اپنی اصل پر باقی ہیں، اس وجہ سے کہ اس سے نکلنے کی کوئی دلیل نہیں ہے اور ان کا مسلم حکومت کے اندر ہونا ضروری نہیں کہ وہ اصل سے خارج ہو جائیں۔ ہمارے نزدیک یہ بات صحیح نہیں ہے، کہ وہ ذمی ہیں، کیونکہ وہ اہل کتاب سے نہیں ہیں اور نہ ہی وہ مستامن ہیں کیونکہ امان کی شرط ایک سال سے تجاوز نہیں کرتی، سوائے کسی ضرورت کے۔ مثلاً دینی ضرورت کی وجہ سے ہندوستان کی حکومت میں انھیں امان ملی ہے۔ حالانکہ وہ کھلم کھلا کفر کرتے ہیں، بتوں کی پوجا کرتے ہیں، شراب پیتے ہیں اور مسلم عورتوں کے ساتھ خواہ وہ سید عورتیں ہوں، فسق و فجور کرتے ہیں۔ وغیرہ وغیرہ

***

آگے انھوں نے ناصب کے بارے میں بحث کی ہے۔ اس کے سلسلے میں دو احادیث ملاحظہ ہوں:۔

(۱) عن ابی عبد اللہ قال خذ مال الناصب حیث ما وجدت وادفع الینا الخمس

(ناصب کا مال لے لو، جہاں چاہو اور ہمارے پاس پانچواں حصہ روزانہ کرو)

(۲) قلت لابی عبد اللہ ما تقول فی قتل الناصب قال حلال

(میں نے پوچھا ناصب کے قتل کے بارے میں کیا خیال ہے؟ جواب دیا حلال ہے)

ناصب کون ہے؟ کہتے ہیں وہ جو مسلمانوں کے ساتھ جنگ کرے۔ دوسرا قول ہے جو اہل بیت سے دشمنی کرے۔ پھر دوسرے قول پر بحث کی ہے۔ آگے چل کر اسلام ایمان کے فرق کو بیان کیا ہے۔

APPENDIX II

Baradaris of Lucknow

The culture of Lucknow has left its impressive footprints on the sands of time. Lucknow has always been seminal and evocative in the development of literature, poetry, dance and music, handicrafts and other fine arts. The city of Lucknow has the distinction of having beautiful, attractive and splendid buildings. The *baradari* was a style of building which was original to Lucknow.

During the ancient Hindu period, *markat mandaps* were constructed inside gardens. Later on, in Rajasthan, they came to be known as *chhatris*. During the Mughal regime buildings such as *Diwan-e-Aam* and *Diwan-e-Khas* were coming into existence in Delhi and Agra. They were buildings of a different genre. *Baradaris* were unknown.

The chain of a novel set of buildings and gardens started in Faizabad, but flourished in Lucknow. Beginning with Asaf-ud-daula and right up to the time of Wajid Ali Shah, Lucknow was the city of beautiful buildings and gardens. Construction of open and airy structures was conceived for enjoyment of these gardens and also for organising cultural activities. An open hall with verandah on all the four sides placed in the centre of the garden was the first thought. Later the verandahs were eliminated. These one-storeyed structures had three *mehrabs* (arched gates) on all the four sides—twelve *dars* or gates in all. Hence these were called *baradaris*, that is, having twelve gates. The idea rhymed very well both with Shia faith and Hindu legend. For Shias the twelve doors of *baradari* had a relevance to the twelve Imams. For Hindus, the ancient rulers of Awadh belonged to the *Suryavanshi* dynasty, who recognised the *surya* or sun as their *kul devata* or family god. The sun passes through twelve *rashis* (Zodiac signs). Hence the number of twelve was considered sacred. As such the *baradari* appealed to popular sentiment. Thus later on *baradaris* were being constructed along with temples, mosques, gardens and fortresses.

These *baradaris* were made of *lakhauri* bricks and lime. At some places, red and white stones were also used. Their *mehrabs* (arched gates) were made in a unique Lucknow style, either in crescent form or in Shahjahani pattern. Later, under European influence, the *mehrabs* in French and Italian styles were also raised. The pillars of the *baradaris* were decorated with floral patterns, superimposed by terracotta or were painted. *Mehrabs* and the ceilings were coated with gold-water or silver foil. The *baradaris* made of stones were decorated with inlays of coloured stone.

In the early days *baradaris* were built with twelve large gates, but later twenty-four and thirty-six gates were also known. Some were constructed in rectangular shape, instead of squares as earlier. Irrespective of the number of gates, these buildings were called *baradaris*. In due course of time all buildings constructed in gardens or orchards with similar designs were commonly known as *baradaris*. These rest-houses were scattered in and around Lucknow. Only a few survive today.

A large number of *baradaris* were built by *nawab* Asaf-ud-daula in Lucknow. Of those, the *baradaris* of Aishbagh, Charbagh and Wazir Bagh are famous. Nishatbagh and Sheesh Mahal were built by *raja* Tikait Rai during the same period. None of them exists today. The ruins of a *baradari* near river Gomti in Moosa Bagh are visible even today. This historical *baradari* was designed by Claude Martin. The pronunciation of *Monsieur* Claude Martin slowly adopted a more native ethos and became *moosa*. *Moosa* in Hindi means rodent. A legend has it that while the *nawab* was driving in his *baggi*, a rodent ran under it and was killed. The large-hearted Nawab named the *baradari* after the rodent, hence Moosa Bagh. The spot later became important during 1857 war. A battle was fought here when Begum Hazrat Mahal personally commanded a regiment riding on a elephant. A memorial of the soldiers who laid their lives is still there—as usual, badly maintained.

The ruins of *baradaris* built by Asaf-ud-daula are also to be found at Chinhat, Banthara, Kasmandi and Malihabad. Asaf-ud-daula had also built a *baradari* in the Tarai of Butwal at Naikot. The *nawab*, along with his *begums* used to visit the place during the summers. When Begum Hazrat Mahal along with Birjis Qadar, left Awadh for Nepal, she stayed here.

The famous Lal Baradari was built by Saadat Ali Khan It was

called *Qasr-ul-Sultan* (Palace of the King). It was the part of the Chattar Manzil complex and was used as Coronation and *darbar* Hall. It was here that the coronation of Ghazi-ud-din Haider took place. The famous European tourist Fanny Perks met the *begums* of the Royal family on the occasion of the first anniversary of the coronation of Nasir-ud-din Haider, at this *baradari*. Another story about this *baradari* is the futile attempt at coronation of Munna Jaan—the minor son of the *nawab*, by Badshah Begum, the widow of Ghazi-ud-din Haider. Later the English converted it into a public library and then a museum. After 1857 Outram built a road between Chattar Manzil and Lal Baradari and destroyed the beauty of the palatial complex. Nowadays it is the office of Lalit Kala Academy.

A *baradari* was built by *nawab* Saadat Ali Khan near Huzoor Bagh. It pillars were covered with silver foil which gave it the name Chandiwali Baradari. During the period of Wajid Ali Shah it became part of the Qaiserbagh Complex and was used as a stage for the opera *Indar Sabha*. The famous *Jogmaya Mela* used to be held here. It was in this *baradari*, that Birjis Qadar, son of Begum Hazrat Mahal, was installed on the throne in July 1857. The silver in this *baradari* was looted during the war of 1857. Later an American library was opened in this building. At present it is the seat of some subordinate courts but is still popularly known as the American Library.

Motijheel Ki Baradari, Dilkusha Ki Baradari, and the *baradari* at Mohammadi (in Lakhimpur District) were built by *nawab* Saadat Ali Khan. Gazi-ud-din Haider built Dil-aram Ki Baradari, Moti Mahal Ki Baradari and Vilayati Bagh Ki Baradari. Most of them lie in ruins. Nasir-ud-din Haider built a magnificent *baradari* at Badshah Bagh with a canal in front of it. This building was made of red stone. During the British period, this complex was given to the *raja* of Kapoorthala. Later Canning College was shifted here and at present it is in the campus of the University of Lucknow. Dil-aram Ki Baradari of old Lucknow was being used as an auditorium in those days. Various cultural functions were organised in this *baradari*.

The Nageenewali Baradari was built by Nasir-ud-din Haider in Qaiserbagh. It was damaged during the War of 1857, but repaired and stands close to the new building of the State Museum in Banarsi Bagh.

Muhammad Ali Shah built a *baradari* on the banks of

Hussainabad *talab*. During the British period, it was renovated and converted into a picture gallery. It houses the portraits of the rulers of Awadh. Sikandar Bagh Ki Baradari was built for Begum Sikandar Mahal. Pattharwali Baradari, built in the Qaiserbagh complex, now houses the Bhatkhande Music College. A magnificent *baradari* of red stones was constructed in Qaiserbagh complex. It was the centre of the activities of Wajid Ali Shah. When Wajid Ali Shah left for Calcutta, Begum Hazrat Mahal used the basement of this structure as a storehouse for her army during the War of 1857. During the British period it was painted white and is now known as Sufaid Baradari.

Baradaris contributed to the art forms of dance and music. The dance was *kathak* and the music *thumri*.

Kathak originated in the recitational style of the stories and legends prevalent in society, *katha*. People say that the way Krishna danced on the hydra headed hood of *kalia* in the Jamuna, was the first rhythmic dance where he avoided the leaping tongues of the serpent and jumped from one hood to the other to create the unison of effect. True to its legendary origin, there is quick movement of steps in this dance form, gathering momentum from original slow beats. The family which gave it a meaningful appearance was that of the *kathak* dancers of *raasdhari* tradition of Braj Bhoomi. From Braj Bhoomi they came and settled in a place called Handia near Allahabad. Since they could not make any impact in the area, they found their way to Lucknow and got the patronage of the *nawabs*. In Lucknow *kathak* found its home and evolved into a classical dance form. In course of time it became a highly polished art with a matchless degree of stylisation and complicated foot work. In the *darbars* it adopted liquid movements, sensuous grace and whirling pirouettes. It was originally a form of *raas leela* and other traditional dance-drama which was nurtured in the temples of Mathura and Vrindaban with the predominant themes of *Krishna leelas*. In the *darbars* of Lucknow it became a sophisticated art, receiving Persian influences. Court traditions gave it polish and glitter. Wajid Ali Shah brought it to blossom with his lavish patronage. He gave seat of honour to his Kathak Guru—Thakur Prasadji. The team of Wajid Ali Shah and Thakur Prasad created the dance-drama operas of *rahas* for which Lucknow became famous. Slowly *bhav-abhinaya* and other embellishments added further glow to the *kathak*.

The *thumri* was the music which complemented *kathak*. They enriched each other. *Thum* or *thumak* means a dance step, and *Thumri* means a small song associated with dance. Initially, *thumris* were always accompanied by *kathak* dance in *abhinaya*. A large number of *thumri* composers flourished in Lucknow. *Kathak* and *thumri* took both aspects in its fold—the religious presentation and the entertainment aspects in the *darbar* and the *mehfils*. *Kathak* adopted a sensuous style and charming dresses and jewellery. *Kathak* is now recognised as a classical dance. The basic groundwork was done during the time of Wajid Ali Shah. Incidentally, the *baradaris* played a prominent role in the presentation of the dance and song combination. Since the audience in Lucknow had become wider and had accepted this evening entertainment as their way of life, the large number of *baradaris* which came up, provided it a fitting setting.

APPENDIX III

Imambaras of Lucknow

Lucknow has always been famous for its *imambaras* constructed during the eighteenth and nineteenth centuries.

The *imambara* virtually is the *azakhana* of Shia sect, which means 'place of mourning'. Religious acts and ceremonies connected with the celebration of Moharram are called *azadari*. Since the *nawabs* of Awadh belonged to Shia community, Lucknow became a city of *imambaras*. Members of the Shia community are ardent followers of Hazrat Imam Hussain, who was a grandson of the Prophet. Imam Hussain laid his life at Kerbala for the sake of the dignity of Islam. His tomb (*rauza*) is situated at Kerbala. During the month of Moharram, replicas of the tomb of the Imam are made and exhibited throughout the country. These replicas are known as *tazias*. These *tazias* are installed in the *imambaras*. During the month of Moharram, religious congregations are also organised in the *imambara*. These congregations are known as *majlis*. The tragedy of Kerbala is the main subject of these *majlises*.

A unique feature of the architecture of *imambaras* is that they always face south with the main entrance on the northern side. All the *imambaras* of Lucknow are south-facing except the Saudagar ka Imambara and Kala Imambara which are east-facing.

Generally, the *imambara* is a rectangular structure with five, seven or nine arched gates (*mehrabs*). These bear a resemblance to Rajput architecture and as such the *imambaras* look like the *thakurdwaras* of Awadh. The interior of the *imambara* is decorated with candle bars, globes and mirrors. Every *imambara* has a raised platform in the interior on the southern side, known as the *shahnashin*. *Tazias* as also *zarih* and *alam* are installed on this *shahnashin*. *Alam* is the replica of the battle flag at Kerbala, whereas *zarih* is the replica of the grave of Imam Hussain. Walls of the interior of the *imambaras* are decorated with suitable designs, Koranic verses and other holy quotations. A large wooden chair with stairs, known as *mimbar* is installed on the eastern side of the hall. The religious preacher, known as *zakir* sits on this *mimbar* while addressing the religious congregations. In some of the *imambaras*, a mosque is also constructed on the western side of the *imambara* for offering *namaz*. During the month of Moharram, and especially on the ninth day of the month, known as *shabe aashur*, there is massive illumination in the *imambaras*.

The Asifi Imambara was built by Asaf-ud-daula and is popularly known as Bara Imambara. The construction of this magnificent *imambara* was started during the famine of 1784. It is said that more than 20,000 people were employed to complete the construction. It helped the famine affected people. The poor would build the structure during the day time, whereas the gentry would demolish it during the night. Thus the entire population affected by the famine would get some help. The real work was done after the famine and the building was completed in 1792 at a total cost of rupees one crore. The architecture of this building was conceived by the famous engineer Kifayat-ul-lah of Shahjahanabad. This is one of the most impressive buildings ever raised in Lucknow.

Outside the Asafi Imambara, there is a grand and massive gate on the western side towards Hussainabad known as Rumi Darwaza. The Rumi Darwaza has been recognised as the signature building of Lucknow. The main building of the *imambara* is situated on a raised platform with two lofty square gates and pavilions on either side of the gate. On the right side of the main building is situated the Asafi Masjid and on the left the *baoli*, a very large and deep well, flanked by seven stories of small rooms and a winding staircase. Perhaps the source of water is directly from the Gomti river. The *baoli* was used as a lodging during the summer season. The interior of the *imambara* consists of three parts. On the southern side, there is a raised *shahnashin*, where *tazias* and *alams* are installed. The central hall, with a length of 163 feet and a breadth of 53 feet has the biggest vaulted roof in the world (with a height of 50 feet). There are no pillars to support it and is built in brick and mortar. The main hall has a square room on the west and an octagonal room on the east. The entire building has been constructed with *lakhauri* bricks and red lime. *Mazars* (graves) of *nawab* Asaf-ud-daula and his favourite wife Shamshun Nisha Begum stand in the central hall. The acoustics are so good that if one tears a paper at one end of the hall, it can be heard at the opposite end. Moharram celebrations and specially *aag ka matam* of the Bara Imambara are very famous and people from far and near gather in large number to see the celebrations and massive illuminations.

On the upper storey of the main building there is network of labyrinthine passages and windows, opening into 489 doors of the same size and design. Any person going unescorted is bound to be confused and lose his way. This is why it is also named the *bhul bhulaian* (the Labyrinth).

The Hussainabad Imambara, also known as Chhota Imambara and Raushni Mahal, that is, the palace of light, was built by Mohammad Ali Shah in 1838. It is situated at few hundred yards on the western side of the Rumi Darwaza. It is the most attractive building of the city because of its interior decoration and outer maintenance. When one enters this complex, one finds a *naubat khana* and a *jilau khana*. The main building of the *imambara*, with a splendid golden tomb is situated on the southern side on a raised platform. In front of this building there is a beautiful canal. The interior of the main hall is decorated with globes, candle bars, and large mirrors set in with golden frames. *Tazias* made of wax, sandal, ivory and silver are installed on the *shahnashin*. The floor of the building is made of black and white stones resembling a chess board. Muhammad Ali Shah is buried here and his grave is surrounded by silver fencing. The *mimbar* installed in this *imambara*, is coated with silver. During Moharram the *imambara* attracts a large number of visitors, specially for its magnificent illumination.

The Shahnajaf Imambara was built by Gazi-ud-din Haider in 1822. He was the Awadh ruler to proclaim himself King. This *imambara* is said to be a replica of the *rauza* of Hazrat Ali (son-in-law of the Prophet) in Najaf. It is constructed on the bank of Gomti and has three entrances. The main building is in square shape with a beautiful tomb over it. A golden sun is installed on the roof of the main building. A replica of the *rauza* of Hazrat Ali, made of silver, is installed on the *shahnashin*. The interior of the building is decorated with candle bars, lamps and pictures with golden frames. Gazi-ud-din Haider and his three wives lie here in eternal sleep.

The Jannat Nashi Imambara was built by Wajid Ali Shah at an estimated cost of ten lakhs for his father Amjad Ali Shah. It is also known as Sibtenabad Imambara. It is situated in Hazratganj, the famous market, which carries its name from the honorific *Hazrat* given to Amjad Ali Shah. After 1857, the British took possession of this *imambara* and converted it into their prayer-hall and a Christian settlement developed here. Today it stands in a very dilapidated condition housing a government office and a furniture workshop. Wajid Ali Shah built an *imambara* at Matiya Burj in Calcutta, also known as Sibtenabad Imambara. *Jan-e-Alam* Wajid Ali Shah lies buried in this *imambara* at Matiya Burj.

A brief description of some other *imambaras* will be of interest. The oldest *imambara* of Lucknow was constructed during the period of *nawab* Safdar Jung, in the year 1745. This was known as *imambara* of Abu Talib. Even ruins of this building are not traceable today. Later on, during the rule of Shuja-ud-daula another *imambara*—of Agha Baqir was built near the Subzi Mandi of Chowk area. The *imambara* of Almas Khwaja Sera is situated near Sarai Malikhana. This 200 years' old magnificent building was famous for its architecture, but today only its ruins tell the story of its glorious past. The *imambara* in *mohalla* Thakurganj, known as *Shia-Bait-ul-Maal*, was built by *raja* Jhao Lal, the Hindu *diwan* of Asaf-ud-daula. The Kala Imambara situated in *mohalla* Peer Bokhara built by Safdar Jang is also unique. It is totally black in colour with Koranic verses *engraved* in white. The famous *baradari* situated in Qaiserbagh was earlier used as Imambara but later it was known as *Qasr-ul-Buka*, that is, place of mourning.

Some important *imambaras* were built by the *begums* of Awadh. The *imambara* of Begum Vilayati Mahal situated in the Residency, the *imambara* of Begum Malika-e-Zamani at Gola Gunj, the *imambara* of Begum Malika-e-Afaq at Makkagunj, the *imambara* of Begum Mughal Sahiba at Wazir Bagh, the *imambara* of Begum Malika-e-Ahed at Ahata-e-Suleman Qadra, the *imambara* of Begum Malika-e-Geti at Talab Gangani Shukal, the *imambara* of Begum Ameer Mahal in *mohalla* Rassi Batan, the *imambara* of Begum Khaqan at Wazirganj, the *imambara* of Begum Chotti Rani of Mehmoodabad at Farrash Khana exist even today.

Some of the courtiers and servants of the rulers of Awadh as also some members of the dancing community also followed their rulers' example and built several *imambaras*. The *imambara* of Agha Mir at Chandi Khana, of Siraj-ud-daula at Chaudhary ki Garhi, of Azeem-ul-lah Nai (Barber) at Chaulakhi, of Darab Ali Khan Khwaja

Sera at Maulviganj, of Chaudhrain at Chowk, and of Tahsin at Akbari Darwaza, are few examples of this category.

The old and historic *imambara* of Gufraan Maab has become a centre of religious activities. It is also famous for the *Majlis-e-Sham-e-Ghariban* held on the evening of the 10th day of Moharram.

No doubt, the rulers of Awadh paid more attention towards the construction, maintenance and decoration of their *aza khana* than their residential buildings and tombs. But a large number of these *imambaras* were destroyed and changed their shape with the lapse of time. The *imambaras* of Fateh-ud-daula, of Ikram-ud-daula, Tajmul Hussain Khan, Saiyed Taqi, of Afzal Mahal, Faiz Baagh and *raja* Darshan Singh are only a few examples of such buildings which live today only in memory.

Some historical and important *imambaras* are also to be found in other cities and towns of Awadh. The *imambara* of Jawahar Ali Khan is situated in Faizabad city near Chowk. It was built by Khawaja Sera (Eunuch) Jawahar Ali Khan, an officer of the palace of Bahu Begum. It is one of the main centres of *azadari* during the Moharram celebrations.

The *imambara* of Miyan Makka was constructed at Khairabad during the period of Nasir-ud-din Haider by the royal tailor Makka. Khairabad is also famous for its *tazia* of 52 bamboos. Likewise the *imambaras* of Mahmoodabad (Sitapur), Mohan, Jahangirabad and Salempur are also famous. The *imambara* of Rudauli (Barabanki) is a beautiful construction of the present century.

APPENDIX IV

Munazirah

Munazirah in Lucknow assumed importance because after a long time the Shia Muslims were trying to find an identity in the intellectual sense. The prime issues under consideration in this series of discussions were *taziadari* and *khilafat*. *Taziadari* was connected with the martyrdom of Hazrat Imam Ali on the battlefield of Kerbala and *khilafat* was the eternal point of discord on the point of succession to the Prophet.

Literally, *munazirah* means keeping an eye on the other and in that eventuality to criticise. The modicum of criticism depended on the level of the persons involved and also the atmosphere prevailing at that time. The legend has it that Khudabanda, the son of Halaku Khan, the great warrior, came in touch with a Shia scholar named Tahir Ibn-e-Mutahir 'Hilli'. The latter was a Shia scholar and he expounded the concepts of Shia thought and philosophy before Khudabanda who was greatly impressed. Encouraged, the scholar put all his thoughts together in a book named *Manhaz-us-Sidque*. This became very popular and was the harbinger of Shia concepts in Central Asia. Khudabanda was greatly enamoured of the Shia philosophy and Shiaism became the official religion in his empire. After some time, a Sunni scholar—Fazl Ibn-e-Rozbahan gave a fitting reply to the book of Tahir. His book was named *Ibtal-e-Batil*—meaning to prove wrong, what is wrong. The objective of the book was to prove Shia religion wrong.

Fazl Ibn-e-Rozbahan came to India during the reign of Emperor Akbar and inspired Badauni—a courtier of Akbar to write a book *Muntakhab-ut-Tawarikh*. On the other hand Faizi, one of the *nine pearls* of the court of Akbar was a Shia, and he called Qazi Noor-ullah Shustri to India, to undo the prevailing influence of Rozbahan and Badauni. Qazi Noor-ul-lah Shustri wrote a very scholarly discourse on the Shia religion and philosophy and the book was published under the title *Ihqaq-ul-Haq*. This book was an effective answer to the Sunni books. This was what Faizi had desired and during the reign of Akbar he succeeded.

After Jehangir came to the throne, a Sunni divine Sarhindi, opposed Din-i-Ilahi and the Shia religion. He upstaged Jehangir and had it conveyed to Jehangir that if he failed to remove these obduracies his throne would be in danger. Rozbahan challenged Shustri to come to India. People advised Shustri not to come because his life will be in danger. But he replied that if his blood were shed, religion would be strengthened. When Shustri came to India, a case was framed against him, and he was flogged to death. Even his dead body was subjected to unseemly treatment. Noor Jahan, a Shia, stopped the inhumanity and Shustri was buried in Agra. There is an annual *Urs* at his mausoleum, and he has been given the honorific Shaheed-i-Salis—the third martyr, after Hazrat Imam Hassan and Hussain. After this incident the Shia-Sunni dialogue came to a halt for some time.

During the time of Asaf-ud-daulah, Ghufran Ma'ab was trying to build up a Shia identity. His first book—*Imayad-ul-Islam* (Pillars of Islam) made a great impact. He wrote five very scholarly books—*Kitab-ul-Tauhid* (on monotheism), *Kitab-ul-Adal* (on justice), *Kitab-ul-Nabuwwat* (on Prophethood), *Kitab-ul-Imamat* (on Imams) and *Kitab-ul-Ma'aad* (life after death). These gave the Shia religionists, students and scholars plenty of literature and points of discussion. Shias, who were almost a suppressed class everywhere in India under Sunni kings and rulers, found in Awadh a place where they could cherish their primacy.

Sunni scholars also rose in opposition and wrote scholarly discourses and published books under the rubric *Muntah-ul-Kalam* (The Final Answer) and *Samsam-ul-Islam* (The sword of Islam). Some Other Sunni scholars published learned compendiums: *Zarbat-e-Haidaria*, *Shaukat-i-Umaria* and *Takhrib-ul-Aqaid*. Again in response to these Maulana Sayyad Hussain Moosvi and Maulana Nasir Hussain published *Abaqat-ul-Anwar*. So the *munazirah* in Lucknow functioned at a scholarly level and always addressed itself to the basic dichotomy of Shia and Sunni beliefs.

Munazirah at some stage of time also assumed discussion in lighter vein. Sunnis circulated satirical literature under the heading—*Qabqabb*. In response, the Shias brought out *Kantaap*. As the name suggests it meant a light roughing up. But it did not attract much attention. The rulers did not allow the *munazirah* to assume obnoxious proportions.

The *munazirahs* were also organised in Delhi and Panjab. As an extension of the *munazirah* of Lucknow and Awadh, Maulana Haider Ali Faizabadi, a Sunni Scholar wrote some long essays on the subject. He was the *ustaad* of Mir Anees—the famous *marsiya* writer. He had a good knowledge of the Shia scholastic works, but his essays were effectively answered by Maulvi Rajab Ali in *Rastujah*. Some people went to the extent of calling *munazirah*, the *mubahila* and took it to comic proportions. To decide the finality of right and wrong, it was suggested that two scholars should go on top of the Qutub Minar and jump from there. The one who was right would survive, the other would die. Fortunately, the contest never took place, and *munazirah* survived as a scholarly discussion between the Shias and the Sunnis.

APPENDIX V

List of *Subedars, Diwans and Wazirs* in the Administration of Awadh during Sultanate and Mughal Period

*** - Period not known

From Sultanate Period (1193) to the Sharqi rulers of Jaunpur (1401-52), there had been a number of *subedars*, who looked after the state of affairs from Delhi to Lucknow, and Jaunpur.

Malik Hasam-uddin Ugul Bak	1193-7
Muhammad Baktiyar Khilji	1197-1225
Nasir-ud-din Muhammad	1226-36
Malik Ghias-ud-din Muhammad	1237-40
Malik Nusur-ud-din Taisi and Kamru-ud-din Kuran	1240-5
Tugan Khan	1245-53
Qutlug Khan	1253-5
Malik Taz-ud-din & Irsalan Khan	1255-66
THE REIGN OF BALBAN (1266) [1]	
Haibat Khan	1266-79
Amin Khan	1279-87
THE REIGN OF QAIKUBAD (BALBAN'S SON) (1287)[2]	
Laghera Khan	1287-90
THE REIGN OF THE KHILJIS (1290)[3]	
Amir Ali Sarjandar Hatim Khan	***
Taj-ud-din Kuchi	***
Alauddin	***
Ala-ul-mulk Malik Umar	***
Mangu Khan	***
THE REIGN OF THE TUGHLAQS[4]	
Aainul Mulk Multani & Krishna Brajran	***
Indri—*Subedars* of Ayodhya	***

THE REIGN OF FIROZ SHAH TUGLAQ (1351-88)[5]	
Hasam-ud-din and Malik Saif-ud-din—*Subedars* of Ayodhya-Sandila	***

After Nusratshah Nasir-ud-din (1394-1414)—the last ruler of the Tuglaq dynasty, the administration of Kannauj, Kara, Ayodhya, Sandila, Dalmau, Baharaich etc., came under the control of Sharqi rulers. From the time of Sher Shah (1545) to Akbar, Sikandar Khan remained the *subedar* of Ayodhya. During the reign of Akbar, the entire empire was divided into 18 *subas*, which Awadh was one.

SUBEDARI OF AWADH	
Bazir Khan Hairat	1580-***
Tarsun Muhammad	1581-***
Fateh Ali & Qasim Ali (*Amirs*)	1594-5

THE FIRST *SUBEDAR* OF AWADH	
Jawahar Ali Khan	***-***
Baqar Khan Najsani	1621-***
Mirza Khan Manuchehar	1621-2
Mirza Badi Uzzman Shahnawaz Kkhan	1622-7
Shafi-ul-la Tabiyat Khan	1670-***
Saadat Khan	1675-84
Naamdar Khan	1675-84
Khwaja Mir Khavafi Salavat Khan	1684-5
Naamdar Khan	1685-90
Himmat Khan	1690-4
Jabardast Khan	1698-1700
Khudabanda Khan	1700-3
Shamsher Khan	1703-6
Mirza Khan Alam	1706-***
Abu Nasir Khan	1706-12
Mir Kamru-ud-din Khan-Duran-Khan-Bahadur	1712-13
Mubariz-ul-Mulk Mir Muhammad Sar-buland Khan Dilawar Jang	1713-19
Girdhar Bahadur Nagar	1719-22

Then Awadh came under the rule of the *nawabs*.

Saadat Khan (1722-39)
Diwan— Raja Surat Singh
Munshi Raja Singh
Safdar Jang (1739-54)
Shuja-ud-daula (1754-5)

Asaf-ud-daula (1775-97)

Diwan— Raja Surat Singh
Raja Tikait Rai

Naib— Munshi Raja Lal
Prakashi Bhola Nath

Mukhtar— Hasan Raza Khan
Tafazzul Hussain Khan

Saadat Ali Khan (1798-1814)

Diwan— Raja Tikait Rai
Naseer-ud-daula

Other Heads Munshi Tota Ram
Raja Bhola Nath
Bakshi Hulas Rai
Majlis Rai

King Ghazi-ud-din Haider (1814-19)

Diwan— Raja Deep Krishna
Bakshi Majlis Rai
Ummed Rai
Raja Bhola Nath
Raunak Ali Khan
Raja Bhawani Pandit
Maharaja Newal Krishna
Ifhkhar-ud-daula
Maharaja Mewa Ram

King Nasir-ud-din Haider (1827-37)

Wazir— Fazal Ali Khan
Hakim Mehdi Ali Khan
Roshan-ud-daula

Diwan— Maharaja Bal Krishna
Munshi Raja Ratan Singh

Mohammad Ali Shah (1837-42)

Wazir— Roshan-ud-daula
Zahir-ud-daula

Diwan— Maharaja Bal Krishna
Maharaja Ratan Singh
Raja Babu Chand

King Amjad Ali Shah (1842-7)

Wazir— Ashraf-ud-daula
Ameen-ud-daula
Munawar-ud-daula

Diwan— Raja Ratan Singh
Maharaja Bal Krishna
Raja Kundan Lal
Raja Ratan Chand

King Wajid Ali Shah (1847-56)

Wazir— Ameen-ud-daula
Amir-ud-daula
Ali Naqi Khan

Diwan— Raja Balkrishna

After the take over by the British Crown, Awadh was governed by the Chief Commissioners. Awadh was divided into districts under the charge of Deputy-Commissioners.

NOTES

1. Jiya-ud-din Barni, *Tarikh-e-Firozshahi*, p. 56.
2. Ibid.
3. *Awadh Gazeteer*, p.14 (Chapter III).
4. *Faizabad Gazeteer*, p. 45.
5. Ibid.

Glossary

Abhinaya	stage acting.
Abkari	excise duty on the sale of liquor.
Adab Arz	I convey my respect to you.
Adalat	court of Law, uprightness.
Akhbar-nawis	a newsletter writer.
Alim	scholar.
Amir-ul-Umara	nobles of the court.
Angarkha	large flowing dress worn by the *nawabs* and people in high position.
Arzdast	a memorial to a superior authority.
Asharfi	a gold coin of roughly ten grammes.
Ataleeq	a guardian, tutor, master for moral education.
Bagh	garden.
Badshah	king.
Baggi	horse-drawn carriage.
Bairagee	a Hindu wandering mendicant pursuing religious goals.
Bakshi	a paymaster, especially of military forces.
Bangash	an Afghan tribe living mostly arround Farrukhabad district.
Begum	lady wife.
Bhav	expression.
Bais	a Rajput tribe, living around Baiswara area.
Bande	human being.
Bangla	a large house sorrounded by open space.
Basant	spring season.
Bhagwan	God.
Bhajan	devotional songs.
Burhan-ul-mulk	good administrator.
Butkhana	temple.
Chakla	A district concerning of several *parganas*, under the administrative control of a *Chakladaar*.
Chandan	sandalwood.
Chati	sixth day celebration for a newly born child.
Chattar	an canopy signifying sovereignty.
Chatri	an umbrella.
Chauka	kitchen.

Chauth recovery of one-fourth of the revenues of the state, a levy mostly collected in the areas conquered by the Marathas.

Daftar office.

Dakhin southern part of India.

Dargah the place where a important religious person is buried.

Dariya-dili large-heartedness.

Darogha the Superintendent of a department or institution.

Dars gate.

Darshan 'auspicious sight' given by a deity to his worshipper.

Darvesh a Muslim wandering mendicant pursuing religious goals, often associated with Sufi order.

Data the Giver.

Daulatkhana a place where wealth is stored; also used to describe respectfully for the house of somebody else.

Deorhi the entry point of a main house.

Deva or *Devata* god or gods; *Devi*—goddess.

Devdaasi the female dancer connected with the temples.

Dham abode.

Digambar honorific used for Lord Mahavira, later it became a sect of Jainism.

Diwan (i) the office or official in charge of financial or revenue matters. (ii) a collection of a poet's composition.

Din-i-Ilahi religion of the God, a concept promulgated by emperor Akbar.

Diwan-e-Aam A rulers office, where audience is granted to the general public.

Diwan-e-Khas A rulers office, where people of high position assemble for conferences.

Faqir a muslim mendicant.

Falak sky.

Farmaan a mandate, command, order or royal patent.

Farrash the menial person kept for cleaning and dusting the house.

Firangi alien, also used for Britishers in India.

Faujdar the military commander of a district or administrative unit.

Gaddi a throne, also used for the place where the highest functionary of an organisation sits.

Ganga-Jamuni Tahzib the word used for composite culture, drawn from the concept of the two great rivers—Ganga and Jamuna, coming together.

Geeta the great religious discourse of Hindu philosophy, proclaimed by Lord Krishna to Arjun on the battlefield of Kurukshetra.

Ghat river bank.

Ghazal a lyric poem, usually on amatory themes, consisting of several couplets.

Ghosi a caste engaged in the trade of milch cattle.

Golundaaz the soldier handling canon.

Gopi the female companions.

Goswami a honorific used for learned persons, the most famous being Tulsidas—the author of *Ram-Charit-Manas*.

Gufran Maab	a religious muslim divine whose sins have been pardoned during his life time and he will have an angelic existence in heaven.
Gurkha	people of Nepalese origin.
Gusain	a religious sect, who also started weilding weapons and engaging in religious wars.
Hadith	an oral report transmitted by generations of Muslim scholars going back to the Prophet or Imams, complements the Koran as a source of Islamic Law.
Hakim	Physician in the tradition of "Greek" medicine going back through Avicenna to Galen and Aristotle.
Halal	to slaughter according to Mohammedan Law, an animal that may be eaten or so slaughtered.
Harem	the female appartments of a ruler.
Harzia	a satirical urdu poem.
Haveli	the large residence of the rich and powerful.
Huzoor	an expression of honour.
Ijtehad	The application of reasoned effort to the derivation of a ruling from the spiritual text, sometimes involving a limited sort of syllogism or analogy by *usulis* from the fourteenth century, also the degree in Islamic theology.
Ijrah	a system of collection of land revenues by awarding a contract by the state.
Ikshvaku	the legendary dynasty of Ayodhya, in which Lord Ram was born.
Ilaqa	region.
Imam	a religious divine.
Imambara	place of worship of the Shia sect, where religious acts and ceremonies performed during Moharram.
Indra	the God of the heavens and rains.
Indraprastha	legendary capital of the Pandavas.
Islaq Nawis	a court official, incharge of the accounts of the state.
Itar	perfume.
Jagir	an assignment of land collection rights, given to a *jagirdar*.
Janmastami	the day of birth of Lord Krishna, accompanied with lot of fanfare and decoration of the houses and temples.
Jhanki	decoration connected with the legend and stories connected with the birth of Lord Krishna.
Jihad	Muslim religious war.
Julaha	a caste connected with the textile weaving.
Kaali	an appearance of the consort of Lord Shiva to destroy the evils, She is worshipped during Dussehra.
Kadde-Sahiba	a form of religious writings and proclamations whereby the Shias adore Imam and condemn the three Caliphs after the Prophet.
Kahar	a caste of palanquin-bearars.
Kalam	Dialectical theology, cultivated by the rationalist *usulis* but

	forbidden by the Akhbaris; also rendering of Urdu poetry during literary congregation.
Kayastha	a caste among Hindus, successors of Chiragupta the computer of the God, keeping accounts of good and evils of all souls born in this world; a class of administrators.
Khansaman	Steward.
Khwaja-Sera	the de-sexed male, who were incharge of King's harem. During the *nawabi* times many such persons played an important rule in administration, some of them were also commanders in the army.
Khilat	a robe of honour bestowed by a ruler on his appointees, putatively having already been worn by the ruler and thus imbued with his substance.
Khums	a Muslim religious tax of 20 per cent of certain kinds of income, which, among Shias, is distributed to poor Sayyads. *Usulis* held the income from this tax should go to the religious jurisprudents.
Khutba	prayer read at the Friday congregational in which along with God, the name of the ruler is also recited for the well-being of the state.
Kotha	residence of the dancing girls, comparables with salons of Paris.
Kotwaal	a mixture of police chief and urban administrator.
Kuber	Lord of wealth in the Hindu pantheon.
Kul	pedigree of the household.
Leela	the playful acts of the infant Krishna.
Madarsa	Muslim institution of higher learning, seminary.
Madde-Sahiba	the clever act of the Sunnis by which they shower praise on Hazrat Imam Ali, as well as the three Caliphs; objected by Shias.
Mahabat	a caretaker of the elephants.
Mahra	a class of the household servants.
Majlis	a mourning congregation held for the martyrdom of Imam Hussain.
Mandaps	a canopy.
Mandi	the market place.
Mangli	a person born on Tuesday.
Mansabdar	the grant of status.
Marsiya	elegiac poetry mourning the Shi'i martyrs, including the Imam Hussain, who died at the seventh-century battle of Kerbala.
Marsiya Khawan	a person who renders *marsiya.*
Masghala-e-Sultani & Masghala-e-Nausherwani	the complaint boxes carried by Wajid Ali Shah and also kept outside his palace.
Masnad	the throne of a ruler.
Masnavi	epic poem on a heroic theme.

Matam	self-flagellation in the mourning of the martyred Imam.
Maula	God.
Mazar	grave.
Mazhab	religion.
Mehfil	cultural or literary assembly.
Mehrab	arch.
Mela	fete.
Minar	minaret.
Mujtahid	a jurisprudent who practices *ijtehad*, or legal reasoning.
Mubahila	spoiled form of *munazirah*.
Mufti-e-Adalat	highest officer of the court.
Mulla	a Muslim priest.
Munazirah	a public debate between the Shias and Sunnis.
Mushaira	a literary congregation, organised for public recitation of poetry.
Mutah	temporary marriage, allowed in Shia Law.
Mutawalli	the trustee of a religious trust.
Naib	the "deputy" of a ruler; the office of chief minister to a governor.
Namaskaar	I pay my respects to you.
Namaz	religious prayer of the Muslim.
Naubat Khana	the outer gate of a palace or *haveli*, where the musicians plays religious rhymes.
Navroz	New Year day of the Parsis and also the ninth day of Moharram.
Nawab	the 'deputy' or first minister to a sovereign.
Nazr	a present, usually cash, presented by an inferior to a superior.
Nizam	the common name for an administrator, honorific granted to the Vice-Regent of Hyderabad.
Paap	incurrence of sin.
Pachmehla	the forts of Sheikhzadas of Lucknow.
Panjatan	the five persons—the Prophet, his wife Fatima, Hazrat Imam Ali and his two sons Hassan and Hussain, who are basic symbols of Shia religion.
Parganah	the administrative unit of a district.
Parmatma	God—the highest supreme soul.
Pinda	the religious offering of a Hindu to the souls of his ancestors.
Prakriti	nature, the female counterpart of the creation with the capacity to conceive and bring forth the new generations.
Purush	male part of the nature carrying in him the capacity to sow the seeds of the progeny.
Qatl Ki Raat	the nineth day of Moharram.
Qazi	a notary with minor local administrative, judicial and religious authority.
Raas	the cosmic dance of Lord Krishna with the *gopis*.
Rahas	adaptation of *raas* by Wajid Ali Shah in Urdu as a stage opera.
Raj	a king's authority, used particularly for the British system of administration over India.
Rajya	state.

Ramzan	the days of fasting of muslims before Id. The legend is that during this time the concept and narrative of Koran was revealed to the Prophet.
Rastra	nation.
Rekti	a genre of Urdu poetry, written as if by female poets.
Rekhta	is the form of language which was evolving in the cantonments, with the grammar and syntax of Hindi and ingress of words of Arabic and Persian.
Rishi	a sage.
Riti-kaal	an era of Hindi poetry running between eighteenth and nineteenth centuries, where the romance was the highlight.
Salam Alaikum	a form expression of showing respect to the other person; literal meaning being glory be to God.
Saawan	the rainy season in north India—a romantic time of the year.
Sabha	assembly.
Saheb	a term of respect given in India to persons of rank and to Europeans.
Samiti	council.
Sanad	a document certifying the grant of land or a perpetual stipend.
Sardar	the headman.
Sardesh-mukhi	recovery of revenues by the Marathas in the areas under their sway.
Sati	a hideous custom, where by the widow of a man was put to flames on the pyre of her dead husband.
Satrapies	small principalities.
Savars	cavalry men.
Serpech	sceptre.
Shaheed-i-Salis	the third martyr in the Shia pantheon; an honour given to Noor-ul-lah Shustri whose mausoleum is at Agra.
Shrawan	sanskritised form of *Saawan*—rainy season.
Sidha	a person of attainments.
Sidha-peetha	the abode of *Sidha*.
Sindoor	vermilion.
Sipahsalar	a close army confidant of the ruler.
Soz Khawani	the chanting of dirges, particularly in the remembrance of the Shia martyrs.
Suba	a province in the Mughal empire, under the governance of a *subedar*.
Sufaid	white colour.
Sufi	a muslim mystic, usually part of an established order.
Suryavanshi	the dynasty in which Lord Ram was born.
Tabarra	the Shia practice of publicly cursing the first Caliphs, whom they believe to have wrongfully usurped the leadership of the Muslim community from the Imam Ali.
Takhte-Taus	the emperors throne; Shahjahans throne in which the famous Kohinoor diamond was embedded.

Tahsildar	the district official placed in charge of a *pargana*.
Taksaal	mint.
Taluqdar	a large rural landholder in Awadh.
Tankhwah	an assignment of the revenues from a specified area.
Tawaif	dancing girl.
Tawalla	praising and blessing the Prophet and the Twelve Imams whom Shias believe to be his legitimate successors.
Tazia	replica of Hazrat Imam Ali's masoleum in Kerbala.
Taziadari	showing respect to *tazia*.
Thum or *Thumak*	a dance step of *kathak*.
Thumri	a song associated with *kathak* dance.
Tila	mound or hillock.
Tilanjali	last homage to the dead person by his son or successor.
Udaasi	a sect of mandarins drawing insparation from Saint Kabir.
Unani	a conventional system of medicine originated in Unan.
Ustaad	the teacher and guide.
Urs	the annual celebration on the *mazar* of a religious divine.
Uzbeg	a person coming from Uzbegistaan.
Vaseekadar	the person getting monthly grants out of the endowments created by the kings of Awadh under the security of the East India Company for the king's relations.
Veer Ras	poetry of valour.
Wahabi	a fundamentalist sect of Muslims.
Wazir	the chief political executive of the king.
Wa-Alaikaum Assalam	the respectful response of *Salam Alaikum*.
Wizarat	headship of the chief executive to the king.
Yantra	mystic formula in the worship of the *Devi*.
Yatra	the religious pilgrimage.
Yojan	a distance of approximately ten miles.
Zukaat	a certain proportions of earnings of a Muslim to be used for charity.

Select Bibliography

I. MANUSCRIPT SOURCES

English

Central Record Office, Allahabad
Correspondence of the Agent to the Governor-General at Benares.
Resident's Proceedings, Benares.
Duncan Records.
Records of various Districts of U.P.

India International Central Library, New Delhi
Nicholls, Charles George, *The British Oriental Atlas*.

India Office Library, London
Home Miscellaneous, Vol. 584 (IOR Reg. 4098: Rotograph of Dr. Qureshi: Relevant portions only).

National Archives of India, New Delhi (N.A.I)
Bengal Political Consultations (BPC).
Bengal Political Proceedings.
Begal Public Consultations.
Bengal Secret and Political Consultations (BSPC).
Bengal Secret Consultations (BSC).
Bengal Secret and Political Consultations.
Bengal Select Committee Proceedings.
Bengal Home Department (Educational Branch) Political Proceedings.
Bengal Home Department (Public Branch) Political Proceedings.
Bengal Military Department Proceedings.
Foreign Department, Political Proceedings (FDPP).
Foreign Political Consultations (FPC).
Foreign Secret Consultations (FSC).
Foreign Secret Proceedings (FSC).
Foreign Miscellaneous Vols., 8-12, 41A, 46-47, 75, 78,135, 158, 171, 197A, 197B, 348.
Indian Political and Foreign Consultations (IPFC)
Indian Political Consultations (IPC)
Indian Secret Proceedings (ISP).
Letters to the Court of Directors (Home Public).
Political Letters from the Court of Directors.
Political Letters to the Court of Directors.
Secret Letters from the Court of Directors.

Secret Letters to the Court of Directors.

U.P. State Archives, Lucknow

Board of Revenue, Oudh General Files.

Board of Revenue, Oudh District Files.

Proceedings of the Board of Revenue, at Fort William in Bengal, 1803-7.

Proceedings of the Board of Commissioners in the Ceded and Conquered Provinces, 1807-22.

PERSIAN

Ahad, Abdal, *Waqa-i- Dil Pazir Awadh*. Persian History 461, Hyderabad: Salar Jang Library.

Ahwal-i-Salatin-i-Mutakhirin, Patna: Khuda Bakhsh Oriental Public Library.

Akhbar, Persian MSS OR 4608-09, London: British Library.

Akhbar-i-Deorhi, Muhammad Ali Shah, Lucknow: Lucknow University Library.

Akhbar-i-Deorhi, Jahandar Shah, Allahabad: The Central Records Office.

Akhbar-i-Nadir Shah, Hyderabad: Andhra Pradesh Goverment Oriental Manuscripts Library and Research Institute.

Akhbar-i-Sa'adat Ali Khan, Persian MSS 10 4341-42, London: Commonwealth Relations Office.

Akhbarat-i Nawab Asaf al-Daula, Persian MS 197, Allahabad: Regional Archives.

Akhtar, Muhammad Sadiq Khan, *Risala-i-Subh-i-Sadiq*, Aligarh: Aligarh Muslim University Library.

Alahi, Kundan Lal Ashiqi, *Muntakhab Tanqihul Akhbar*, Rampur: Raza Library.

Alam, Mir, *Hadiqat-ul-Alam*, Hyderabad: Salar Jung Museum.

Ali, Inam, *Ausaf al-Asaf*, Lucknow: State Museum.

Ali, Qasim, *Tarikh-i-Shahiya-i Nishapuriya*, Persian MS 2148, Rampur: Raza Library.

Allahabadi, Khayr Al-Din Muhammad, *Ibrat Nama*. Persian MS 2210, New Delhi: National Archives of India.

Bhatnagar, Ganga Bishan, *Gulshan-i-Bahar*, Calcutta: The National Library.

Baksh, Munshi Faiz, *Ahwal-i-Zindagi-i-Faizbaksh* or *Chashma-i-Faiz*, Calcutta: The Asiatic Society of Bengal.

__________, *Insha-i-Faiz Baksh*, Lucknow: Amiruddaulah Public Library.

__________, *Tarikh-i-Faiz Bakhsh*, Aligarh: Aligarh Muslim University.

Bangash, Muhammad Khan, *Aiziz-ul-Quloob*, Qaimganj, Farrukhabad: Library of Janab Nadim Ahmad Khan Saheb.

Bedar, Sanath Singh, *Majmua Tawarikh-i-Bedar*, Agra: Agra University Library.

Bhan, Chandra, *Chahhar Chaman*, Hyderabad: Andhra Pradesh Goverment Oriental Manuscripts Library and Research Institute.

Bhan, Suraj, *Waqa'i-i Awadh*, Lucknow: State Museum.

Bijnouri, Muhammad Mohsin, *Jauhar-i-Samsam*, Calcutta: The Asiatic Society of Bengal.

Bilgrami, Muhammad Zahiruddin Khan, *Israr-i-Wajidi*, Lucknow: Tagore Library, Lucknow University.

Bilgrami, Murtaza Husayn, *Hadiqat al-Aqalim*, Persian MS 11784, Allahabad: Regional Archives.

Dasturul Amal-i-Awadh, Rampur: Raza Library.

Das, Har Charan, *Muntakhab az Char Gulzar-i Shuja'i.* Rotograph R 35. Aligarh: Centre for Advanced Study, Aligarh Muslim University.

Fragment of a Collection of Reports by a Lakhnau Amil, Persian MSS 10 4530-31, London: Commonwealth Relations Office.

Hasan, Syed Ibn, *Burhan-i-Awadh,* Aligarh: Aligarh Muslim University.

Haydar, Kamal Al-Din, *Tarikh-i Mamulkat-i Awadh,* Persian MS 377, Allahabad: Regional Archives.

——————, *Tarikh-i Sawanihat-i Salatin-i Awadh,* Photograph, Aligarh: Centre for Advanced Study, Aligarh Muslim University.

Hazin, Sheikh Ali, *Swaneh Umri Sheikh Ali Hazin,* Lucknow: Dar-ul-uloom Nadwatul Ulema.

Hazrat, Mufti Ghulam, *Kawaif-i-Zila Gorakhpur,* Aligarh: Aligarh Muslim University.

Hikayat Fateh Nadir Shah, Calcutta: The Asiatic Society of Bengal.

Husain, *Hayat-i-Khusnaveesan,* Hyderabad: Salar Jung Museum.

Hussaini, Imad-ud-din, *Hussain Shahi* or *Tarikh-i-Ahmad Shah Durrani,* Calcutta: The Asiatic Society of Bengal.

Intikhab-i Akhbarat, Persian MS Add.16721, London: British Library.

Intikhab Darbar-i-Mullah wa Mahaji Sindhia Babtah, Hyderabad: Salar Jung Museum.

Iqbalnamah or *Tarikh-i-Wazir Ali Khan* and *Tarikh-i-John Shore,* Aligarh: Aligarh Muslim University.

Iqbalnamah, Rampur: Raza Library.

Karim, Abdul, *Gulshan-i-Hind,* Allahabad: The Central Records Office.

Kashiraj, *Karzar-i-Sadashiv Bhau wa Shah Ahmad Abdali,* Calcutta: The National Library.

Kashmiri, Khwaja Abdul Karim Khan, *Bayan-i-Waqai,* Hyderabad: Salar Jung Museum, or *Tarikh-i-Nadir Shah,* Hyderabad: Andhra Pradesh Goverment Oriental Manuscripts Library and Research Institute.

Kashkol, Rampur: Saulat Public Library.

Khan, Ghulam Hussain, *Tarikh-i-Benaras,* Patna: The Khuda Bakhsh Oriental Public Library.

——————, *Balwand-Namah,* Persian MS 2210, N.A.I.

Khan, Hafiz Rehmat, *Khulasat-ul-Insab,* Rampur: Raza Library.

Khan, Khafi, *Muntakhab-ul-Lubab,* Persian Text, Calcutta: The Asiatic Society of Bengal, Vol.II.

Khan, Kunwar, *Tarikh-i-Chaghtai,* Amir MS, Lucknow: Amir-ud-daula Public Library.

Khan, Mir Karim Ali, *Muzaffar Nama,* Hyderabad: Salar Jung Museum Library.

Khan, Muhammad Mustajab, *Gulistan-i-Rehmat,* Rampur: Raza Library.

Khan, Mahdi Ali, *Dastur al-Amal,* Persian MS 83, Allahabad: Regional Archives.

Khan, Muhammad Khalil Al-Din, *Manazil-i Hindustan.* Abd al-Salim collection MS 492/13, Aligarh: Aligarh Muslim University.

Khan, Najbat Hussain, *Sawaneh Lucknow,* Patna: Patna University Library.

Khan, Saadat Yaar, *Gul-i-Rehmat,* Rampur: Raza Library.

Khan, Saqi Dad, *Kitab-i-Malfoozat-i-Soofiya-iKiram wa Ashar-i-Nasayeh Sobra-i-Ali-Muqam,* Quimganj, Farrukhabad: Library of Janab Nadeem Ahmad Khan Saheb.

Khan, Shah Nawaz, *Maasir-ul-Umara,* Persian Text, Vol.III, Culcutta: The Asiatic Society of Bengal.

Khan, Syed Ahmad, *Jam-i-Jum*, Rampur: Raza Library.

Khan, Sayyid Ghulam Ali, *Imad al-Sa'adat*. Qutb al-Din Collection MS 95/15, Aligarh: Aligarh Muslim University.

Kitab Akhbar Deorhi Badshah-i-Awadh, Lucknow: Tagore Library, Lucknow University.

Lahori, Muhammad Qasim, *Ibarat Maqal*, Patna: Khuda Baksh Oriental Public Library.

———, *Ibrat Nama*, Patna: Khuda Baksh Oriental Public Library.

Lal, Awadhi, *Mansurul Maktubat*, Lucknow: Tagore Library, Lucknow University.

Lal, Bihari, *Ahwal-i-Najib-ud-daulah Amir-ul-Umara Sabit Jung*, Hyderabad: Salar Jung Museum.

Lal, Mendu, *Lucknou* 1253 *Hijjri Men*. Farsi Tarikh MS 2241, Hyderabad: Andhra Pradesh Central Library.

Lalji, Munshi, *Mirat-ul-Auza*, Rampur: Raza Library.

———, *Sultan-ul-Hikayat*, Rampur: Raza Library.

Lucknawi, Shiv Das, *Shah Nama-i-Munawar Kalam*, Rampur: Raza Library.

Majmua-i Khutut, Persian MS 10915, Allahabad: Regional Archives.

Majmua-i Khutut-i Muntakhab Sarkar Kampni Angrezi Bahadur Muta'alluq Suba Awadh, MS 529, Hyderabad: Andhra Pradesh State Archives.

Majmua Khutut Muntakhib Sarkar Company Angrez Bhadur Mutalliq Suba Awadh, Hyderabad: Andhra Pradesh State Archives.

Maktub-i Shah-i Awadh. Abd al-Salam Collection MS 505/26, Aligarh: Aligarh Muslim University.

Maktubat-i Sarkar Kampni benam Wajid Ali Shah. Library of the Raja of *Muntakhab-ul-Insha*, Patna: Patna University Library.

Mahumadabad, Lucknow, Persian and Urdu.

Miskin, Tahmasp Khan, *Qissa-i-Miskin*, Calcutta: The National Library.

Muhammad, Qazi Faqir, *Jamey-ut-Tawarikh*, Rampur: Saulat Public Library.

Muhammad, Sayyid, *Dastur al-Amal-i Awadh*, Persian MS 2241, Rampur: Raja Library.

Muhammad, Khairuddin, *Alam-i-Ashob*, Benares: Library of the Maharaja of Benares.

———, *Ibrat Nama*, Rampur: Raza Library.

Najm, Syed Muhammad Raza, *Asarul Mehshar*, Rampur: Raza Library.

Parshad, Munshi Shital, *Mir'atal-Auza*, Persian MS 2149, Rampur: Raza Library.

Parshad, Shiv, *Tarikh-i Faiz Bakhsh*, Persian History 115, Hyderabad: Salar Jang Museum.

Qadir, Moulvi Abdul, *Roznamchah Abdul Qadir Ghamgin*, Rampur: Raza Library.

Rai, Bhupat, *Insha-i-Roshan Kalam*, Tagore Library, Lucknow: Lucknow University.

Rai, Khushlal, *Nadir-us-Zamani*, Amritsar: Khalsa College Library.

Rizvi, Hashim Ali, *Mir'at al-Bilad*, Persian MS 2551, Allahabad: Regional Archives.

Raghib, Munshi Inamullah, *Ausaf-ul-Asaf*, Aligarh: Aligarh Muslim University.

Rifat, Ghulam Jilani, *Durr-i-Manzoom*, Rampur: Saulat Public Library.

Ruz-namcha-i-Darbar-i Abu Muzaffar Ghazi al-Din Haydar, Farsi Tarikh MS 702, Hyderabad: Andhra Pradesh Central Library.

Shadan, Busawan Lal, *Amir Nama*, Hyderabad: Andhra Pradesh Goverment Oriental Manuscripts Library and Research Institute.

Shafiq, Lakshmi Narain, *Bisatin Chanaim*, Hyderabad: Andhra Pradesh Goverment Oriental Manuscripts Library and Research Institute.

———, *Maasir-i-Asafi*, Hyderabad: Andhra Pradesh Goverment Oriental Manuscripts Library and Research Institute.
Shah, Wajid Ali, *Ishq Namah*, Lucknow: Library of Dr. Nayyar Masud.
———, *Soot-ul-Mubarak*, Rampur: Raza Library.
Shambhunath, *Miftah-i-Khazain*, Benares: Library of the Maharaja of Benares.
Shoq, Maulvi Qudratullah Siddiqi, *Jam-i-Jahan Numa*, Rampur: Raza Library.
Singh, Bahadur, *Yadgar-i Bahaduri*, Persian MS 255, Allahabad: Regional Archives.
Singh, Kalyan, *Khuasat-ut-Tawarikh*, Patna: Khuda Bakhsh Oriental Public Library.
Singh, Ratan, *Sultan al-Tawarikh*. Persian MS 11777, Allahabad: Regional Archives.
Shustri, Abdul Latif, *Tuhfat al-alam*, Allahabad: Regional Archives.
Tarikh-i Ahmad Shah. Persian MS OR 2005, London: British Library. Miscellaneous Collections.
Yamani, Abdul Razzaq, *Mazahir-ul-Asrar*, Rampur: Raza Library.
Yusufi, Ahmad Mirza Muhammad, *Jinanul Firdaus*, Rampur: Raza Library.

URDU

Aali, Syed Muhammad Rafey Rizvi, *Tarikh-i-Benaras*, Rampur: Raza Library.
Afsar-ut-Tawarikh, Lucknow: Library of Dr. Nayyar Masud.
Ali, Abbas, *Tawarikh ma'Tasawir-i Rajagan wa Ta'alluqdarn-i Awadh*, Allahabad: n.p. 1880 (Urdu and English).
Ali, Muhammad Ahmad, *Maraqqa-i Awadh* (title page missing) 1912.
Ali, Muhammad Azmat, *Maraqqa-i-Khusravi*, Lucknow: Tagore Library, Lucknow University.
Aftab-i Awadh (title page missing), Lucknow: Library of Dr. Nayyar Masud.
Ansari, Muhammad Raza, *Bani-i Dars Nizami*, Lucknow: Nami Press, 1963.
Bakhash, Husayn, *Baharistan-i Shadi*, Lucknow: n.y., 1853-4.
Chand, Munshi Purn, *Tarikh-i Suba-i Awadh*, Lucknow: Tamanni Press, 1963.
Das, Balaqi, *Guldasta Awadh*, Delhi: Muir Press, n.d.
Ghani, Najm Al-, *Tarikh-i Awadh*. 5 Vols., Lucknow: Newal Kishore, 1919.
Hasan, Ali, *Mahumadabad Ki Tarikh*, 5 Vols., Lucknow: Library of the Raja of Mahmudabad.
Hasan, Sayyid Aqa, *Ihsan al-Tawarikh*, 3 Vols., Lucknow: Jang-Bahduri Press, 1863-5.
Haydar, Kamal-Din, *Qasar al Tawarikh*, 2 Vols., Lucknow: Newal Kishore, 1879.
———, *Sawanihat-i Salatin-i Awadh*, Lucknow: Newal Kishore, 1879.
———, *Tarikh-i Awadh*, 2 Vols., Lucknow: Newal Kishore, 1907.
Husayn, Sulayman, *Lakknau ke Chand Namwar Shri'ara*, vol. 1, Lucknow: Sarfaraz Qaumi Press, 1973.
Ibrat Kada-i Sami'an, Lucknow: Library of Dr. Naiyar Masud.
Jan, Mirza, *Hadiqa-i Shuhda* (title page missing), available in Madwa Academy Library, Lucknow.
Khan, Muhammad Hasan, *Akhbar-i-Hasan*, Rampur: Raza Library.
Khan, Muhammad Imam Ali, *Asar-i Yadgar*, Lucknow: Tasawir-i Alam, 1901-2.
Khan, Muhammad Sadral-Din, *Sawarikh Umri*, Lucknow: n.p., 1911.
Khan, Siyadat Hasan Syed Jalaluddin, *Afsana-i-Lucknow*, Lucknow: Library of Dr. Nayyar Masud.

———, *Shikwa-i-Firang*, Lucknow: Library of Dr. Nayyar Masud.
Kishore, Newal, *Tarikh-i Nadr al-'Asr,* Lucknow: Newal Kishore, 1863.
Parshad, Hut, *Tawarikh-i Awadh*, Urdu MS 141, Rampur: Raza Library.
Parshad, Durga, *Tarikh-i Ajodhya,* Lucknow: Newal Kishore, 1902.
Rizwi, Muhammad, *Taj wa Nishan* (title page missing), 2 Vols., 1906.
Rai, Bhupat, *Insha-i-Roshan*, MS, Lucknow: Tagore Library, Lucknow University.
Shah, Wajid Ali, *Jawabat-i Shukuk Mundarijah Awadh Blu Buk,* Library of the Raja of Mahmudabad.
———, *Risala Wajidya Sultani*, Lucknow: Library of Dr. Nayyar Masud.
———, *Sibat-ul-Quloob*, Calcutta: Ittihadya Library.
Sahai, Munshi Ram, *Ihsan al-Tawarikh*, Lucknow: Tamanni Press, 1876.
Shamsulla, *Tarikh-i Hind*, Urdu MS 12046, Allahabad: Regional Archives.
Shara, Abd Al-Halim, *Guzishta Lakhnau Mashriqi Tammadun Ka Akhri Namona*, New Delhi: Maktab Jami Limited, 1971.
Singh, Indar Bahadur, *Tarikh-i Raja Balrampur*, Lucknow: Newal Kishore Press, 1909.
Taqi, Mirza Muhammad, *Tarikh-i Aftab-i Awadh*, Lucknow: University Library.
Tarikh-i-Firaq, Khuda Bakhsh Oriental Public Library, Patna.
Tarikh-i-Mumtaz, Lucknow: Library of Dr. Nayyar Masud.
Tarikh-i-Noor, Patna: Khuda Bakhsh Oriental Public Library.
Tarikh-i Salatin-i Awadh (No title page), Lucknow: Nadwa Academy Library.
Tasleem, Amirullah, *Tarikh-i-Badei*, Rampur: Saulat Public Library.
Viqai Khandan-i-Bangash, Qaimganj: Library of Janab Nadim Ahmad Khan Saheb.
Waji al-Arz of Mahumdabad Village, Mahmudabad: District Record Office.
Yavar, Sheikh Imad Ali, *Bayaz-i-Yavar*, Lucknow: Library of Dr. Nayyar Masud.

ARABIC

Kinturi, Sayyad Ijaz Husayn, *Shudhur-al'iqyan fi tarajim al-a'yan*, Bukar Collections (An unpublished Arabic Source, Calcutta National Library.

FRENCH

Modave's Journal du Voyage, Paris MS, Calcutta: Copy in National Library.

II. OTHER PRINTED CONTEMPORARY, NEAR CONTEMPORARY AND LATER CONTEMPORARY SOURCES

ENGLISH

A Short History of English Transactions in the East Indies, Cambridge, 1776.
Addison, G.A., *Indian Reminiscences or the Bengal Moofussil Miscellany*, London, 1837.
Ali, Meer Hasan, *Observations on the Mussulmans of India*, London, 1832.

Argyll, Duke of, *India under Dalhousie and Canning*, London, 1865.

Arnold, E., *The Marquess of Dalhousie's Administration of British India*, 2 Vols., London, 1865.

Asiatic Annual Register, Or A View of the History of Hindustan, and of the Politics, Commerce and Literature of Asia, for the Year 1803, London, 1804.

Auber, Peter, *Rise and Progress of the British Power in India*, 2 Vols., London, 1837.

Bell, E., *Retrospects and Prospects of Indian Policy*, London, 1868.

Benett, W.C., *Report of the Final Settlement of the Gonda District*, Allahabad, 1878.

————, *A Report on the Family History of the Chief Clans of Rai Bareilly District*, Lucknow, 1870.

Beveridge, H., *A Comprehensive History of India*, 3 Vols., London, 1867.

Brand, J., *A Refutation of the charge brought against the Marquess of Wellesley on account of his conduct to the Nabob of Oude*, London, 1807.

Broome, Arthur, *History of the Rise and Progress of the Bengal Army*, Vol. I, Calcutta, 1850.

Broome, Ralph, *An Elucidation of the Articles of Impeachment preferred by the Late Parliament against Warren Hastings Esq., Late Governor General of Bengal*, London, 1790.

Butter, Donald, *Outlines of the Topography and Statistics of the Southern Districts of Oudh and of the Cantonment of Sultanpur-Oudh*, Calcutta, 1839.

Campbell, Sir George, *History of Modern India*, London, 1852.

Capper, John, *The Three Presidencies of India*, London, 1853, Reprinted under the title *The Real India*, Delhi, 1972.

Carnegy, Patrick, *Notes on the Land Tenures and Revenue Assessments of Upper India*, London, 1874.

————, *Fyzabad: Settlement Reports*, Nos. II & III, Lucknow, 1865.

————, *Fyzabad Zilah Fyzabad*, Lucknow, 1870.

Davis, J.F., *Wazir Ali Khan and the Massacre of Benaras*, London, 1844.

Dorn, Bernard, *History of the Afghans*, 2 Vols., London, 1829.

Dow, Alexander, *The History of Hindostan*, 2 Vols., London, 1868.

Edwards, William, *Reminiscences of a Bengal Civilian*, London, 1866.

Elliott, Charles Alfred, *The Chronicles of Oonao, A District in Oudh*, Allahabad, 1862.

Elphinstone, M., *Cabul: An Account of the Kingdom of Cabul and its Dependencies in Persia, Turkey and India etc.*, London, 1842.

Ferrar, M.L., *The Regular Settlement and Revised Assessment of the District of Sitapur*, Lucknow, 1875.

Forbes, W.E., *Report on the Revenue Settlement of the Partabgarh District*, Lucknow, 1877.

Francklin, W., *The History of the Reign of Shah Aulum, the Present Emperor of Hindostan*, First published in London in 1798, Lucknow (rpt.) 197?.

Gazetteer of the Province of Oude, Allahabad, 1877.

Grand, G.F., *The Narrative of the Life of a Gentleman long Resident in India*, ed. by W.K. Firminger, Calcutta, 1910, First published at Cape of Good Hope in 1814.

Grant, Robert, *A Sketch of the History of the East India Company from its first Foundation to the Passing of the Regulating Act of 1773 etc.*, London, 1813.

Hamilton, Charles, *An Historical Relation of the Origin, Progress and final Dissolution of the Government of the Rohilla Afghans in the Northern Provinces of Hindostan*, London, 1787.

Hamilton, Walter, *A Geographical, Statistical and Historical Description of Hindonstan and the adjacent countries*, 2 Vols., originally published in 1820. Reprinted from Delhi, 1971. There is no difference in the paginations of both the editions.

Hastings, Warren, *The Minutes of what was offered by Warren Hastings Esq. Late Governor General of Bengal at the Bar of the House of Commons*, London, n.y.

Imperial Gazetteer, Uttar Pradesh, Faizabad, 1905.

Jackson, Sir Charles, *A Vindication of the Marquis of Dalhousie's Indian Administration*, London, 1865.

Kaye, John, *History of Indian Mutiny*, London, 1888.

Kaye, J.W., *The Administration of the East India Company, History of Indian Progress*, London, 1853.

Kaye, J.W. & Malleson, G.B., *History of the Indian Mutiny of 1857-58*, 6 Vols., London, 1906.

Kirkpatrick, William, *An Account of the Kingdom of Nepal*, London, 1811.

Knighton, William, *The Private Life of an Eastern King or Elihu Jan's Story or The Private Life of an Eastern Queen*, London, 1855 & O.U.P., 1921.

Lewin, Malcolm, *Has Oudh Been Worse Governed?*, London, 1857.

Macandrew, I.F., *Report of the Settlement Operations of Rae-Bareily District*, Lucknow, 1872.

Macandrew, I.F., *Settlement of the Land Revenue of the Sultanpur District*, Lucknow, 1873.

—————, *On some Revenue Matters chiefly in the Province of Oudh*, Calcutta, 1876.

Macfarlane, C., *Our Indian Empire*, London, 1848.

Maddock, *An Abstract view of the State of Oudh as gathered from the Persian papers etc.*, London, 1834.

Malcolm, John, *The Political History of India*, Vol. I, London, 1826,

Marshman, James Clark, *The History of India from the Earliest Period to the Close of Lord Dalhousie's Administration*, 2 Vols., London, 1867.

Martin, R. Montgomary, *History of the Possesssions of the Honourable East India Company*, 2 Vols., London, 1837.

Masihuddin, M. Muhammad, *Oude: Its Princes and its Government Vindicated*, ed. by Safi Ahmad, Meerut, 1969.

Mill, James, *History of India*, London, 1858.

Orme, R., *A History of the Military Transactions of the British Nation in Indostan*, 3 Vols., London, 1806.

Prinsep, H.T., *History of the Political and Military Transaction in India during the Administration of the Marquess of Hastings 1813-1823*, London, 1825.

Prior, James, *Memoirs of the Life and Character of the Right Honourable Edmund Burke etc.*, London, 1826.

Raikes, Charles, *Notes on the North Western Provinces of India*, London, 1852.
Rajas and Nawabs of the North-Western Provinces, Allahabad: North-Western and Oudh Government Press, 1877.
Report Census Oudh, Vol.I., Allahabad, 1869.
Roberts, Emma, *Scenes and Characteristics of Hindoostan*, London, 1835.
Rouse, G.H. (ed.), *Lucknow Album*, Calcutta: Baptist Mission Press, 1874.
Rousseau, S., *A Dictionary of Mohammedan Law, Bengal Revenue Terms, Shanscrit, Hindoo and other words used in East Indies*, London, 1802.
Scott Major John, *A short Review of the Transactions in Bengal during the Last ten years*, London, 1782.
Selections from Revenue Records, North Western Provinces 1822-33, Allahabad, 1872.
Selections from Revenue Records, North Western Provinces, Allahabad, 1873.
Shore, H.F.J., *Notes on Indian Affairs*, 2 Vols., London, 1837.
Sleeman, W.H., *Rambles and Recollections of an Indian Official*, London. 1893.
———, *Journey Through the Kingdom of Oudh*, London, 1858.
Spencer, Alfred, *Memoirs of William Hickey, 1775-1782*, 2 Vols., London, 1919
Spry, H.H., *Modern India*, London, 1837.
Stocqueler, J.H., *The Life of Field Marshall the Duke of Wellington*, Vol. I, London, 1852.
Taylor, W.C., *A Popular History of British India*, London, 1842.
The Bengal Obituary, Calcutta, 1848.
The East India Military Calendar, 3 Vols., London, 1823, 1824,1826.
Thornton, Edward, *The History of the British Empire in India*, 3 Vols., London, 1842.
Trevelyan, G.O., *Caunpore*, London, 1865.
Trotter, L.J., *The History of the Indian Empire*, 3 Vols., London, n.y.
Walsh, Rev. J. Johnston, *A Memorial of the Fattehgurh Mission and the Martyred Missionaries with some remarks on the Mutiny in India*, London, 1859.
White, William, *The Prince of Oudh Mirza Kaiwan Jah or the Dethroned King of Oudh in Chains*, London, 1838.
Williams, Capt. John, *An Historical Account of the Bengal Native Infantry*, London, 1817.
Wilson, H.H., *The History of British India*, London, 1845.

Persian

Akhtar, Muhammad Sadiq, *Guldasta-i-Mohabbat*, Lucknow, 1824.
———, *Mahamid-i-Haidri*, Lucknow, 1823.
Ashraf, Syed Imam, *Tuzuk-i-Shahi*, Lucknow, 1854.
Beale, Thomas William, *Miftah-ut-Tawarikh*, Kanpur, 1867.
Behari, Munshi Kunj, *Insha-i-Rahat-i-Rooh*, Lucknow, 1287 H.
Diwan-i-Viqar, Kanpur, 1269 H.
Hussein, Murtaza, *Hadiqat-ul-Aqalim*, Lucknow: Newal Kishore Press, n.y.
Khan, Amir Ali, *Wazir Nama*, Kanpur: Nizami Press, 1876.
Kasmiri, Muhammad Ali, *Najum-as-sama takmilah*, Lucknow: Matba-i-Jafri, 1302/1884-5.

Mirat-ul-Ashbah Salatin-i-Asman Jah, Matba-i-Sultani, 1852,
Mubahisab Bain-ul-Nafs wa Al-Aql, Calcutta, 1291 H.
Naqvi, Ghulam Ali, *Imaad-us-Saadat*, Lucknow, 1897.
Qalandar, Shah Turab Ali, *Mujahidat-ul-Auliya* (Defective).
Shah, Wajid Ali, *Behr-ul-Hidayat*, Lucknow, n.y.
———, *Jauhar-i-Urooz*, Calcutta, 1290 H, 1292 H.
———, *Malik Akhtar*, Calcutta, 1296 H.
———, *Namah-i-Akhtari*, n.p. & n.y.
———, *Nasaih Akhtari*, Lucknow, 1275 H.
———, *Sahifa-i-Sultanyah*, Calcutta, 1289 H.
———, *Soot-i-Mubarak*, Lucknow, 1269 H.

URDU

Jan, Mirza *Hadiqa-i-Shohda*, n.p., 1856.
Jang, Mohtashim-ud-daulah Ghaus Muhammad Khan Bahadur Shaukat, *Sair-ul-Mohtashim*, Javrah, 1851.
Lal, Hakim Jawahar, *Muntakhab-ut-Tawarikh*, Lucknow, 1860.
Parshad, Shiv, *Jam-i-Jahan Numa Khurd*, Lucknow, 1862.
Shah, Syed Muhammad Abdul Hasan, *Ayinah-i-Awadh*, Kanpur, 1869.
Shah, Wajid Ali, *Bani*, Calcutta, 1295 H.
———, *Chanchal Naznin*, Calcutta, 1297 H.
———, *Dulhan*, Calcutta, 1290 H.
———, *Irshad-i-Khaqani*, Lucknow, 1269 H.
———, *Malazul Kalmat*, Calcutta, 1297 H.
———, *Najo*, Calcutta, 1286 H.
———, *Nazm-i-Namwar*, Calcutta, 1287 H.
———, *Qamar Mazmoon*, Calcutta, 1281 H.
———, *Riyaz-ul-Quloob*, Calcutta, 1302 H.
Shah, Syed Ahmad Ali, *Tawarikh-i-Gorakhpur*, Mirzapur, 1859.
Sharar, Molana Abdul Halim, *Jan-i-Alam*, Lahore, n.y.
Tarikh-i-Jadooliya, Lucknow: Newal Kishore Press, 1853, Agra, 1854.

HINDI

Charan, Surajmal, *Vamsbhaskar*, Jodhpur, n.y.

III. UNPUBLISHED THESIS

ENGLISH

Anon., *Ghazi-ud-din Haider: The First King of Oudh, 1814-1827*, Lucknow: Tagore Library, Lucknow University.
Ahmad, Muhammad Taqi, *Naseeruddin Haydar, King of Oudh, 1827-1837*, Lucknow: Tagore Library, Lucknow University.

Qureshi, Hamid Afaq, *Nawab Wazir Ali Khan: Life and Career, 1780-1817*, Author's Typed Script.
Rizvi, Syed Najmul Raza, *A Study of Zamindars of Eastern U.P. in the Eighteenth Century*, Allahabad : Allahabad University.

HINDI

Gupta, Usha, *East India Company Ki Bhartiya Rajyon Kai Sath Nirhastakshep Ki Niti, 1786-1798*, Lucknow: Tagore Library, Lucknow University.
Siddiqi, Nafees Ahmad, *Saadat Ali Khan Kai Adhipatya Main Awadh, 1798-1814*, Author's Typed Script.

IV. JOURNALS, MAGAZINES, PAMPHLETS AND NEWSPAPERS

Ahmad, Safi, 'The Treaty of 1837', *Medieval India—A Miscellany* 2 (1972).
Amini, Faraq, *Babri Masjid Tathayon Ke Prakash Mein* (Hindi Pamphlet), Delhi: Union Printing Press, n.y.
Anon., *Shree Ram Janam Bhoomi Ka Pramanith Itihas* (Hindi Pamphlet), Ayodhya: Shri Ram Janam Bhoomi Mandir, Ayodhya Dham, n.y.
Askari, Sayyad Hassan, 'The Political Significance of Hazin's Career in Eastern India', *Bengal Past and Present*, 63(1943).
Datta, Kalikinkar, 'Raja Jhow Lal of the Oudh Court', *Journal of the Bihar and Orissa Research Society*, 23, Part 4(1937).
Diskalkar, D.B., 'Foundation of an Observatory at Lucknow', *Journal of the U.P. Historical Society* 10, pt.1 (July, 1937).
Dixit, R.S., 'Avadh: An Historico Geographical Analysis', *The Avad Geographer*, Vol.I, Lucknow, 1975.
Fisher, Michael H., 'The Imperial Coronation of 1819', *Modern Asian Studies* 19 (1985).
Irvine, William, 'The Later Mughals', *Journal of the Asiatic Society of Bengal*, 1894, 1896, 1903, 1904 & ed. by J. Sarkar, Calcutta and Reprinted from Delhi, 1971.
————, 'The Bangash Nawabs of Farrukhabad', *Journal of the Asiatic Society of Bengal*, 1878-9.
Muhammad, B. Saiyid Abu, 'Some Autographs of King Nasiruddin Haydar'. *Journal of the U.P. Historical Society* 12, pt.1 (July 1939).
Mukherjee, A., 'King Nasirud Din Haidar of Awadh (1827-1837)', *Journal of Indian History* 45, pt. 2 (August 1967).
Praveen, Yogesh, 'Nawabene Awadh', *Dharamyug*, 20 May, 1979.
————, 'Shahane Awadh', *Dharamyug*, 27 May, 1979.
Raza, Moonis, 'Delimiting Suba Awadh—1550-1605: A Study in Historical Geography', *The Avad Geographer*, Vol.I, Lucknow, 1975.
White Paper on Ayodhya, Govt. of India, 1993.

V. LATER AND MODERN WORKS

ENGLISH

Anon., *A Short History of Hind-Pak*, Karachi, 1960.
Adams, W.H. Davenport, *Episodes of Anglo-Indian History*, London, n.y.
Ahmad, Safi, *Two Kings of Awadh, Muhammad Ali Shah and Amjad Ali Shah*, 1837-1847, Aligarh, 1971.
———, *British Residents at the Court of Avadh, 1764-1856*, Lucknow, 1968.
———, *British Aggression in Awadh*, Meerut, 1969.
———, *Two Kings of Awadh: Muhammad Ali Shah and Amjad Ali Shah — 1837-1847*, Aligarh, 1971.
Aitchison, C.U., *A Collection of Treaties, Engagements and Sunnads Relating to Indian and Neighbouring Countries*, Calcutta: Foreign Office Press, 1909.
Alavi, Seema, *The Sepoys and the Company: Tradition and Transition in Northern India—1770-1830*, New Delhi: O.U.P., 1985.
Ali, Abdullah Yusuf, *Life and Labour of the People of India*, London, 1907.
Ali, Mirza Azhar, *King Wajid Ali Shah of Awadh*, 2 Vols., Karachi, 1982.
Ali, Shahamat, *The History of Bhawalpur*, London, 1848.
Alli, Darogha Ubbas, *The Lucknow Album*, Lucknow, 1894,
———, *Historical Album of the Rajas and Taluqdars of Oudh*, Lucknow, 1880.
Altekar, A.S., *Benaras: Past and Present*, 1943.
Anderson, G. and Subedar, M., *The Expansion of British India 1818-1858*, London, 1918.
Arbuthnott, Sir Alexander John, *Lord Clive*, London, 1899.
———, *Maj. Gen. Sir Thomas Munro*, London, 1889.
Archer, Mildred, *Company Drawings*, London, 1972.
Archer, Mildred & William G. Archer, *Indian Paintings for the British, 1770-1880*, Oxford, 1955.
Aspinall, A., *Cornwallis in Bengal*, London, 1931.
Atkinson, Edwin T., *Statistical, Descriptive and Historical Account of the North Western Provinces of India*, Allahabad, 1875-6.
Baden-Powell, B.H., *The Land Systems of British India*, 3 Vols., Oxford, 1892.
———, *A Short Account of the Land Revenue and its Administration in British India, with a sketch of Land Tenures*, Oxford, 1913.
Bahadur, M. Maseeh-ud-din Khan, *British Aggression in Oudh*, Lucknow, 1964.
Bailey, T. Graham, *History of Urdu Literature*, Calcutta, 1932.
Ball, Charles, *The History of the Indian Mutiny*, 2 Vols., London, n.y.
Banerjee, A.C., *Rajput Studies*, Calcutta, 1944.
———, *The Rajput States and the East India Company*, Calcutta, 1951.
———, *Lectures on Rajput History*, Calcutta, 1962.
———, *The Rajput States and British Paramountcy*, New Delhi, 1980.
———, *Peshwa Madhav Rao*, Calcutta, 1943.
Barat, A., *The Bengal Native Infantry: Its organisation, discipline, 1796-1852*, Calcutta, 1962.

Barnett, R.B., *North India Between Empires: Awadh, the Mughals and British, 1720-1801*, Berkeley & Los Angeles, 1980.

Basu, B.D., *Rise of the Christian Power in India*, 4 Vols., Calcutta, n.y.

Basu, P., *Oudh and the East India Company, 1785-1801*, Lucknow, 1943.

Batra, H.C., *The Relations of Jaipur State with East India Company, 1803-1858*, Delhi: S. Chand and Company, 1958.

Bayly, C.A., *Rulers, Townsmen and Bazaara: North Indian Society in the Age of Expansion—1770-1870*, New Delhi: O.U.P., 1983.

Beaglehole, H., *Thomas Munro and the Development of Administrative Policy in Madras, 1792-1818*, Cambridge, 1966.

Beale, Thomas William, *The Oriental Biographical Dictionary*, Calcutta, 1881.

Bhanu, Dharam, *History and Administration of the North Western Provinces, 1803-1858*, Agra, 1970.

Bhargava, P.N., *Who's Who in India*, Lucknow, 1911.

Bhatnagar, G.D., *Awadh under Wajid Ali Shah*, Varanasi, 1968.

Bhatnagar, C.P. (ed.), *Studies in the Social History of Modern India*, Allahabad, 1964.

Bhattacharya, A., *A Dictionary of Indian History*, Calcutta, 1971.

Bhattacharyya, Sukumar, *The Rajput States and the East India Company from the close of 18th Century to 1820*, New Delhi, 1972.

Bird, R.W., *Dacoitee in Excelsis, or the Spoilation of Oude by the East India Company*, Allahabad, 1924 & Lucknow (rpt.), 1971.

Blacker, J.F., *The ABC of Indian Art*, Delhi (rpt.), 1975.

Blunt, E.A.H., *The Caste System of Northern India*, Madras, 1931.

Brown, Percy, *Indian Architecture*, Bombay, n.y.

Browne, E.G., *A Literacy History of Persia*, Cambridge, 1928

Burgess, B.K.R., *The Chronology of Modern India for four hundred years from the close of the Fifteenth Century 1494-1894*, Edinburgh, 1913.

Burmon, B.K.R., *Muharram in Two Cities: Lucknow and Delhi*, New Delhi, 1965.

Burton, R.G., *The Mahratta and Pindari War*, Simla, 1910, Delhi, 1975 (There is no difference in the pagination of the two editions).

Butter, S.H., *Oudh Policy Considered Historically and with reference to the present political situation*, Allahabad, 1896.

Callahan, Raymond, *The East India Company and Army Reforms 1783-1798*, Cambridge, 1972.

Cardew, F.G., *Sketch of the Services of the Bengal Native Army to the year 1895*, Calcutta, 1903.

Caroe, Olaf, *The Pathans, 1550-1957*, London, 1964.

Carter, E.H., *Pioneers of the Modern World*, London, 1958.

Cavenagh, Gen. Sir Orfeur, *Reminiscences of an Indian Official*, London, 1884.

Chailley, Joseph, *Administrative Problems of British India*, London, 1910.

Chand, T., *The Administration of Oudh*, Calcutta, 1972.

Chand, T.P., *The Administration of Awadh*, Varanasi, 1971.

Chandra, Satish, *Parties and Politics at the Mughal Court, 1707-1740*, Aligarh, 1959.

Chatterji, Nand Lal, *Verelst's Rule in India*, Allahabad, 1939.

__________, *Clive As an Administrator*, Allahabad, 1955.

__________, *Glories of Uttar Pradesh*, Lucknow, 1957.

Chaudhuri, S.B., *Civil Disturbances During the British Rule in India, 1765-1857*, Calcutta, 1955.

Chowdhury, H.C. Roy, *Political History of India*, Calcutta,1972.

Cole, J.R.I., *Roots of North Indian Shi'ism in Iran and Iraq: Religion and State in Awadh —1722-1859*, Madras: O.U.P., 1989.

Compton, Herbert, *A Particular Account of the European Military Adventurers of Hindustan from 1784 to 1803*, London, 1892.

Cotton, J.S., *Mountstuart Elphinstone*, Oxford, 1892.

Coupland, Sir Reginald, *India, A Re-Statement*, London, 1945.

Crooke, William, *An Ethnographical Hand Book for the North Western Provinces and Oudh*, Allahabad, 1890.

Crooke, William, *The Popular Religion and Folklore of Northern India*, London, 1896.

__________, *North-Western Provinces of India*, Varanasi, 1971.

__________, *The Tribes and Castes of North-Western Provinces and Oudh*, 4 Vols., Calcutta, 1896.

Curzon of Kedleston, the Marquis, *British Government in India, the Story of the Viceroys and Government Houses*, 2 Vols., London, 1925.

Datta, K.K., *Anti-British Olots and Movements before 1857*, Meerut, 1970.

__________, *Reflections on the Mutiny*, Calcutta, 1967.

__________, *Survey of India's Social Life and Economic condition in the Eighteenth Century, 1707-1813*, Calcutta, 1961.

__________, *History of the Freedom Movement in Bihar*, Vol. I, Patna, 1957.

__________, *Shah Alam II and the East India Company*, Calcutta, 1965.

Davie, Sir James, *The Panjab, North-West Frontier Provinces and Kashmir*, Delhi, 1974.

Davies, A. Mervyn, *Warren Hastings, Maker of British India*, London, 1935.

__________, *Clive of Plassey*, London, 1939.

Davies, C.C., *Warren Hastings and Oudh*, London, 1939.

Davis, J.F., *Vizier Ali Khan or the Massacre of Benares, A Chapter in British Indian History*, London, 1844.

De, Barun (ed.), *Perspectives in the Social Sciences: Historical Dimensions*, Calcutta, 1977.

Desai, Z.A., *Centres of Islamic Learning in India*, New Delhi, 1978.

__________, *Mosques of India*, New Delhi, 1979.

Devi, Rithambhari, *Indian Mutiny 1857 in Bihar*, Delhi, 1977.

Dewar, D., *Notes on the English Pre-Mutiny Records in the United Provinces* (Defective).

__________, *In the Days of the Company*, Calcutta, 1920.

__________, *Bygone Days in India*, London, 1922.

Dictionary of National Biography, London, n.y.

Dighe, V.C., *Baji Rao I and Maratha Expansion*, Bombay, 1944.

Diwakar, R.R., *Bihar through the Ages*, Delhi, 1958.

Dodwell, Henry, *Dupliex and Clive, the Beginning of Empire*, Gorakhppur, 1962.

Dunbar, Sir George, *India and the Passing of Empire*, London, 1951.

Edwardes, Michael, *Glorious Sahibs*, London, 1968.

————, *King of the World*, London, 1970.

————, *The Orchid House*, London, n.y.

Elphinstone, M., *The Rise of the British Power in the East*, ed. by Sir Edward Colebrooke, London, 1887.

————, *History of India*, London, 1878.

Elliot and Dawson, *The History of India As Told By Its Own Historians*, 8 Vols., Allahabad, 1964.

Elton, Lord, *Imperial Commonwealth*, London, 1945.

Embree, Ainslie Thomas, *Charles Grant and British Rule in India*. London, 1962.

English, Barbara, *John Company's Last War*, London, 1971.

Feiling, Keith, *Warren Hastings*, London, 1955.

Fergusson, James, *History of Indian and Eastern Architecture*, revised and ed. by James Burgess and P. Spiers, Second Indian Reprint 1972.

Fernandes, Proxy, *Storm Over Seringapatam, the Incredible story of Hyder Ali and Tipu Sultan*, Bombay, 1969.

Ferrier, J.P., *History of the Afghans*, London, 1858.

Festing, Gabrielle, *When Kings Rode to Delhi*, London, 1928.

Fisher, Michael H., *A Clash of Cultures: Awadh, the British and the Mughals*, Delhi, 1987.

Forrest, G.W., *Cities of India*, London, 1903.

————, *Life of Lord Clive*, 2 Vols., London: Cassel & Co., 1918.

Fortesscue, John, *Wellington*, London, 1925.

Foster, William, *The English Factories in India*, Oxford, 1912.

Fox, Richard G., *Kin, Clan, Raja and Rule: State-Hinterland Relations in Pre-Industrial India*, Berkeley,1971.

————, *Realm and Region in Traditional India*, Durham, 1977.

Fraser-Tytler, W.K., *Afghanistan*, London, 1950.

Frazer, R.W., *British India*, London,1898.

Frykenberg, R.E. (ed.), *Land Control and Social structure in Indian History*, Wisconsin, 1969.

Gamon, Richard B., *Warren of Oudh*, London, 1926.

Gauba, K.L., *His Highness or the Pathology of Prince*, London, 1930.

Gazetteer: Besides the Imperial Gazetteer of India, Gazetteer for the various districts of U.P..

Gilliant, Edward, *Heroes of Modern India*, Delhi, 1971.

Gleig, G.R., *The Life of Robert First Lord Clive*, London, 1907.

Graint, James, *Cassell's Illustrated History of India*, 2 Vols., London, n.y.

Greaves, Edwin, *Kashi, the city Illustrious or Benares*, Allahabad, 1909.

Gribble, J.B.B., *History of the Deccan*, 3 Vols., London, 1896.

Griffin, Lepel, *The Rajas of the Panjab*, Lahore, 1870.

Gupta, H.R., *History of the Sikhs*, 3 Vols., Calcutta and Lahore, 1939-44.

————, *Studies in Later Mughal History of the Panjab, 1707-1793*, Lahore, 1944.

Gupta, S.C., *Agrarian Relations and Early British Rule in India*, London, 1963.

Hamilton, A., *Afghanistan*, London, 1906.
Handbook for India and Egypt, London, 1941.
Harcourt, E.S. & Hussain, Fakhir (trs.), *Lucknow, the last phase of an Oriental Culture*, London, 1975.
Hardinge, C.V., *Rulers of India: Viscount Hardinge*, Oxford, 1891.
Hardy, P., *The Musalmans of British India*, Cambridge, 1972.
Hasan, Mohibbul (ed.), *Historians of Medieval India*, Meerut, 1968.
Hasan, Syed Masud, *Urdu Drama and Stage*, Lucknow, 1957.
Havell, E.B., *Indian Architecture*, London, 1927.
Hay, Sidney, *Historical Lucknow*, Lucknow, 1937 & 1939.
Hill, S.C., *Major General Claud Martin*, Calcutta, 1901.
Hilton, E.H., *The Tourists Guide to Lucknow*, Lucknow, 1913.
Hodson, V.C.P., *Historical Records of the Governor General's Body Guard*, London, 1910.
Hoey, William, *A Monograph on Trade and Manufacture in Northern India*, n.p. & n.y.
Hollister, J.N., *The Shia of India*, London, 1953.
Holt, P.M., *Cambridge History of Islam*, Cambridge, 1970.
Hunter, W.W., *The Marquess of Dalhousie*, Oxford, 1880.
Hussain, Asad, *British India's Relations with the Kingdom of Nepal, 1857-1947*, London, 1970.
Hussain, Mahmood, *A History of the Freedom Movement*, Karanchi, 1957.
Hussain, Shaikh Tasadduq, *The Lucknow Guide*, Lucknow, 1936.
Hussey, Christopher, *English Country Houses*, London, 1956.
Hutchinson, Lester, *The Empire of the Nabobs, A Short History of British India*, London, 1937.
Hutton, W.H., *Marquess Wellesley*, Delhi, 1978.
Ikram, S.M., *History of Muslim Civilization in India and Pakistan*, Lahore, n.y.
Innes, P.R., *History of the Bengal European Regiment*, London, 1885.
Irwin, H.C., *The Garden of India or Chapters on Oudh History and Affairs*, London, 1880.
Jain, A.C., *Lucknow, the City of Nawabs*, Delhi, n.y.
Jafri, S.H.M., *The Origins and Early Developments of Shia Islam*, London, 1979.
Jarrat, H.S. and Sarkar, J., (trs.), *Ain-i-Akbari*, Calcutta, 1942.
Jones, Rosie Llewllyn, *A Fatal Friendship: The Nawabs, the British and the City of Lucknow*, New Delhi: O.U.P., 1985.
——————, *A Very Ingenious Man: Claude Martin in Early Colonial India*, New Delhi: O.U.P., 1992.
Kaye, John William, *History of the War in Afghanistan*, Vol. I, London, 1857.
——————, *A History of the Sepoy War in India, 1857-58*, Vol. I, London, 1865.
——————, *Memorials of Indian Government*, London, 1853.
——————, *The Life and Correspondence of Maj. Gen. Sir John Malcolm*, 2 Vols., London, 1856.
——————, *History of the Indian Mutiny*, London, 1888.
Keene, H.G., *History of India*, Vol. I, Edinburgh, 1906.
——————, *Hindustan under Free Lancers*, London, 1907.

———, *The Turks in India*, London, 1879.
———, *A Handbook for Visitors to Agra and its neighbourhood*, Calcutta, 1874.
———, *Madhav Rao Sindhia*, Lucknow, 1968.
———, *The Fall of the Mughal Empire*, London, 1876.
Keightly, Thomas, *A History of India*, London, n.y.
Khan, Syed Ahmad, *Review on Dr. Hunter's 'Indian Musalmans'*, Benares, 1872.
Khan, Mohibbul Hasan, *History of Tipu Sultan*, Calcutta, 1951.
Khan, Yusuf Hussain, *Nizam-ul-Mulk Asaf Jah-I*, Mangalore, 1936.
Khatak, Sarfraz Khan, *Shaikh Muhammad Ali Hazin: His Life Times and Works*, Lahore, 1944.
Khosla, R.P., *Mughal Kingship and Nobility*, Allahabad, 1934.
Kidwai, Ikramuddin & Qanungo, K.R., *Lucknow, Past and Present*, Lucknow, 1951.
Kincaid, C.A. & Parasnis, D.B., *A History of the Maratha People*, Vol. III, Oxford, 1925.
King, R.M., *Report of the Land Revenue Settlement of the Pertapgarh District*, Lucknow, 1869.
Kopf, David, *British Orientalism and the Bengal Renaissance*, Calcutta, 1969.
Kulkarni, V.B., *British Statesmen in India*, Bombay, 1961.
Lal, D.C., *The Rise of British Power and the Fall of Marathas*, Lucknow, 1972.
Latif, Syad Muhammad, *History of the Panjab from the Remotest Antiquity to the Present Time*, Calcutta, 1891.
Latif, Syad Muhammad, *Agra Historical and Descriptive*, Calcutta, 1896.
Laurie, W.F.B., *Sketches of some Distinguished Anglo-Indians*, London, 1888.
Lawson, Sir Charles, *The Private Life of Warren Hastings*, London, 1905.
Lee-Warner, W., *Life of the Marquess of Dalhousie*, 2 Vols., London, 1904.
Lockhart, L., *Nadir Shah*, London, 1938.
Love, H.D., *Vestiges of Old Madras, 1640-1860*, London, 1913.
Ludlow, John Malcolm, *British India, its Races and its History*, 2 Vols., Cambridge, 1858.
Lyall, Alfred, *The Rise and Expansion of the British Dominions in India*, London, 1894.
———, *Warren Hastings*, London, 1891, 1907.
Macaulay, *Warren Hastings*, ed. by S. Holes, Longman, Green & Co., 1906.
Macfarlane, Charles, *History of British India from the Earliest English Intercourse*, London, 1958.
Mackintosh, J.S., *Rajas and Nawabs of the North-Western Provinces*, Allahabad, 1877.
Majumdar, R.C., *The Sepoy Mutiny and the Revolt of 1857*, Calcutta, 1957.
———, *History of the Freedom Movement in India*, Vol. I, Calcutta, 1971.
———, *History and Culture of Indian People*, Bombay, 1968.
Malcolm, Sir John, *Life of Robert, First Lord Clive*, 3 Vols., London, 1832.
Malik, Zahiruddin, *The Reign of Muhammad Shah, 1714-1748*, New York, 1977.
———, *A Mughal Statesman of the Eighteenth Century Khan-i-Dauran, Mir Bakhshi of Muhammad Shah, 1719-1739*, Delhi, 1973.
Malleson, G.B., *French Struggles in India*, Delhi, 1977.

——————, *Essays and Lectures on Indian Historical Subjects*, London, 1866.
——————, *The Decisive Battles of India*, New Delhi, 1969.
——————, *Life of Warren Hastings, First Governor General of India*, London, 1894.
——————, *History of Afghanistan from the Earliest Period to 1878*, London, 1879.
——————, *Rulers of India, Lord Clive and the Establishment of the English in India*, Oxford, 1900.
Manners, Victoria & Williamson, G.C., John Zoffany, R.A., *His Life and Works, 1735-1810*, London, 1920.
Marchant, William, *Romantic India*, London, 1897.
Marriott, John A.R., *The English in India*, Oxford, 1932.
Marshall, P.J., *The Impeachment of Warren Hastings*, Oxford, 1965.
——————, *Problems of Empire: Britain and India*, London, 1968.
——————, *East Indian Fortunes: The British in Bengal in the Eighteenth Century*, Oxford, 1976.
Martin, R.M., *The History of the Indian Empire*, 3 Vols., London, n.y.
Mehta, M.S., *Lord Hastings and the Indian States 1813-1823*, Bombay, 1930.
Meray, Viscount, *The Viceroys and Governors General of India 1757-1947*, London, 1949.
Metcalf, T.R., *Land, Landlords and the British Raj: Northern India in the 19th Century*, London, 1974.
Mill, James & Wilson, Horace Hayman, *The History of British India*, 10 Vols., London, 1858.
Miller, A.F., *Report on the Land Revenue Settlement of Fyzabad District*, Allahabad, 1880.
Minney, R.J., *Clive*, London, 1931.
Misra, G.S., *British Foreign Policy and Indian Affairs, 1783-1815*, Bombay, 1963.
Misra, Rekha, *Women in Mughal India*, Allahabad, 1967.
Montgomerry, Robert, *Statistical Report of the District of Cawnpoor*, Calcutta, 1849.
Moon, Penderel, *Warren Hastings and British India*, London, 1947.
Morris, Henry, *The Governors General of India, First Series*, Madras, 1894.
Morrison, J.L., *Lawrence of Lucknow*, London, 1934.
Mukherjee, Ramkrishna, *The Rise and Fall of the East India Company*, Berlin, 1958.
Mukherjee, Rudrangshu, *Awadh in Revolt 1857-1858: A Study of Popular Resistance*, Delhi, 1984.
Murray, J., *A Hand Book for Travellers in India, Burma and Ceylon*, London, 1911.
Muir, Ramsay, *The Making of British India 1756-1858*, London, 1917.
Narain, V.A., *Jonathan Duncan & Varanasi*, Calcutta, 1959.
Neale, W.C., *Economic Change in Rural India —Land Tenure and Reform in Uttar Pradesh 1800-1955*, Yale, 1962.
Nesfield, John, *A Brief View of the Caste System of the North-Western Provinces and Oudh*, Allahabad, 1885.

Nilsson, Sten, *European Architecture and India 1750-1850*, London, 1968.
Oldhamk, Wilton, *Historical and Statistical Memoir of the Ghazeepoor District*, Allahabad, 1870.
Oswell, G.D., *Sketches of Rulers of India*, 4 Vols., Delhi, 1972.
Owen, S.J., *The Fall of the Mughal Empire*, London, 1912.
————, *The Mussalman, the Maratha and the European: Rise of the English Power in India*, London, 1869.
Owen, S.J., *India on the Eve of the British Conquest: A Historical Sketch*, London. 1872.
Palmer, Julian, *Sovereignty and Paramountcy in India*, London, 1930.
Phillips, C.H., *The East India Company*, Manchester, 1940.
Panikkar, K.M., *The Determining Periods of Indian History*, Bombay, 1962.
————, *The Evolution of British Policy Towards Indian States, 1774-1858*, Calcutta, n.y.
————, *Asia & Western Dominance*, London, 1955.
Parkaash, Ram, *The Foreign Policy of Warren Hastings*, Hoshiarpur, 1960.
Pearson, R., *Eastern Interlude*, Calcutta,1933.
Pemble, John, *The Raj, the Indian Mutiny and the Kingdom of Oudh, 1801-1859*, New Delhi, 1977.
Prasad, Ishwari, *Indian in the Eighteenth Century*, Allahabad, 1973.
————, *A History of Modern India*, Allahabad, 1951.
Prasad, S.N., *Paramountcy under Dalhousie*, Delhi, 1964.
Praveen, Yogesh, *Lucknow Monuments*, Lucknow, 1989.
Qidwai, Ikramuddin, *Lucknow Past and Present*, n.p & n.y.
Qureshi, I.H., *The Muslim Community of the Indo-Pakistan Subcontinent*, Hague, 1962.
Qureshi, H.A., *Some Aspects of Harem of the First Four Nawabs of Avadh*, Privately circulated Mimeograph, Lucknow, 1981.
————, *Saadat Ali of Avadh: Life till Accession*, Privately circulated Mimeograph, Lucknow, 1981.
————, *Degeneration of the Army of Avadh under Shuja-ud-daulah and Asaf-ud-daulah*, Lucknow, 1982.
Raghuvanshi, V.P.S., *Indian Society in the Eighteenth Century*, New Delhi, 1969.
Rahim, M.A., *Lord Dalhousie's Administration of the Conquered and Anexed States*, Delhi, 1963.
Raikes, Charles, *Notes on the North Western Provinces of India*, London, 1869.
Raj, Jagdish, *The Mutiny and British Land Policy in North India 1856-1868*, Bombay, 1965.
Ranade, Mahadeo Govind, *Rise of the Maratha Power*, New Delhi, 1974.
Rapson, E.J., *The Cambridge History of India*, Delhi, 1955.
Rashid, Abdur, *Najibuddaulah*, Aligarh, n.y.
Reeves, P.D. (ed.), *Sleeman in Oude: An Abridgement of W.H. Sleeman's A Journey through the Kingdom of Oude in 1849-1850'*, Cambridge, 1971.
Regmi, D.R., *Modern Nepal*, Calcutta, 1961.
Richards, Donald Sidney (ed.), *Islam and the Trade of Asia*, Philadelphia, 1970.
Richards, John F. (ed.), *Kingship and authority in Sourth Asia*, Wisconsin, 1978.

Rizvi, S.A.A., *Shah Wali-Allah and HGis Times*, Australia: Ma'Rifat Publishing House, 1980.
Rizvi, S.A.A. and Bhargava (ed.), *Freedom Struggle in U.P*, Vols.I & II, 1957.
Roberts, P.E., *India under Wellesley*, Gorakhpur, 1961.
———, *History of British India under the Company and the Crown*, Oxford, 1938.
Ross of Blanderberg, Major, *The Marquess of Hastings*, Oxford, 1900.
Russell, Ralph and Islam, Khurshidul, *Ghalib—Life and Letters*, London, 1969.
———, *Three Mughal Poets*, London, 1969.
Sachedina, A.A., *Islamic Messianism: The Idea of the Mahdi in Twelver Shi-ism*, Albany, 1981.
Sadiq, M., *A History of Urdu Literature*, London, 1964.
Sankhdar, Brijendra Mohan, *Sambhal: A Historical Survey*, New Delhi, 1971.
Santha, K.S., *Begums of Oudh*,Varanasi, n.y.
Sardesai, G.S., *New History of the Marathas*, Bombay, 1948.
Sarkar, J., *Fall of the Mughal Empire*, 4 Vols., Vol. I, Calcutta, 1949, 1971, Vol. II, Calcutta, 1934, 1950, Vol.III, Calcutta, 1960, Vol. IV, Orient Longman, 1972.
———, *India of Aurangzeb*, Title pages missing.
———, *Nadir Shah in India*, Calcutta, 1973.
Saxena, Ram Babu, *European and Anglo-Indian Poets of Urdu and Persian*, Lucknow, 1941.
Saxena, R.K., *Maratha Relations with the Major States of Rajputana, 1761-1818*, New Delhi, 1973.
Sen, Sailendra Nath, *Anglo-Maratha Relations during the Administration of Warren Hastings, 1772-1785*, Calcutta,1961.
———, *Anglo-Maratha Relations*, Madras, 1974.
Sen, Surendra Nath, *Eighteen Fifty Seven*, Delhi, 1957.
Sen, S.P., *The French in India 1765-1816*, Calcutta, 1958.
Seton Karr, W.S., *The Marquess Cornwallis*, Oxford, 1898.
Shah, S.I.A., *Modern Afghanistan*, London, n.y.
Shejwalkar, T.S., *Panipat, 1761*, Poona, 1946.
Sheppard, E.W., *Coote Bahadur*, London, 1956.
Sherring, M.A., *Benares, the Sacred City of the Hindus*, Delhi, 1975.
Shirvani, Zaynu'l Abidin, *Riyad-as-Siyahah*, Moscow, 1974.
Siddiqi, A., *Agrarian Change in a Northern India State, Uttar Pradesh, 1818-1833*, Oxford, 1973.
Sikander, Raza (ed.), *Wajid Ali Shah and Monuments of Awadh*, Lucknow, 1974.
Singer, Milton & Bernard S. Cohn, *Structure and Change in Indian Society*, Chicago, 1968.
Singh, Ganda, *Ahmad Shah Durrani, Father of Modern Afghanistan*, London, 1959.
Singh, Kaur Lachman, *Historical and Statistical Memoir of Zila Bulandshahar*, Allahabad, 1874.
Singh, Raghubir, *Indian States and the New Regime*, Bombay, 1938.
Singh, Nagendra, *Juristic Concepts of Ancient Indian Polity*, Delhi, 1980.
Sinha, Surendra Nath, *The Mid-Gangetic Region in the Eighteenth Century: Some observations of Joseph Tieffenthaler*, Allahabad, 1976.

Sinha, H.N., *Rise of the Peshwas*, Allahabad, 1931.
Sinha, R.K. & Hasan, M., *Glimpses of Faizabad*, Delhi, 1975.
Smith, V.A., *The Oxford Student's History of India*, Oxford, 1911.
Spear, Percival, *Master of Bengal: Clive and His India*, London, 1975.
————, *The Oxford History of Modern India*, Delhi, 1976.
————, *Twilight of the Mughals*, Cambridge, 1951.
Springer, A., *Report on the Researches into the Muhammadan Libraries of Lucknow*, Calcutta, 1896.
————, *Catalogue of the Libraries of Kings of Oudh*, n.p & n.y.
Srinivasachari, C.S., *The Inwardness of British Annexations in India*, Madras, 1951.
Srivastava, A.L., *The First Two Nawabs of Awadh*, Agra, 1954.
————, *Shuja-ud-daulah of Awadh, 1754-1775*, 2 Vols., Agra, 1961, 1974.
Steel, Flora Annie, *India Through the Ages*, London, 1908.
Stephen, J.F., *The Story of Nuncomar and the Impeachment of Sir Elijah Empey*, 2 Vols., London, 1885.
Strachey, John, *India, its Administration and Progress*, London, 1888.
————, *Hastings and the Rohilla War*, Oxford, 1892.
Suri, V.S., *Some Origfinal Sources of Panjab History*, n.p & n.y.
Sykes, P., *History of Afghanistan*, 2 Vols., London, 1940.
————, *History of Persia*, 2 Vols., London, 1922.
————, *The Marquess of Dalhousie: Rulers of India Series*, Oxford, 1890
————, *The Origin, Rise and Consolidation of the Indian States—A British Assessment*, First Published by the Government of India in 1932 for private circulation only, Delhi (rpt.), 1975.
Tholal, Bishambhar Nath, *History of the Sombansi Raj and Estate of Partabgarh in Oudh*, Allahabad, 1899.
Thompson, E. & Garratt, G.T., *Rise and Fulfilment of British Rule in India*, London, 1935.
Thornton, James Howard, *Memories of Seven Campaigns*, Westminster, 1895.
Tilby, A. Wyatt, *The English People Overseas*, 2 Vols., London, 1911.
Titus, Murray, T., *Indian Islam: A religious History of Islam in India*, London, 1930.
Torrens, W.M., *Empire in Asia: How We came by it: A Book of Confession*, London, 1872.
————, *Wellesley: The Marquess Wellesley: Architect of Empire: An Historic Portrait*, London, 1880.
Trotter, L.J., *History of India from the Earliest Times to the Present Day*, London, 1889.
————, *History of India under Queen Victoria, 1836-1880*, 2 Vols., London, 1888.
————, *Earl of Auckland*, London, 1905.
————, *Warren Hastings*, London, 1892.
Tupper, Charles Lewis, *Our Indian Protectorate*, London, 1893.
Verma, Birendra, P., *English East India Company and the Afghans, 1757-1800*, Calcutta, 1968.
Verma, D.C., *Plassey and Buxar: A Military History*, New Delhi, 1976.
Wallace, C.L., *Fatehgarh Camp*, Lucknow, 1934.

Walsh, Major J.H. Tull, *A History of Murshidabad District, Bengal, with Biographies of some of its Noted Families*, London, 1902.
Watt, W.M., *The Formative Period of Islamic Thought*, Edinburgh, 1973.
Weitzman, Sophia, *Waren Hastings and Philip Francis*, Manchester, 1929.
Wellington's Compaigns in India, Calcutta, 1908.
Wilks, *History of Mysoor* (Defective).
Williamson, George C., *Life and Works of Ozias Humphry, R.A.*, London, 1918.
Wilson, C.R., *Old Fort William in Bengal*, 2 Vols., London, 1906.
Wilson, H.H., *Glossary of Indian Terms*, London, 1885.
————, *A Glossary of Judicial and Revenue terms of British India*, London, 1875.
Wilson, Sir Charles, *Lord Clive*, Ambala, 1972.
Woodburn, J., *Pargana Manglasi*, Lucknow, n.y.
Wylly, Col. H.C., *A Life of Lt. Gen. Sir Eyre Coote*, Oxford, 1922.

PERSIAN

Al-Ahad, Abd, *Tarikh Badshah Begum alias Waqa i-idil Pazir*, tr. by Muhammad Taqi Ahmad, Allahabad: Indian Press, 1938.
Alvi, Shah Himayat Ali, *Noor-ul-Raib*, Lucknow, 1332 H.
Asi, Abdur Bari, *Tazkirah Khandah-Gul*, Lucknow, n.y.
Azfari, Ali Bakht, *Vaqiat-i-Azfari*, ed. by T. Chandrashekharan, No. 65, Madras: Madras Govt. Oriental Manuscript Series, 1957.
Bilgrami, Mir Ghulam Ali Azad, *Maasir-ul-Kiram*, Agra, 1910.
Ghubar, Ghulam Ali, *Ahmad Shah Baba-i-Afghan*, Kabul, 1944.
Haidar, Kamaluddin, *Taqveem Bait-us-Saltanat Lucknow*, Matba-i-Sultani, n.y.
Haidrabadi, Nasiruddin Naqsh, *Tazkirah Uroos-ul-Azkar*, ed. by Afsar Siddiqi Amrohvi, Karachi, 1975.
Khan, Mirza Afsar Ullah, *Dastan-i-Tuzuk Tazan-i-Hind*, 4 Vols., Bombay, 1307 H.
Khan, Syed Muhammad Amir Ali, *Amirnamah*, Calcutta, 1870.
Prasad, Durga, *Bostan-i-Awadh*, Lucknow, 1892.
————, *Gulistan-i-Hind*, 4 Vols., Sandilah, 1310 H.
————, *Hadiqa-i-Ishrat*, Sandilah, 1893.
Shushtri, Aqa Syed Muhammad Abbas *Kitab Nujoo-mus-0Sama-fi-Tarajim-ul-Ulema*, Matba-i-Jafri, 1297 H.

URDU

'Adeeb', Masud H., *Lucknau ka Shahi Stage*, Lucknow, 1957.
Ahmad, Iqbal, *Ayinah-i-Masoodi*, Kanpur, n.y.
Alam, Molvi Muhammad Ikram, *Haqiqat-i-Rampur*, Badaun, 1960.
Ali, Muhammad Ahd, *Muraqqa-i-Awadh*, Lucknow, 1919.
Ali, Sabir, *Saadat Yar Khan Rangin*, Karachi, 1954.
Azad, Muhammad Hussain, *Tazkirah-i-Ulema-i-Hind*, Lahore, 1922.
Azmi, Khan, *Amir-ul-Mujahidin*, Rudauli, 1977.
Bari, *Company Ki Hukoomat Hindostan Main*, Lahore, n.y.

Baro, Shyam Sunder Lal, *Bahar-i-Sukhan*, Sitapur, n.y.
Bismil, Muhammad Rafiuddin, *Kanz-i-Tarikh*, n.y.
Das, Bulaqi, *Dar-ur-Riyasat Mustafabad Urf Rampur*, Delhi, n.y.
———, *Guldasta-i-Awadh*, Delhi, 1887.
Fazal, Molvi Hafiz Muhammad, *Asar-i-Badaun*, Badaun, 1915.
Ghafoor, Munshi Muhammad Abdul, *Muraqqa-i-Salatin alias Aasar-ul-Mutakhirin*, Delhi, 1874.
Hashmi, Noorul Hasan, *Dilli Ka Dabistan-i-Shairi*, Lucknow, 1971.
Hasan, S.M., *Tarikh-i-Benares*, 2 Vols., Vol. I, Benares, 1916, Vol. II, Benares, 1926.
Hussain, Inayat, *Futuhat-i-Hind*, Lucknow, 1873.
Hussain, Sajjad, *Sawaneh Shah-i-Awadh*, Meerut, n.y.
Hussain, Shaikh Tasadduq, *Begmat-i-Awadh*, Lucknow, n.y.
Inayatullah, Molana Molvi Muhammad, *Tazkirah-i-Ulema-i-Firangi Mahal*, Lucknow, 1928.
Karim, Molvi Abdul, *Gum-Gashtah Halat-i-Ajodhya*, Lucknow, 1927.
Kazmi, Tamkeen, *Tazkirah-i-Rekhti*, Hyderabad, 1934.
Khan, Amjad Ali, *Tarikh-i-Awadh Ka Mukhtasar Jaiza*, Lucknow, 1978.
Khan, Hakim Muhammad Hussain, *Allama Najmul Ghani Khan*, Rampur, n.y.
Khan, Hakim Molvi Muhammad Hussain, *Farman Ravayan-i-Rampur*, Rampur, 1972.
Khan, Ikhlar-ud-daulah Syed Ahmad Hussain, *Halat-i-Madarsah-i-Qaisryah*, Lucknow, 1890.
Khan, Najmul Ghani, *Tarikh-i-Awadh*, 5 Vols., Lucknow, 1919.
Khan, Raja Muhammad Imam Ali, *Asar-i-Yadgar*, Lucknow, 1302 H.
Kishore, Munshi Newal, *Tawarikh-i-Nadir-ul-Asr*, Lucknow, 1863.
Lal, Diwan Roshan, *Khulasah Tarikh-i-Awadh*, n.p & n.y.
Lal, Munshi Mohan, *Khatoon-i-Awadh*, Lucknow, 1925.
Malihabadi, Jafar, *Goya, Sahib-i-Saif wa Qalam*, Lucknow, 1978.
Masood, Khan Bahadur Syed Masood Hasan, *Andalib-i-Tawarikh*, Allahabad, 1963.
Mehar, Ghulam Rasul, *Atharah-so-Sattawan*, Lahore, n.y.
Mehdi, Muhammad Agha, *Tarikh-i-Sultan-ul-Ulema*, Karachi, 1930.
Nadvi, Syed Abul Hasan Ali, *Islami Dunya Par Musalmano Kai Uroj Wa Zawal Ka Asar*, Lucknow, 1974.
Nami, Syed Aqa Hasan, *Hasan-ut-Tawarikh*, 3 Vols., Matba-i-Jang Bahaduri, 1279 H.
Naqvi, Sibte Muhammad, *Amjad Ali Shah*, Lucknow, 1976.
Nizami, Nizamuddin Hussain, *Karam-i-Rampur*, Rampur, 1919.
Nomani, Molana Abdus Salam, *Asar-i-Benares*, Benares, 1963.
Parshad, Durga, *Tawarikh-i-Sandila*, Lucknow, 1915.
———, *Tarikh-i-Ajodhya*, Lucknow, 1902.
———, *Baharistan-i-Awadh* (Defective).
Parshad, Munshi Gaya, *Risala-i-Jugrafiyah Zilah Bareilly*, Akhbarabad, 1860.
Parshad, Shiv, *Ayinah-i-Tarikh Numa*, Allahabad, 1873.
Rai, Lala Daulat, *Char Hasas Mai Naqshjat*, Lahore, n.y
Rizvi, Syed Afzal Hussain, *Hayat-i-Dabir*, Lahore, 1913.
Sabit, Syed Afzal Hussain, *Durbar-i-Hussain*, Delhi, 1921.

Sarwar, Munshi Ghulam, *Gulzar-i-Shahi*, Lahore, 1873.
Sharar, Molana Abdul Halim, *Guzishta Lucknow*, Delhi, 1971.
————, *Jan-i-Alam*, Lahore, 1951.
Shayan, Tota Ram, *Tarikh-i-Sitara-i-Hind*, Lucknow, 1299 H.
Shad, Munshi Shakatha Prasad, *Kayasth Raj Tarangini* Vol. I, Jaunpur, n.y.
Siddiqi, Abu Layyas, *Lucknow Ka Dabistan-i-Shairi*, Delhi, n.y.
Siddiqi, K.A., *Rekhti Ka Tanqidi Mutalah*, Lucknow, 1974.
Siddiqi, Rashid Ahmad, *Ashufta Bayani Mir*, Delhi, 1960.
Sindhi, Abaidullah, *Shah Waliullah aur Unki Siyasi Tehrik*, Lahore, 1944.
Sitapuri, Syed Nadim, *Allama Sitapur*, Delhi, n.y.
Tamanna, Ram Sahai, *Afzalut Tawarikh*, Lucknow, 1879.
Umar, Muhammad, *Atharhavin Sadi Main Hindustani Maashrat*, New Delhi, 1973.
Zutshi, Pandit Manohar Lal, *Guldasta-i-Adab*, Allahabad, 1933.
Zaidi, Chaudhari Syed Ali Muhammad, *Barahbanki*, Barabanki, 1984.
Zaidi, Syed Ali Muhammad *Apni Yadain Rudauli Ki Batain*, Lucknow, 1977.

HINDI

Bajpai, Krishna Datt, *Braj Ka Itihas*, Mathura, 1958.
Bhartiya, Tabassum Nizami, *Lucknow Janpad Ka Rashtriya Itihas*, Lucknow, 1961.
Chand, Moti, *Kashi Ka Itihas*, Varanasi, 1985.
Debral, S.P., *Uttarakhand Ka Itihas*, 4 Vols., Garhwal, 1928.
Diwakar, B.M., *Bharat Main Company Raj Kai Karnamai*, Jaipur, 1979.
Hussaain, Ehtisham, *Urdu Sahitya Ka Alochnatmak Itihas*, Allahabad, 1969.
Pandey, Rajendra, *Awadh Ki Loot*, Lucknow, 1966.
Praveen, Yogesh, *Bhar-e-Awadh*, Lucknow, 1987.
Misr, Brij Kishore, *Avadh Kai Parmukh Kavi*, Lucknow, 2017 VS.
Mishra, Jagganath, *Adhunik Bharat Ka Itihas*, n.p. & n.y.
Ram, Lala Sita, *Shri Awadh Ki Jhanki*, Allahabad, 1933.
Sen, Surendra Nath, *Atharoh So Sattavan*, Delhi, 1957.
Sahai, Jagdish, *Awadh Mein Nawabi Shasan Ka Itihhas*, n.p. & n.y.
Shukla, Ram Chandra, *Hindi Sahitya Ka Itihas*, Kashi: Nagri Pracharini Sabha, 1994.
Singh, Pawan Kumar, *Shahar-e-Lucknow*, Lucknow, 1990.
Srivastava, Kanhaya Lal, *Behraich Janpad*, Bahraich, n.y.
Sunderlal, Pandit, *Bharat Main Angrezi Raj*, 2 Vols., Delhi, 1976.
Tewari, Gore Lal, *Bundelkhand Ka Sanshipt Itihas*, Kashi, 1990.
Varhaspati, Acharya, *Musalman aur Bhartiya Sangit*, Delhi, 1974.
Verma, Paripurnanand, *Wajid Ali Shah aur Awadh Raj Ka Patan*, Prayag, 1959.
Zaidi, Shailash, *Bilgram Ke Musalman Hindi Kavi, 1600-1800*, Varanasi, 1969.

Index